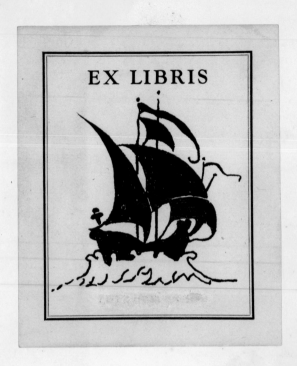

IT'S THE IRISH

IT'S THE IRISH

—————————— BOB CONSIDINE

Foreword by JAMES A. FARLEY

DOUBLEDAY & COMPANY, INC. GARDEN CITY, NEW YORK, 1961

Special acknowledgment is made to the following, who have granted permission for the use of copyrighted material from the books and sources listed below:

"Pat Malloy" from IRISH TAVERN FOLIO OF HUMOR SONGS. Copyright 1947 by Chas. H. Hansen Music Corp. Reprinted by permission.

JOHN KENNEDY: A POLITICAL PROFILE by James MacGregor Burns. Copyright © 1959, 1960 by James MacGregor Burns. Reprinted by permission of Harcourt, Brace & World, Inc.

TO THE GOLDEN DOOR by George Potter. Copyright © 1960 by Erna Constance Potter. Reprinted by permission of Little, Brown & Company.

Eight lines of poetry by Bernard Shaw, and an extract from JOHN BULL'S OTHER ISLAND by Bernard Shaw, reprinted by permission of the Public Trustee and The Society of Authors.

Excerpt from *America* (p. 684, issue of February 25, 1961)

*For Michael, Barry and Dennis Considine . . . who will carry a
Clare name, and light hearts, into the Age of Space . . .*

ACKNOWLEDGMENT

The author owes a considerable debt of gratitude to two resourceful young working journalists, James P. Aldrich and James Harper for helping to make this volume possible.

Messrs. Aldrich and Harper, keen students of Ireland's tremendous contributions to the growth and strength of America, left no Blarney stone unturned in searching out or editing the material contained herein.

B.C.

LIST OF ILLUSTRATIONS

CONTENTS

CONTENTS

[x]

FOREWORD

No Irishman ever publicly boasts that people of our strain possess a monopoly on wit, wisdom, good humor, and the ability to rise above any oppression, repression, or depression. Modesty, a characteristic trait of the Irish, forbids such a proud posture.

But at a time when a young man named John Fitzgerald Kennedy rises to the highest office the Free World has to offer, the Presidency of the United States, it is time to take another look at the all but incredible contributions the Irish have made to this country and to the world in general. One would be hard pressed to find a field of endeavor in which men and women of Irish background have not excelled in the United States and elsewhere. Yet Ireland itself is but a pinpoint on the map of the world, and her people have known persecution and poverty of terrible scope.

It is easy to agree with the basic premise of a speech the elder Henry Cabot Lodge made in 1888 before the New England Society of Brooklyn:

"Let every man honor and love the land of his birth and the

race from which he springs and keep their memory green. It is a pious and honorable duty. But let us have done with British-Americans and Irish-Americans and German-Americans, and so on, and all be Americans . . .

"If a man is going to be an American at all let him be so without any qualifying adjectives; and if he is going to be something else, let him drop the word American from his personal description."

That is sound advice for British-Americans, German-Americans, and Italian-Americans. But the counsel can hardly apply to Americans fortunate enough to trace their ancestry back to Ireland. It is not that we are any less American; a list of the heroes and casualties in any war since the Revolution will attest to that. It is, I think, simply the enchantment of having a root that reaches back into a land as dear and as enduring as the Emerald Isle. Ireland cast a flickering but unquenchable light over a whole section of the world during the Dark Ages. Her teachers, philosophy, prose, poetry, music, chivalry, character—yes, and her Faith —are treasures to point to with pride.

Few, if any, nations can be said to have prevailed in the face of such prolonged adversity. But we are not here to pity Ireland and her far-flung people. We are here to salute Ireland and thank her for, among many other achievements, helping to make America as great as our country is today. If there had been no famine or persecution afflicting Ireland, millions of us would never have seen and coped with the challenge of the New World.

Forgive me if I re-stress the presence of an American of Irish Catholic ancestry in the White House. It is only to illuminate the remarkable buoyancy of the race. In his outstanding biography, *John Kennedy: A Political Profile*, James MacGregor Burns gives us a dramatic picture of the conditions under which the great-grandfather of the President, lived in the Ireland of the 1840s:

" . . . The blight rotted the potatoes with terrifying speed—

in a single night, some said. A priest traveling from Cork to Dublin one day rejoiced at the rich harvest in the making; returning a week later he saw 'one wide waste of putrefying vegetation.'

"Misery lay on the land like a pall. Some families took to the road, wandering from blighted field to blighted field, leaving the old and the young dying in the ditches. Others waited quietly in their cottages to die. Some survived near-starvation to perish of typhus, which was spreading through the drifting population. Others had only one dream—to leave this land on which God seemed to have laid a curse and escape to another country, to America, land of gold and milk and honey. . . .

"When the flight from famine was at its peak, young Patrick Kennedy deserted his thatch-roofed home in New Ross and joined the great migration of the hungry and the helpless. Doubtless he boarded a Cunarder at Cork or Liverpool and crossed the Atlantic in the crowded steerage. He was lucky to be able to raise the fare—$20, including provisions—and lucky, too, to avoid the epidemics that sometimes decimated the shiploads of immigrants on the long passage."

To repeat, there's something about the Irish. And a lot of the answers are contained in this volume.

James A. Farley

1 ON PARADE:

America's "Fellow Immigrants"

Some years ago, my wife and I rented a summer place on the Sound of Long Island at Mamaroneck, New York. It was late afternoon of a sunny and pleasant day by the time the moving van departed. Our things were more or less in order, and it was the appropriate time to raise a glass to the coming holiday period.

Then I noticed for the first time that the place next to ours was occupied, and that a lad of approximately Michael's age—six or seven—had come to the hedge that separated the two properties. Somewhere farther in the distance, I could see a man of about my own age—a tweedy, suburban type—puttering in his garden. The father of the child, surely.

Here, clearly, was an opportunity to strike up a friendship, a neighborly rapport that could blossom into all sorts of rewarding entanglements.

I quickly mixed a jar of very dry martinis, opened a fresh bottle of Scotch and one of Irish, set these things on a tray with glasses, ice, and lemon peel and started resolutely toward the hedge—a communal barrier that has for ages untold separated man, nations, and notions. Mike preceded me and now was staring at the other child at the close and silent range that, in older males, might indicate the prelude to a fight.

"Hello, son," I said to the lad in the other yard, as I balanced the tray with what passed for a professional air. "That your father over there in the garden?"

"Yeah," the kid said, "and he's one of the biggest furriers in New York. We're worth $500,000."

The pronouncement nearly caused the disaster of a toppling tray. I had that day received an impersonally printed note from my bank stating, quite personally, that I was overdrawn $28.40.

"Good for him," I said when I had control of the tray. He came over to the hedge himself now, the father did, and holding the goodies with one hand I extended the other, shook his hand, and introduced myself. I did not expect him to leap with joy at the sound of the name, but on the other hand I was not quite prepared to have him just stand there and wait for me to continue.

"I was thinking," I continued wildly, "that it will sure be nice, living next to you this summer. That's a fine little son you have there. He and Mike will have lots of fun playing, swimming . . . you know." My voice was beginning to trail off.

He met this prediction with inscrutable mien.

"Ah, the drinks," I went on, as if Bacchus had suddenly appeared from wherever he and his cirrhosis reside and had magically placed the tray in my hand. "I thought we'd have a drink: I rather pride myself on my martinis, or would you like a highball? . . . something on the rocks . . . ?"

"Don't drink," my neighbor said. "I've never touched it."

I offered him a cigarette, but it developed that his lips had never been stained by the foul weed. There followed a painful little monologue in which I said, in effect, that some of my best friends were furriers but that I happened to be a newspaperman.

"Never read them," he said. "I prefer to get my news from radio."

The ice was beginning to melt. But only in the drinks. We nodded and went to our respective points of interest—my neighbor back to his garden, myself to the bar.

After a bit, Mike came in the house and I called out to him, "How did *you* make out?"

"Oh, fine," Mike said, going about his business. "He said that thing about them being so rich again, but I shut him up."

"How?" I asked, thinking uneasily of the $28.40 overdraw.

"I told him, 'Aw, that's nothing. *My* father drinks a quart of whisky every day!'"

It must have stereotyped the Considine clan in the mind of the nice neighbor and his family for we saw precious little of them throughout the remainder of that fine season. They seemed to remain away from the hedge rather studiously as if fearing total immersion in a flood of rum. There was never any way to get through to them to say that it really was not a quart a day; and that the principal liquid consumed in the house was milk—cow's and mother's, for Barry had just been born.

But we lived in peace, side by side in the New World, his family whose roots reached principally back to old Russia and my family whose forebears were mostly Irish. And both as American as Paddy's and Ivan's pig!

And that, as you've known since birth, is the pride and power of America. Our forebears had to come to America. Nobody brought America to us.

It is, too, a point about which we must be occasionally reminded, particularly those among us who tend now and then to conclude the land is theirs by divine right. Franklin Delano Roosevelt, of Dutch immigrant stock, speaking to a convention of the Daughters of the American Revolution commenced his address:

"Fellow immigrants!"

[3]

Some of the dear ladies who prided themselves on being able to spot a first-generation American at twenty paces, managed to choke back their cheers for this "betrayer of his class."

But there was applause on a similar subject, for example, when F.D.R. appeared during the 1944 campaign in Boston, tradition-steeped gateway to America.

"All of our people, except full-blooded Indians, are immigrants, or descendants of immigrants," he said at a rally. "Including those who came over on the *Mayflower*," he added, which was regarded locally as a crushing blow against the Republicans—though history does not record there were any members of the G.O.P. aboard that ship.

The wartime President might have added that he was not making a pitch for the Indian vote; that indeed, the Indians probably had come up out of Asia in the long ago, waited until what is now the Bering Strait was properly jelled and trekked across the ice and down this side of the world as far as Tierra del Fuego.

Why? Why does anyone move? How can the human being, with all his frailties and hunger for peace and quiet at almost any price go out into a hostile world and seek a new place to live? . . . a place filled with physical danger, prejudices, exotic customs, odd languages, strange and perhaps revolting food, alarming climate, menacing beasts and maladies?

Each great ethnic group, great national group, has provided its own reason for its peoples' cutting ancient ties and setting out for far places. And each family, too, can tell a story. How often has a father stared at a murky ceiling through the far hours of the night, dreaming of a land where his plow would probe more fecund earth, where his kind could throw off the shackles of the past and be more than serfs, peasants, second-class citizens? How many have yearned to pull stakes and be gone—wherever: in some fragile bark upon a tempestuous sea, a covered wagon from the East of the United States to the West, across the hazard-filled prairie, in a rattling jalopy from Oklahoma's dust bowl to California . . . or in the stinking hold of an immigrant ship bound for the Promised Land of America, where, as everyone once knew, the streets were paved with gold.

The Irish who came to America, eventually like a tidal wave, were unique in two respects. They were the first people here to be called "foreigners." They were the first, really, to suffer segregation and discrimination. And, of course, they were the first to do something about a symbolic and neatly printed sign they read in the shop windows of Boston, New York and elsewhere: MAN WANTED. NO IRISH NEED APPLY.

In time, the scenes and faces of the old land fade from the mind, seem, indeed, as if they might have occurred in another incarnation. Soon, by some chemical change, the migrant discovers that he belongs.

It's something akin the change that occurs in a new New Yorker. Because New York is a big city, offering endless opportunities, young people move there from all over, in search of a break. Would-be artists from Ashtabula, dancers from Denver, salesmen from Spokane, and actors from everywhere crowd to the place. For a year or so, they think of themselves as Ashtabulans or Denverites who just happen to be living in New York. Then suddenly one day they wake up and, without knowing when or how it happened, they discover they are New Yorkers who just happen to have come from Ashtabula or Denver. They're still proud of the old home town, still correspond with the folks back in Ohio and Colorado, but they no longer are part of it or one of them. They are, of a sudden, New Yorkers, full of the lore of subways, the Broadway shows, the right restaurants, the "characters" of the columns.

It's much the same with the new American. It may be a trivial incident that causes his spiritual naturalization. He may get an advertisement in the mail addressed to him, and suddenly he knows he's no longer "Hey, you," but Mr. Michael Pinsinski,

American. Oh, he's not about to quit the Polish-American Society, or stop sending money to his sister back in the old country. But, all of a sudden, he's no longer a Pole living in America but an American of Polish descent.

Such a transformation has happened to every one of us—or to one of our forebears. Suddenly, we're American, no longer Polish, or Irish, or British. After all, the waters of the Amazon, the Thames, and the Hudson—flowing into the Atlantic—in time are no longer Amazon, Thames, Hudson, but part of the vast ocean.

In this book, we'll follow one of the rivers that makes up the great ocean of America from its headwaters to the sea. There will be storms and sunny days along the route, and the scenery may shift from swamps to grassy uplands. The river will twist and turn upon itself, and occasionally dwindle to a dismal trickle only to tumble and surge through violent rapids. And in the end, as it rushes to meet the sea, it runs strong and deep.

Some twenty million Americans, perhaps more, trace their ancestry to Ireland, while the population of the homeland itself, which hit a peak of eight million in the mid-nineteenth century, now stands at only about four million.

The Irish migration differed from all others. The half-million Greeks who came to America left multitudes of Greeks behind. Italy, overflowing with people, hardly missed the 4,776,884 Italians who settled in the United States. A total of 6,248,529 Germans—largest immigrant group of all—entered the melting pot over a 130-year period, causing no major change in the course of events in Germany.

Not so with the Irish, who never do anything by half measures. During the sixty years of the heaviest Irish emigration, more people left than stayed behind. The United States, the destination for the vast majority of those people, like Ireland itself, will never be the same. America now has four times as many people of Irish descent as the Emerald Isle itself. In a century of so-called population explosion, Ireland, whose Catholicism sternly bans birth control, nevertheless has seen its number sink by half.

Not only did the enthusiastic Irish come in quantity, they came early. The tide of Irish immigration reached its crest in 1851—31 years before the peak for Germany, 56 years before the high tide for Italians, 37 years before that for Britain, and 60 years before the Poles came in greatest numbers.

For all these reasons, the 4,617,485 immigrating Irishmen—ranking third in number behind the Germans and Italians—nevertheless formed a unique parade, for the Irish immigrated as the Irish fight, love, talk, and live—with gusto. No major immigrant group, from the Germans at the top to the Czechs (in 26th place with 128,360), embraced their new nation with more ardor.

The Irishman never lost sight of the fact that he was an Irishman. He never forgot his beginnings. The Irish originally dwelt in clans, and the Irish remain clannish to this day. Of all the immigrant groups, none was so cohesive. Long after other foreign-born blocs had split on issues, there still was, within each community, a solid Irish vote. Long after the German and Italian had dropped out of their moribund nationality clubs and joined the Elks, their Irish neighbor was attending weekly meetings of the Hibernian Society.

This one-for-all, all-for-one spirit goes back to the old country. In neglecting the Catholic Irishman's education and barring his political and economic advancement, England kindled not only his undying hatred of all things English, but also his imperishable pride in all things Irish.

When the Irish moved to America, their tendency to cluster was fanned by two factors—the troubles they themselves were having in the new land and the troubles their relatives were having in the old. By sticking together, the immigrant Irish helped one another over often disheartening barriers. By sticking together they managed to help the homeland struggle out of the grasp of England.

So strong was this unifying hatred of Britain that it sent one group of fighting Irish-Americans off on a wild goose invasion of English Canada and another to South Africa to battle on the side of the Boers. So strong was it, in fact, that many of the sons of those two groups donned uniforms with mixed feelings when America joined England in two world wars.

The Irish also kept together through their religion. Because it originally was a faith strange to many Americans it set the Irish apart and thus made them cling closer together. Also, in discouraging marriage outside Catholicism, it discouraged wandering from the Irish clan. And, in establishing parochial schools, colleges, charitable organizations, and clubs, it limited the contact of the Irish with outsiders. Thus, the "Irishness" of the Irish has remained comparatively little diluted over the years.

When an Irish voice is lifted in Irish song, our typical Celt, though separated by many generations from the immigrant ship, nevertheless will contribute a tear or two to the memory of a land he has never seen. He may have trod the streets of neither Dublin nor South Bend, yet he will turn first to the sports pages each Sunday during the football season to see how the Fighting Irish of Notre Dame have done.

The tide of Ireland, flowing into the vastness of America, has given it a green tint it will never lose. All the rest of us—the Finklesteins, the Buckhalters, the Thorndikes, and the Krctrakowskys alike—are a little Irish because the Irish are here, because their sprightliness and flair are highly contagious.

In the pages that follow, we will see why this is so. From a vantage point above time and space we'll watch the unfolding of a wondrous drama. But first, we'll look at the setting of our opening act—the lush land of Ireland itself, so beautiful, yet sometimes so deathly. We'll visit it during its golden age, when it serves as the schoolhouse of the civilized world. Then we'll watch in sorrow as, through the centuries, it slides into an abyss of poverty and despair. And thrill to its emergence as a free nation.

As our drama unfolds, we'll see the English with incredible cruelty reduce the Irish to a nation of ragged, landless laborers. The excesses of Oliver Cromwell, a man who practiced dictatorship before the word was coined, may seem to the reader a preview of Nazi terrorism.

The travail of the Irish suddenly becomes twofold, not only political, but economic as well. Throughout the land, the Irishman's fare, the round plump potato, begins to come out of the earth shriveled and black. Over twenty years, our actors gradually turn into a gaunt, stumbling multitude, animated by one thought: to find food.

Down to the beaches they stream (like the Allies at Dunkirk long after), intent on getting away from this country before it kills them. We'll watch tearful dockside scenes as the Irish leave the land where they've lived since the dawn of recorded time. Then we'll ride with them in the holds of immigrant ships, amid a stench as thick as an Irish fog. And finally we'll go ashore with them in America.

Here, our scene changes, but not the tenor of the story. The Irishman, like the desert traveler following a retreating mirage, finds to his deepest dismay that America is not the answer—at least, not the automatic answer. Redemption is not won that easily. The Gaels, who have suffered the ordeals of famine and loss of homeland, must undergo still further trials. For the new land presents a new problem—prejudice. Because of it, jobs are not so easy for an Irishman to come by. And some jobs—on the railroad and canal gangs—only an impoverished Irishman would accept.

Many of the older Americans, scions of the Reformation English, are less than enthusiastic about the tide of Catholicism ris-

[9]

ing around them. An "Irishman Go Home" spirit sweeps the land.

But in the end, time—and the indomitable spirit of the Celt —change the course of our drama. Without becoming one whit less Catholic, one whit less Irish, the Catholic Irish become American. Perhaps the best kind—Irish-American.

Thus, our drama is framed by two great parades. The first is a parade of gaunt men and women, the smell of steerage still clinging to their rags, struggling up out of the holds of immigrant ships and across the docks of our cities, to the jeers of pierside idlers. For decades that tattered parade continued— 48,000 or more a year—until it seemed it would never end, that America could never absorb them all. Finally, when Ireland at last had lost the surplus it could not support, the flow thinned out.

As that grim parade dwindles, another comes into focus. It is last St. Patrick's Day, and the Irish are out in force. The flags are flying, the bands are playing, the whole town is there to cheer. No ragged ill-fed band this, clinging to its few pitiful possessions, but strong, proud, prosperous Americans. The parade means only one thing. The saga knows its climax. The long ordeal of the Irish is over. After centuries of sorrow and strife, victory is here. And as they pass, wave on wave, a mighty cheer goes up: "It's a Great Day for the Irish."

2 DOWNTRODDEN IRISH:

The Centuries of Troubles

My own first trip to Ireland possessed elements of stealth.
W. R. Hearst, Jr., and I touched down at Foynes on a long,
slow flight from wartime London to New York. It was November 1943. As the lumbering Sunderland flying boat neared the
neutral Emerald Isle—which was as gray and chilled as an
onion that day—we changed out of our American war correspondent uniforms and into business suits. We had been told that
Ireland might intern us if we appeared in uniform.

The passengers on the plane queued up and inched slowly
past the desk of an old gentleman—whose name turned out
to be Fergus—who scrutinized each passport and, upon due deliberation, stamped the edge of a page.

I was last in line. The old man's impersonal air changed when
he read my name. He looked up at me, measuring me in a kindly
way, and said one of the dearest things I've ever heard.

"I was in jail with many a Considine," he said.

Several passengers within earshot burst into laughter and the raucous noises they made offended the old man. He silenced them with a stare.

"It was an honor to be in jail during the T(h)rouble," he said with great dignity. And, of course, he was right. Not to have a jail record was for a long time a handicap for any true Irishman, for it implied indifference to a great and glorious crusade for freedom or, worse, submission to powerful pressures working against that ambition.

He took me out of the stuffy little terminal and pointed across the misty wastes.

"Ennis, in Clare, is over that way," he said, pointing. "Your people came from there. Some of them are still in the trees."

(I discovered on subsequent trips into Ennis that this was a villainous canard on the part of the old guy. Most of the Considines in Ennis are respectable saloonkeepers, butchers, confectioners.)

There was a delay at Foynes, and Fergus had some time off. Not only that, he was willing to introduce a re-immigrant to the land.

Our car meandered through towns and villages, past Ballycotton, until we reached the fishing village of Cloyne. We followed a sign pointing to Castlemary Demesne, and a few minutes later we stopped. Fergus said: "This is the beginning."

He pointed and I saw three huge stones supporting a third stone across their tops—a kind of giant stone bench. It reminded me of the mysterious stone circles at Stonehenge in England. "This is called a dolmen," said Fergus, "and it's a very good one. No one knows who built this or other dolmens in Ireland, or why they were built, but some people believe they may have been the altars of sun worshipers. In any case, they probably date back to about the year 2000 B.C. There are some rock scribblings, graves, and pottery from that same era but the people who left these marks of civilization failed to tell us when they arrived on this island and where they came from."

"And before they arrived," I asked, "this place was deserted?"

"Well," Fergus said, "there is a story written somewhere that a granddaughter of Noah, a lady named Cessair, arrived forty days before the Flood. The ark was fully booked, so she brought her husband, father, brother, and retinue of servants here to escape the rising waters. But Cessair became angry at Noah and threatened to give up his God for an idol. The Flood came and they were all drowned. According to some Irish historians, this happened in the year 2242 in the history of the world. But they had their own way of counting. That's not the same as 2242 B.C."

"Then, who did come to Ireland to live?"

Fergus cited an ancient manuscript, *The Book of Invasions*. This account, written sometime in the thirteenth century, but probably started much earlier, tells of five great invasions of Ireland. Hordes from Spain, Greece, and other parts of Europe overran the island in successive waves. There were great battles which provided many a song and story for the minstrel of later years.

"Were these invasion stories true?"

He shrugged. "Who can say? No doubt some truth is mixed with the mythology of ancient heroes. We know that Aristotle wrote of Ireland, calling it 'Iernia.' Plutarch referred to it as 'Ogyia' or 'most ancient.' They probably had heard of those 'barbarians' who lived beyond the edges of civilization. It seems certain, though, that Ireland's main colonizers were Gaelic Celts from France and the north of Spain. They pushed—or were driven here—about 350 before Christ. The Druid traditions they brought with them were superimposed on the paganism of the people already here. For example, the old Celtic name for Ireland was 'Everio' or 'Eriu.' Now, Eriu was the sun goddess— so it is possible that the island was named for the sun worshipers who lived here and built dolmens like this one. From Eriu we got the modern name for Ireland of Eire, so these pagan influences are still with us.

"In the years of the Celts," Fergus continued, "Ireland became much more than a forest. It had the richest gold deposits in the European area. Skilled artisans turned out beautiful works in gold, bronze, and brilliant white bronze."

"It was strange," I said, "that the Romans never came to conquer."

"They never did," he said. "Agricola, the invader of Britain, was told he could have that little island across the water by dispatching one legion. Maybe he decided it wasn't worth the effort. Anyway, Ireland went its own way, drifting through the centuries. It was rural—no big cities. The family, or sept, was the basic unit of the society. It held property in common. Each community was called a tuath and was ruled by no less than a king. Perhaps there were one hundred or more kings in Ireland at any one time—a rather high number considering the limited terrain. But even without a powerful central government, Ireland did have one special quality which we think distinguishes it from other countries in those early days—cultural unity. I mean, we were the first to turn our language into a distinctive form of literature, native to us, reflecting our legends and our way of life."

"Yes," I said, "and Gaelic has survived even Latin as a spoken language."

"Before the Irish adapted Gaelic to the Latin alphabet," said Fergus, "they had an alphabet of their own called Ogham. Twenty letters or sounds were represented by combinations of vertical or slanting lines. I'll show you some inscriptions on stone pillars. It's read from top to bottom like Chinese, looks a little like shorthand, and can be turned into sign language."

He held his two index fingers at right angles to form a T. "This," he said, "had the sound of B and the whole alphabet can be done this way with the hands—something we can't do with the alphabet we use today.

"So much for the ancients," said Fergus. "This Druid, pagan business has a strange fascination and will hypnotize you if you let it. Let's go. There is so much more to see—centuries more."

The sight of those strange rocks did stir my curiosity about this island and its people. I wanted to see as much, hear as much, read as much about them as I could.

Three other stops on that tour brought us into another era— a "new beginning" for the Irish people. We climbed the rugged Croagh Patrick rising out of the Mayo plain, crowned by a small chapel. It was on that peak, the scholars tell us, that St. Patrick was granted the power to drive the snakes and/or toads from Ireland.

There is the island on Lough Derg in Donegal, where St. Patrick had his vision of purgatory. An incorrigibly enduring story surrounds this place. It's said that in the twelfth century, a knight in the service of King Stephen of England, crawled through a cave on the island, crossed a bridge and found himself in purgatory. The word spread, and soon pilgrims from many lands were searching for the cave. Finally, Pope Alexander VI ordered the pilgrimage abandoned and the cave filled in. This was done on St. Patrick's Day in 1497. But soon another cave appeared nearby, and the pilgrims resumed their journeys. Other attempts were made to ban what were thought to be heathen superstition, but it took an act of the English Parliament in the eighteenth century to close the second cave. A chapel named for St. Patrick was built there, and the island now has a church and hostels for tourists. Still they come.

A third compelling look at the past is a treasure stored in the library of Trinity College in Dublin. There, in a glass case, is the Book of Kells, a magnificently illustrated volume of Gospels, inscribed sometime in the sixth century by St. Columba or other gifted craftsmen. From time to time, the pages are turned so

[15]

that sunlight will not dim the coloring of the rich ornamentation. It is with justification that some medieval scholars call this the "most beautiful book in the world."

This trio in a sense sums up a brilliant period in Ireland's history. It opens in the year 432 A.D. with the arrival of St. Patrick. Actually, he was probably making his second trip to Ireland. Scholars say he lived in western Britain as a youth, was seized by the Irish King Niall in a raid and brought to Ireland as a slave. After six years, he escaped, went to France to study and then returned, ordained, to bring Christianity to the people who had once been his masters. One source says his arrival was greeted by a volley of stones from the hostile natives, and that later, at Tara, home of the High Kings, he was attacked by King Laoghaire, (pronounced Leary). If true, the wonder is not that this missionary had resistance to overcome, but that so little resistance was offered, that pagan leaders encouraged him and even offered land on which to build his churches. It was as though the Irish were waiting for Patrick.

The possibility of conflict was lessened by the fact that the teacher was no zealot intent on replacing the old order with the new. What Patrick did was to build Christianity on the framework of the existing society. Pagan rites, Gaelic customs were cloaked with new meaning. Seasonal feasts were observed in honor of saints, and church relics took the place of magic charms. When Patrick died in 461, it was obvious that his mission had been a stupendous success.

The Church brought Latin to Ireland, with the cultural nourishment of writers and philosophers of other times and places. Formerly, knowledge and traditions were passed from one generation to another by the spoken story. Now it was necessary to read to study the Bible. Learning and teaching captivated the dynamic, imaginative Gaelic mind, and soon Ireland became a literary country. Scholars laboring in monasteries produced such wonders as the "Book of Kells." Christianity drew them to Rome,

[16]

and along the way they preached in market places and taught in schools. Ireland became known as the isle of saints and scholars. Its missionaries helped keep alive the flickering light of learning during an age that promised to return man to the cave.

In this golden age of Ireland, spearmakers turned to artisans, warriors to farmers, kings to cattle raisers. The island prospered, military traditions withered, and this storehouse of learning felt itself safe from the barbarians beyond the seas. Alas! This peaceful land became a tempting target of the warlike, plundering Norsemen. About 800 A.D., the Swedes, Norwegians, and Danes began their raids on homes and monasteries. At first, they attacked and fled with what they could carry. Later, some remained to settle on river banks. In the year 852, they built a fort on a hilltop and a town grew around the fort. It was near a "dark pool"—in Gaelic, *dubh linn*—and the town, founded by the Danes, became the city of Dublin.

The Norsemen also settled Wicklow, Waterford, Cork, and Limerick, giving Ireland its first towns. The invaders made one other important contribution. Their presence brought unity and leadership. And the Irish learned from them. From north Munster came the greatest of the Irish kings, Brian Boru, to give his people a unified command for the first and last time in the Gaelic world. In battle after battle, Brian defeated the Norsemen, delivering the final blow at the Battle of Clontarf on Good Friday in the year 1014. Two hundred years of Norse domination had ended. The invaders lost Ireland, but Ireland lost Brian Boru. The King was killed at Clontarf. Warring factions picked up their quarrels where Brian had stopped them, and one historian wrote: "The hundred and fifty years that followed . . . remain practically a blank in Irish history."

For Ireland, the golden age was over.

The long and historic troubles with neighboring England began in the next century. In 1155, it's said, the writer and churchman, John of Salisbury, was sent by the Plantaganet King of England, Henry II, to Pope Adrian IV. The Pope, Nicholas Breakspeare, the only Englishman ever to be Pontiff, granted Ireland to Henry who said he would reform its Church and put an end to the constant fighting among miscellaneous kings.

One of the troublemakers, Dermot MacMurrough, King of Leinster, had been pushed out of Ireland in a power feud with two other kings, and took refuge in England. The thought of treason did not interfere with his desire for revenge, and King Henry was only too glad to take advantage of this local rivalry. Henry also was having his problems with some ambitious Norman barons in Wales. Here was an opportunity of great promise. Henry sent Dermot to see the Earl of Pembroke, nicknamed "Strongbow" by his friends and foes on the battlefield. The turncoat Irish king offered Pembroke his daughter's hand in marriage, and the right to succeed to the throne of Leinster, if Pembroke would help him crush those who had expelled him from Ireland. The deal was made, and a new invasion of Ireland was on.

In 1170, the forces of Dermot and Pembroke captured Dublin. Soon after this victory, Dermot died and Pembroke claimed the throne which had been promised him. When the news reached England, Henry was anything but pleased. One of the Norman barons he feared gave all indications that he planned to take over all of Ireland with its resources and manpower. That alarmed Henry so much that the following year, he led his own invasion of Ireland, and nearly all the kings pledged their support to him and agreed to pay tribute. The English Pope was, of course, on the side of the King of England. The Archbishops and the Bishops were told they must support Henry. The Church must be strengthened and the sinful natives reformed.

Historians, with hindsight's 20-20 vision, have bemoaned the fact that the Earl of Pembroke was not allowed to conquer all Ireland, or that King Henry, having put Pembroke in his place, failed to do so. They reason that under strong rule, Ireland might have been united, peaceful, and eventually prosperous again. As it was, Ireland was not conquered. For decades, king fought king, natives battled the Norman nobility, and everyone resisted the English colonists. After more than two hundred years of this, England's King Richard II described Ireland as divided among "the wild Irish, English rebels and the obedient English."

England's control was confined to areas she could physically protect—the Pale, it was called. Beyond the Pale were the terrible Irish natives and rebels not fit to live in a proper society. England wanted to make certain that its culture and people were not "contaminated" by any contact with these undesirables. Separation of peoples and the superiority of one nation to another were ordered by law. In 1366, the Statute of Kilkenny made it a crime for those within the Pale to marry an Irish person, use the Irish language, follow Irish law or custom, or even dress like the Irish. If one had an Irish name, he was instructed to drop it forever and take another indicating his vocation, town, or background. Irish priests were barred from English cathedrals and monasteries. Irish poets and minstrels were banned. The Statute of Kilkenny was a ruthless attempt to put an ancient culture in quarantine. But as bad as it was, it was only a beginning.

While the rest of the world moved forward, the native Irish moved backward. A nation of chiefs, warriors, artisans, farmers, teachers became a pitiful assemblage of cowherds, woodcutters, laborers, servants, and ignorant peasants. The only important elements of their lives left to them were their religion and Celtic traditions.

The meaning of religion to the Irish is examined in a later chapter, but it should be said here that Catholicism played a great role in the political history of the day. The Anglo-Normans whose ancestors had invaded Ireland several generations back had little use for the native Irish, who were considered to be barbarians. But in time, a strange thing happened. Instead of the Irish becoming like the Normans, the Normans became (in that well-known phrase) more Irish than the Irish.

When Henry VIII broke with Rome and England turned to the Protestant Reformation, the Normans were drawn even closer to the native Irish because they shared the same religion. That unity, in turn, frightened England. Policy toward Ireland grew tougher, and the Irish resistance stiffened. The scene was set for an all-out struggle.

King Henry II had claimed a Lordship over Ireland by a grant from the Pope. Now, King Henry VIII claimed the same authority while denouncing the power of a later Pontiff. More than that, the often-married monarch decided to give himself the title of "King of Ireland." He was already Supreme Head of the Church of England. He wanted to become Supreme Head of the Church in that country, and he ordered the Irish to stop sending money to Rome. The Irish clergy thundered defiance. But Henry concentrated on trying to win over clan chiefs by promising them lands and new titles. In any country, there are those who will work with foreign invaders for a profit, and Henry found several in Ireland. These favors bought some stanch support. But when England's king made a direct attack on the church, closed monasteries and donated some of their lands to the newly titled aristocracy, Church and people fought back with valor.

The resistance continued through the reign of Henry's successor, Edward VI.

Then, a Catholic returned to the throne of England. The oppressed Irish certainly hoped for mercy, if not sympathy from Queen Mary. But she was more English than Catholic as far as her policy toward Ireland was concerned.

It was Mary Tudor who introduced the hated policy of plantation. That meant, simply, the confiscation of Irish lands by English settlers. The native Irish were told they must give up two-thirds of their property to newcomers from England. The settlers would have English servants and English soldiers to guard them. Mary began by confiscating the territories of Leix and Offaly, and renaming them Queen's County and King's County. The lands of the O'Mores, O'Conors, and O'Dempseys were seized, and the occupants moved out to barren bog land. But the Irish fought back with such determination that some confiscations occurred only on paper, and eventually the policy was modified and some leaders were even handed back their lands.

Obviously, it occurred to the Irish that they might be able to throw out the English if they had support from European powers. Naturally they turned to the Catholic powers—France, Spain, and Rome. When a group of English cavaliers asked the Queen's permission to seize thousands of acres held by the Desmonds in south Ireland, the Desmonds rallied support from Italy and Spain. But the Irish and their small band of foreign soldiers were crushed. The Desmonds lost most of their land.

One historian of the time, Philip Wilson, made the prediction that if Queen Mary had lived twenty years and continued her policies toward fellow Catholics in Ireland, the Irish would have turned into the most violent Calvinists in Europe!

When Queen Elizabeth I took the throne, Irish resistance was frenzied, and the English force grew more ruthless. It called forth the now familiar "scorched earth" policy. Crops were burned and cattle slaughtered in a deliberate attempt to drain Ireland of all resources and weaken the people by starvation and futility.

Queen Elizabeth continued the practice of plantation. In 1586, she confiscated thousands of acres in Munster and handed them to "undertakers," so named because they undertook to import tenants from England to settle on the land. But these colonial agents had trouble convincing their fellow Englishmen that Ireland was the correct place to live and bring up their children. So, the undertakers finally had to resort to placing Irish tenants on the seized land. That proved a financial failure and Queen Elizabeth finally gave up on plantation.

She faced three serious rebellions. The biggest threat to England's power came from Hugh O'Neill, Earl of Tyrone. For nine years, O'Neill and a kinsman, Hugh Roe O'Donnell, battled the English from their stronghold in Ulster. It looked as though the Irish might be able to hold on indefinitely despite an English blockade. But a Spanish expedition sent to help O'Neill landed in the south of Ireland and was hemmed in by the English. The Irish broke through and went to the aid of their allies. On Christmas Eve in 1601, the Irish and their Spanish friends were defeated. In the next few years, O'Neill and other Gaelic leaders who held the title of Earl fled to the Continent and never returned. English law supplanted Gaelic law. Gaelic land divisions were outlawed. Gaelic literary and social traditions began to disappear. An ancient civilization was crumbling. Gaelic Ireland was dead.

The "flight of the Earls" opened the way for the greedy seizure of more Irish lands. The first of the Stuarts, King James I, inherited the English throne and with it the problem of Ireland. He was relieved to learn that O'Neill and O'Donnell had left Ulster for Europe and he hoped that with the leaders gone, this difficult province would settle down and cease to be a threat. How could he make certain? Perhaps plantation was the answer, but this time it must be done wisely, avoiding past mistakes.

It was easy enough to take over the lands of all absent Earls. When a minor chief caused trouble, the English used the incident as an excuse to confiscate six counties of Ulster—more than half-a-million acres. The land was turned over to the "undertakers" again with instructions that the tenants must be English or Scottish Protestants. This time, plantation was a success—from the English point of view. Joint enterprises sprang up—with headquarters in London. The plantation of Derry was renamed Londonderry. Both England and Ulster prospered from new trade.

The native Irish, stung by the land-grab, looked on sullenly. As Ulster grew richer, and new measures made them poorer and more miserable, their anger mounted to fury. In 1641, the Irish swooped down on the Ulster Protestants in what the Puritans call the "Great Massacre." Some accounts say 10,000 were killed, some say 100,000. In any case, England sent troops to fight the rebellion, and offered more Irish lands to persons contributing money to the campaign. In 1642, the Irish chiefs and English Catholics in the Pale joined forces in the Confederation of Kilkenny, and Presbyterians, angry at Episcopalian intolerance, supported the Catholic alliance. The Irish rebels were encouraged by strife within England, and hopeful of better things when King Charles I lost his head.

Once again, changes in England brought even darker days to Ireland. This time, a new ruler spelled disaster. It was the ruthless despot, Oliver Cromwell. He had marked Ireland for destruction. As soon as he was able to do so, he devoted his full energies to the task. Cromwell decided there had been entirely too much leniency in dealing with the Irish and that the "nonsense" of rebellion had gone on long enough. The Irish rebels must be crushed, the whole country brought under the control of the English Parliament, and Catholicism eradicated.

In 1649, Cromwell and his troops landed in Ireland and began a merciless slaughter. At Drogheda, he wiped out a garrison which had surrendered—soldiers, priests, and civilians, including women and children. And praised God!

"It hath pleased God to bless our endeavours at Tredah," he reported. "After battery, we stormed it. The enemy were about 3000 strong in the town. They made a stout resistance, and near 1000 of our men being entered, the enemy forced them out again. But God, giving a new courage to our men, they attempted again, and entered, beating the enemy from their defences. The enemy had made three entrenchments, both to the right and left of where we entered; all which they were forced to quit. Being then entered, we refused them quarter; having the day before summoned the town. I believe we put to the sword the whole number of the defendants. I do not think thirty of the whole number escaped with their lives. Those that did, are in safe custody for the Barbadoes . . . I wish that all honest hearts may give the glory of this to God alone, to whom indeed the praise of this mercy belongs."

The next year, Kilkenny, capital of the Irish resistance, surrendered, and a few months later, Cromwell was able to return to England, leaving mopping-up operations to his son-in-law, Ireton. Guerrilla fighters kept up the struggle in the west for a few years, but the cause was hopeless. Disease and hunger took over where the conquering soldiers left off. Population figures are only estimates, but it's said that warfare and pestilence reduced Ireland's number to about half a million.

Earlier overlords had taken large tracts of land from the Irish as war spoils and punishment for resistance. But Cromwell was not a believer in half measures. The English Parliament declared that all Ireland was forfeited. Protestants were handed the lands of Catholics in Ulster, Leinster, and Munster. The poor working people of Ireland were pardoned and told they could remain where they were to be of service to the new privileged class of foreign settlers and adventurers. Wealthier or land-owning Roman Catholics suspected of any rebel sympathies were ordered to move themselves and their families across the River Shannon into County Clare and desolate Connacht. Their harsh fate is recalled for succeeding generations by the phrase "to hell or Connacht."

For others, defeat meant banishment or virtual slavery. Roman Catholic officers and those who fought with them were allowed, and even encouraged, to leave the country. Thirty-four thousand of them marched off to serve in the armies of Catholic powers in Europe—France, Spain, Austria, and the little Republic of Venice. Young and potentially effective leadership was lost to Ireland when she needed it most.

The orphans of war, young boys and girls and young women were led from poor houses and country huts and herded aboard ships bound for the plantations of the West Indies. Colonial planters offered to pay by the head for healthy, young field hands and servants, maids, household managers, and companions. It was good business for the dealers in human cargo. For many of the six-thousand forced emigrants, the move also proved to be a good one. It put them and their descendants close to the New World, and many took advantage of the steppingstone.

Cromwell died in 1658, and after a year of indecision, England looked to royalty for the splendor, sanity and stability of by-gone days. Charles II, the Stuart heir to the throne who had been in exile in Holland, was invited to claim the royal scepter, and when he entered London in late May 1660, he was cheered like a conquering hero. Immediately, the King's backers turned on the Puritans for revenge. Those responsible for the execution of Charles I were marked for punishment and several were put to death. The new group in control went so far as to drag Cromwell's body from the tomb, and order it suspended by chains from the gallows for a whole day. Even Cromwell's Irish victims could hardly derive much satisfaction from such revolting vengeance.

Once again, the Irish waited in vain for signs of mercy and toleration from a new reign in England. Charles II was followed by his brother, James II, an avowed Catholic, but the Stuarts had meant nothing but trouble for Ireland and James played his role along with the rest. He was forced to flee England in the bloodless revolution of 1688, the throne being offered to the Dutch Protestant, William of Orange. A year later, with the support of France, James tried to fight his way back to England. He landed in Ireland, rallied English-hating Catholics around him and the battle was on. For two years it raged. Finally, at the Boyne and at Aughrim, William's forces scored decisive victories. James slipped back to France, leaving the Irish and their allies to pay the penalty for picking the wrong side in another English power struggle. For Ireland, it was another costly mistake.

The Irish commander, Patrick Sarsfield, surrendered in 1691 at Limerick. His field commanders and their troops left their homes as others had done a half century earlier and sailed to join the armies of Catholic nations in Europe. In all, Ireland lost another fourteen thousand men whose courage and intelligence were sorely needed.

Despair and degradation awaited those who remained. They were punished with a final, sweeping act of confiscation. An English writer, Arthur Young, in 1780 put it this way: "Nineteen-twentieths of the kingdom changed hands from Catholic to Protestant. The lineal descendants of great families, once possessed of vast property, are now to be found all over the kingdom in the lowest situation, working as cottars."

The treaty signed at Limerick promised the Catholics religious toleration, but the agreement was only a scrap of paper powerless to resist the new penal code. This series of statutes was designed to crush the Irish Catholics once and for all with severe limitations on land holdings and disposals, inheritance, education, and business activities, bans on keeping weapons, holding public office, or voting.

The penal laws are examined in greater detail in the chapter on religion. For the time being, we can note two results: these harsh measures only succeeded in driving the Catholic Irish underground, but not in shaking their devotion to religion.

All the Irish, Catholics and Protestants alike, felt the effects of English economic oppression. Parliament first halted the sale in England of Irish cattle, sheep, and hogs. Then it banned Irish trade with the colonies. The heaviest blow came in 1698 with the ban on the prosperous woolen industry. In effect, England made Ireland grazing farmland and set back its development by several centuries while other nations were preparing for the new age marked by the Industrial Revolution.

The Catholics struggled under the penal code and the Protestants under economic restrictions, and eventually both groups made some progress. In 1745, Lord Chesterfield deliberately overlooked some of the religious laws, and because the English needed manpower, Catholics were allowed to join the English Army.

In the 1760s, both the Catholics in the south and the Presbyterian dissenters in the north formed secret societies to resist outrageously high rents and the collection of tithes to support the Church of England. Catholics donned white shirts to disguise themselves on enforcement missions and prevent any one man from being singled out by the clothes he wore, and so they were called Whiteboys. In the north, these resistance groups were named Hearts of Oak Boys, and later Hearts of Steel Boys. Despite their common economic problem, the Protestants continued to be suspicious of Catholic motives and the possibility of Catholic gains. An organization known as Peep-o-Day Boys raided Catholic homes, looking for weapons, usually striking early in the morning. Gangs also tried to prevent Catholics from bidding on property or gaining any sort of business control. The Catholics, in turn, formed about 1785 their own protective society called The Defenders and the government seized every opportunity to promote feuding between the rival groups to keep Ireland divided and obscure the economic issues. But there were many examples of unity for a common cause.

A Protestant, Henry Grattan, was the leader of the battle for freedom and rights for all Catholic Irish.

The newly independent Irish legislature, meeting first in 1782, swept away all the remaining penal laws with one exception: Catholics were still barred from Parliament.

In the 1790s, the Catholic Committee for Irish Freedom joined forces with the Society of United Irishmen, formed by Protestants in Belfast. Both groups yearned for a united Irish Republic and were forced to go underground by the government.

By this time, both the American and French revolutions had set examples to the freedom-minded victims of oppression throughout the world, and it was the French cry of "Liberty, Equality, Fraternity" which captured the imagination of a young Presbyterian barrister, Theobald Wolfe Tone. He was a revolutionary who wanted to throw England out of Ireland on behalf of the Rights of Man. (Ironically, Wolfe Tone was the descendant of a planter sent to Ireland by Cromwell.) The French were excited by Tone's plan and sent three separate fleets with troops to aid the Irish in their uprising of 1798. Each one met with disaster.

Even with foreign help, the Irish never were able to dislodge the English, though the attempt was made several times. The suppression of this rebellion was just as bloody, just as efficient as the stamping out of previous struggles against land seizures, crop burning, and religious persecutions.

The English had spies operating within the United Irishmen, who kept the government informed of every meeting, every plan. Ringleaders were rounded up in a series of arrests. Police and troops battled the rebels in fierce engagements, and, in some areas, the peasants were led into battle by priests. But the strength of the government was too great.

Tone was captured. A court-martial denied his request that he face a firing squad like any soldier convicted of treason, and sentenced him to be hanged and disemboweled. Tone cheated the hangman by taking his own life, and the rebellion of 1798 ended in tragedy for him and for thousands of Irishmen whose only crime had been a desire for freedom and the willingness to fight for it.

The price of the unsuccessful rebellion was paid in still another way—the end of Parliamentary independence for Ireland. The Act of Union in 1800 followed the pattern set by the fusion of the English and Scottish Parliaments a hundred years before. Irish Protestants were permitted to send representatives to London, and the government took the new title of the "United Kingdom of Great Britain and Ireland."

Ten years before the outbreak of the rebellion, during the American struggle for freedom, George Washington had written: "Patriots of Ireland! Champions of liberty in all lands—be strong in hope! Your cause is identical with mine!"

Some of the refugees of 1798 found their way to the United States. Not only did the newly independent nation offer them escape, it symbolized the hope of the Catholic Irishman for political and religious toleration, the hope of all for economic opportunity, the chance to make a fresh start.

In addition, the United States had the distinction of success in a struggle against England. For three hundred years, the Irish had looked to Spain, France, and Rome for physical and spiritual help in their fight. Aid had been offered, but in the phrase of a later day, usually turned out to be "too little and too late" or geographically misdirected and badly co-ordinated. Perhaps the United States, by its example or with concrete aid and counsel could help Ireland along the same path.

3 EARLY AMERICAN IRISH:

Fighters of the Revolution

No one knows when the first Irishman reached the shores of the New World, and there is no statue in his honor. He may have been the "William from Galway" listed among the crew of Christopher Columbus. Or, he may have beaten William and Columbus by more than nine hundred years! A Vatican manuscript tells the romantic story of St. Brendan of Clonfert, who sailed westward from Ireland sometime in the sixth century A.D., and sighted land not found on any maps of the day. The story, true or not, was so widely circulated that for hundreds of years, nearly every map maker drew an "Insula Sancti Brendani" somewhere in the unknown waters west of Europe.

Another strange and interesting point is the reference to the American continent in old Norse writings as "Greater Ireland" —a curious name for a land touched by the Norse hero, Leif Ericson.

As fascinating as these foggy footnotes to history are, it would be straying from our main story to weigh the evidence in the case of St. Brendan or trace the ancestry of William from Galway. It would be equally time-consuming to search old records for the name of the first Irish person to settle permanently in North America and the year he or she arrived. For years, scholars have been thumbing through marriage and baptismal certificates, land grants, tax and rent lists, wills, deeds, ship passenger lists, and the like. Some have consulted such weighty and all-enveloping publications as: John Hotten's *Original Lists of Persons of Quality; Emigrants; Religious Exiles; Political Rebels; Serving Men Sold for a Term of Years; Apprentices; Children Stolen; Maidens Pressed; and Others Who Went from Great Britain to the American Plantations, 1600–1700.* These documents fail to give a conclusive answer, and the answer is not vital to our story.

The important point is: there were Irish in the American colonies from the first settlements. One of the earliest descriptions of life in Virginia known to scholars was written in Gaelic by a Francis Maguire, and dated 1609. A few years later, the first recorded Irish settlement grew up on the present site of Newport News. One of New York's provincial governors was Irish-born Thomas Dongan. Many familiar Irish names turn up in chronicles of Colonial life in New England. But the North was not the only stronghold of these first Irish immigrants. In that first official census of 1790, the number of persons born in Ireland, not counting those of Irish descent, is set down as 44,000. Of these, more than half lived south of Pennsylvania.

Many of the earliest Irish immigrants were exiled during Cromwell's reign of terror, and shipped off to sugar plantations in the West Indies. Years later, some bought their freedom and others escaped to find refuge in the Carolinas and Virginia. Some Irish were landholders of wealth who resented the restrictions placed upon them because they were Catholics. They sold their estates and joined with Catholics from England to found the colony of Maryland. The Carroll family of Carrollton is the best example of an early Irish dynasty. The first Carrolls arrived in Maryland before 1700. One became governor of Maryland,

and his grandson Charles Carroll was a signer of the Declaration of Independence and later a United States senator. Another member of the family, John Carroll, became the first American bishop and the first Catholic Archbishop of Baltimore.

Pennsylvania also attracted large numbers of Irish by its reputation for encouraging freedom of conscience. Some of William Penn's chief advisers and the colony's most influential citizens came from Ireland. South Carolina's port city of Charleston saw Irish immigrants set their first foot on the relatively free ground of the New World.

Up North, there were enough Irish in Boston to hold a formal celebration of St. Patrick's Day in 1737. In New York, the first recorded observance of any size was in 1762, although smaller celebrations could have been held earlier.

It is impossible to pursue the story of this era very far without running straight into the controversy which has been labeled "Scotch-Irish" versus "Mere Irish."

A generation or more ago, it became fashionable among some groups of historical writers to view the settlement of the American colonies and the struggle for freedom as a virtual monopoly of the English. The Bradfords, Cabots, Smiths, and others with an Anglo-Saxon ring to their names were prominently featured in the saga—and rightly so. But when a Maguire or O'Donnell distinguished himself, these writers generally referred to him as "Scotch-Irish."

The line of reasoning went like this: most of the people who came here from Ireland before 1820 were from Ulster, and the people who lived in Ulster were transplanted Presbyterians from Scotland; therefore, these early emigrants should be called "Scotch-Irish" to separate them from the torrents of plain Irish, most of them Catholic, who streamed across the Atlantic after 1820.

Professor Wayland Dunaway of Pennsylvania State college elaborates on this point of view in his book *The Scotch-Irish of*

Colonial Pennsylvania, published in 1944. He writes that the term (Scotch-Irish) "has been the customary usage in the nomenclature of American history and literature for so long a time, and is commonly understood by the people, that it appears to be straining a point to challenge it at this late day." Professor Dunaway cites a number of sources, including an English clergyman who referred in a letter dated 1728 to "the Irish (who usually call themselves Scotch-Irish). . . ."

The claim that the term was in "customary usage" is disputed by other writers with Irish ancestors.

Shaemas O'Sheel of New York, a poet and third generation Irish-American, contended that no member of the Scotch-Irish faction had ever quoted a single written or spoken line in which the phrase was used by a so-called "Scotch-Irishman" during Colonial or early Revolutionary times.

As for the argument that the first Irish in America were from Ulster and nearly all Presbyterian Scots, O'Sheel said his relatives lived in Ulster before St. Patrick arrived, stayed there through the immigration from Scotland and England and remained Catholic. Ulster never was without its "Old Irish" families, whether they were landowners, tenants, field workers, or servants.

It's true that the flow of people from Ulster to the American colonies increased to about twelve thousand a year between 1725 and 1750. But many of the immigrants had family roots in Ireland for four or five generations, and if one of them had been asked where he came from, it's doubtful that he would have said anything but "Ireland." In fact, a small group of Irish met in Boston in 1737 to form a charitable society. They met on St. Patrick's Day and the name they chose was "The Irish Society." They were Presbyterians.

What this controversy boils down to is: Just who are the Irish, anyway? Are they only the descendants of the Gaelic Celts who were in the reception committee for St. Patrick when he arrived?

What of the Danes and Swedes who sailed in on Viking ships to establish Ireland's first towns? What of the French and the Spaniards who stepped off invasion ships and stayed on to become husbands and fathers? For that matter, what of the English planters Cromwell put on confiscated Irish land whose descendants became heroes of the Irish freedom movements like Wolfe Tone's? What of the Irish forced to drop obviously "Irish" names by the English Parliament in 1465, in favor of towns, colors, and professions, becoming Whites, Browns, Smiths, Taylors, and Butlers? Among these groups, is one more Irish than another?

We never hear of the Danish-Irish, the Spanish-Irish, or the English-Irish, yet some writers insist on crediting the "Scotch-Irish" with any and all accomplishments in the American colonies. Some, like William Clemens, scanned early marriage records and came to the startling conclusion that nine-tenths of the colonists in New England and Virginia were English. One-tenth he allotted to the Dutch, Swedes, and Germans. Where were the Irish? Hiding, apparently, for when Michael J. O'Brien looked over the records a few years later, he discovered names such as Callahan, Lynch, and O'Hogan. They *could* have been English or German, but it's not very likely.

In a letter to Louis Adamic, published in Adamic's A *Nation of Nations*, O'Brien mentions John Alden and Priscilla Mullens as two colonists who did not deny their Irish heritage. Governor John Winthrop of the Massachusetts Bay Colony wrote that "Darby Field, an Irishman" had discovered the White Mountains. The date—about 1632. Records show that "Irish and Scottish gentlemen" settled along the Merrimack River two years later. In 1654, the ship *Goodfellow* arrived in Boston with four hundred people from Ireland. Even then, some natives wondered whether the Irish were trying to take over the country and there were calls for a halt to Irish immigration.

O'Brien also notes that new settlements were springing up

with Old World names like Belfast and Limerick in Maine, Londonderry in Vermont, Dublin and Antrim in New Hampshire, and Waterford in Connecticut.

Names, of course, can be misleading—especially as written in early records. For example, the overseer of the Dutch settlement of Beverwyck in New York in 1645, is listed at that time as "Jan Andriessen" but right after that name is: "de Iersman van Dublingh." He was John Anderson from Dublin! Similarly, other Dutch records contain references to a "Willem" or "Jan" who turn out to be "William" or "John" from "Irlandt."

Church records also can be misleading. Occasionally, one comes across the statement that New York City, for example, had few Irish before the 1800s because there were no Catholic churches there. The Irish population—so the argument goes— must have been limited to Maryland and Pennsylvania, where Catholic churches existed.

This viewpoint overlooks the evidence carved into weatherbeaten gravestones in Protestant churchyards, written in fading ink on marriage registers in Protestant churches, and set down on baptismal certificates. Hundreds of names identifiable as Irish are preserved for all time in the City of New York alone, and the records of Protestant churches in other early settlements confirm the presence of Irish. The fact is, those early immigrants from Ireland arrived before their church. Few towns had even one Catholic priest, so it was the Protestant church which performed the vital religious services of baptism, marriage, and burial. Certainly not all the Irish in the Colonies were Catholic, but many of the faith of Patrick found themselves turning to Protestant churches as the only houses of worship open to them, and the main center of decent social contact with their neighbors. Occasionally, the Catholics carried their prayerbooks and rosaries to the Protestant services, to the dismay of the clergyman.

Ship records give us some idea of the heavy traffic between

Irish and Colonial ports. In 1716–18, newspapers in New York and Philadelphia noted the arrivals of ships from Dublin, Waterford, and Cork with passenger lists running from 50 to 150 names.

A decade later when Pennsylvania levied an entrance duty on immigrants, ships' captains landed their human cargo at Burlington, New Jersey, and Newcastle, Delaware. The port tax failed to discourage newcomers. In fact, one newspaper noted that about two thousand Irish had arrived at Newcastle during one week in 1729, and another paper reported that more than five thousand had checked into the Colonies through Philadelphia that same year—about ten times the number arriving from other countries.

As the years rolled on, the Irish tide rose until James Logan, secretary to William Penn, and himself a Protestant Irishman noted with alarm the "crowds of foreigners, Irish Papists and convicts" walking down the gangplanks. One foreigner was worried by the arrival of other foreigners. Logan wrote: "It looks as if Ireland is to send all her inhabitants hither, for last week, not less than six ships arrived, and every day two or three also arrive."

So the number of Irish trying their luck on new shores increased from about twelve thousand per year in the mid-1700s to thirty-five thousand annually just before the Revolution. Many of them arrived just in time to shoulder a musket in a battle against their former homeland's ancient foe, England.

The Irish contribution to the struggle for independence is properly part of our chapter on "Fighting Irish," but let it be noted here that our Revolution, like most others, was the work of a determined minority. Many wealthy Tory colonists, businessmen, and landowners openly supported the British in the war, and even before the fighting started, many Colonial leaders considered talk of independence from England as the rantings of a lunatic fringe. When the bullheaded King George III allowed the rift with the Colonies to become an open break and the fight was on, General George Washington found many loyal, hard-fighting soldiers among the Irish. John Adams, who once blamed the Boston Massacre on a mob of "Irish Teagues," must have been grateful later for the mobs of Teagues, Connors, and Mulligans who joined Washington's army.

The Kellys actually outnumbered all the other clans with 695 listed on the muster rolls—more than any other name, including Smith.

Most estimates say that fully one-third of Washington's army was Irish, new or older generation.

The Irish not only fired muskets at the red coats, but helped create the very spirit of the Revolution. Four signers of the Declaration of Independence were born in Ireland: Colonel James Smith, George Taylor, Edward Rutledge, and Matthew Thornton. Five signers had Irish parents or grandparents: Thomas McKean, George Read, Robert Treat Paine, Charles Carroll, and Thomas Lynch, Jr. The section of the Declaration listing the wrongs inflicted upon the Colonies was mainly the work of John Sullivan, a member of the Continental Congress and one of the first agitators for independence.

The Sullivans were quite a family. Five of them were officers in Washington's army, and Mother Sullivan boasted later that when she had plowed, a future governor, judge, and attorney general of New Hampshire and a future governor of Massachusetts—her children—had tagged along after her.

John Rutledge, whose father was born in Ireland, wrote much of the final draft of the Constitution, and Alexis de Tocqueville said that the document bore "a personal stamp; one man made it and it was Rutledge." In 1795, this framer of the Constitution became Chief Justice of the United States, but during the blackest days of the struggle for independence, Rutledge was forced to shelve his belief in government by law. In 1780, when the British were at Charleston's door, the state's General Assembly voted Rutledge dictatorial powers. Other men in American history have held great authority in their cities, counties, or states, but no one has ever wielded such power as Rutledge and yielded it so readily when the danger had passed.

The McCarthy family can claim with great justification to be one of America's First Families. Five McCarthys were second cousins to George Washington and often visited Mount Vernon. When the first President was near death, he dictated the names of those who would be honorary pallbearers at his funeral, and three of the eleven names on the list were McCarthy.

Washington, who had few personal friends to relax with, seemed to enjoy the company of a witty, well-informed innkeeper, Patrick O'Flinn of Wilmington, Delaware. O'Flinn had been a captain in Washington's army, and whenever the former commander came to town, he'd spend the evening with the tavern owner, retelling wartime experiences.

Washington had reason to be fond of the Mulligan brothers in New York. Hugh was an export-import provision merchant, and Hercules a tailor and clothier. Both were friends of Alexander Hamilton, and after the British seized New York, Hamilton recommended the appointment of Hercules as Washington's confidential agent. The brothers remained in business, pretended to serve the British well with uniforms and provisions and were in a position to deliver valuable information to the Revolutionary forces. They provided the tip that helped save Washington from capture by the British on a trip to Newport in 1781. Naturally, some activities of the Mulligans aroused the ire of patriots in New York, and Washington felt obliged to save their reputations by inviting them to breakfast when the war had ended and the British were pulling out of New York.

The Irish who came to the Colonies and helped build the new nation were fighters, lawyers, public officials, merchants, physicians, teachers, writers, inventors, and explorers.

In 1765, Robert Fulton was born of poor Irish parents at

[38]

Little Britain, Pennsylvania. His formal education was limited to reading and writing, but he studied on his own time while apprenticed to a jeweler in Philadelphia and had a natural talent for portrait and landscape painting. It was not until his late twenties that Robert Fulton turned to mechanics. He invented flax and rope making machines, the *Nautilus*, a submarine designed to fire torpedoes, and finally a small steamboat. In 1807, Fulton launched the larger steamship, *Clermont*, on the Hudson and thousands of spectators were astonished as it started off toward Albany at the hair-raising speed of five miles per hour.

A colleague, Christopher Colles, shares with Fulton the honor of fathering the American canal system. Colles was director of navigation on the River Shannon before coming here in 1766. He introduced a lock system for canals and projected a plan for the Erie Canal before the Revolution began, halting further consideration of the ambitious venture. Colles drew the plans for the Croton Reservoir, source of New York City's water supply, and wrote the first road atlas published in the United States.

An Englishman who traveled in this country just after the Revolution, one J. Kent, is quoted as saying: "An Irishman, the instant he sets foot on American ground, becomes *ipso facto*, an American; this was uniformly the case during the whole of the late war. Whilst Englishmen and Scotsmen were regarded with jealousy and distrust, even with the best recommendation of zeal and attachment to their cause, a native of Ireland stood in need of no other certificate than his dialect. . . . Indeed, their conduct in the late Revolution amply justified this favourable opinion, for whilst the Irish emigrant was fighting the battles of America by sea and land, the Irish merchants . . . laboured with indefatigable zeal, and at all hazards . . . to increase the wealth and maintain the credit of the country; their purses were always open, and their persons devoted to the common cause. On more than one occasion, Congress owed their existence, and America possibly her preservation, to the fidelity and firmness of the Irish."

Another tribute came from historian David Ramsay, writing in 1789: "The Colonies which now form the United States may be considered as Europe transplanted. Ireland, England, Scotland, France, Germany, Holland, Switzerland, Sweden, Poland and Italy furnished the original stock . . . and are generally supposed to have contributed to it in the order named. For the last seventy or eighty years no nation has contributed nearly so much to the population of America as Ireland."

Although Ramsay did not foresee it, the main Irish contribution to America's population was still to come. In Ireland, new and terrible disasters would drive thousands more from their tiny homes and cottages, and send them in desperation to the United States where great opportunities awaited and a nation was straining to young manhood.

4 IMMIGRATING IRISH:
Out of the Land of Famine

"*Let any man go down to hell and open an Irishman's heart* there, and the first thing writ across it was land." The author is unknown, but his point is sound. For centuries, the Irishman had struggled to hold onto what little land he had and it was a losing battle. Wave after wave of invaders confiscated fertile fields and herded the native into desolate wastelands where he could not hope to produce enough to support a family. People died young, but families grew, adding mouths to feed. One estimate put the population of Ireland in 1791 at 4,753,000. In the next half century (before the potato famine), at least 1,750,000 left for America and other havens, but the census of 1841 revealed an amazing increase to 8,175,000 persons in Ireland: still more people in a country that had been condemned to agriculture and forbidden to join world commerce and industry.

The Irishman would raise cereal crops and livestock and then watch hungrily as the products of his toil were shipped off to England to pay the landlord. While others ate well on meat and wheat, he was forced to exist—and barely so—on the one crop which provided the greatest food yield per acre, the potato. The hard-working man of the family might consume as much as seven pounds of potatoes at each meal. He had them at morning, at noon, and at night. A family of five or six would devour a barrel of potatoes a week, eating them three times a day with a little salt and washing them down with skimmed milk, if times were good, or water if times were bad. In one year, an acre of good ground would yield about sixty barrels of potatoes, or a little more than the average family needed for its own table, but that was under ideal conditions. The possibility of plant failure or bad weather always hung over the farmer's head, and 1822 and 1831 were bad years for potato growers, imposing great hardship upon their families.

The potato just barely enabled the peasant to get along—not only in Ireland but throughout Europe—and those forced to base their incomes and their very lives upon it had to accept the bare minimum of housing, clothing, and the few luxuries of life then available. In Ireland, a vicious circle began with larger families leading to smaller inheritances for the children, greater dependence upon the potato, worn-out land, more poverty, still more people trying to live on land which would grow only potatoes, and so on. As time went on, said one historian, only revolution or catastrophe could break the sequence.

Still the Irishman never would allow hard times to interfere with the many pleasures of family life. Bishop James Doyle said at the time that Irishmen felt that marriage would not make them worse off, but might give them a companion for their suffering. As one poor farmer put it: "If I had a blanket to cover her I would marry the woman I liked; and if I could get potatoes enough to put into my children's mouths I would be as happy and content as any man."

That kind of human devotion has kept Ireland alive through war, disease, revolution, and natural disasters of all descriptions.

The Irishman's troubles were compounded by absentee landlords. Only about eight thousand persons held property in Ireland, and most of them lived in England or in countries farther away. In England and other countries, it was the custom of landlords to keep up their property with repairs and new additions as required, but in Ireland things were quite different. The tenant was expected to build or rebuild the structures on the land he rented, make all repairs, erect fencing, and have his own implements, and the return for his trouble was a higher rent due to the improvements he had made when the lease was ready for renewal. Or, worse yet, he could be ousted from the land he had worked on by someone else who offered higher rent—bitterly called "the grabber."

The real villain of the piece was not always the landlord, but his agent in charge of renting the property, who could be, and often was, a racketeering middleman. When it came time to renew the brief lease, the agent expected to collect a bribe from the poor tenant in the form of money or goods for himself and for his wife and family. The agent was out to get everything he could. Churchmen and public-minded citizens condemned the ruthless middlemen as "scavengers among the poor," as oppressors, as cruel moneylenders. Still they flourished.

The landlord also hired overseers and stewards who were detested with even greater fervor because they did the real dirty work—the actual seizing of crops or possessions when rents went unpaid, ordering the poor to make improvements they could ill afford, evicting tenants and wrecking their cabins to force them out. Under all these layers of authority was the Irish peasant, trapped, his life being squeezed out for the profit of others.

In the 1820s, when Ireland's pitiful economy was the victim of dropping grain prices and more and more tenants failed to pay their rents, landlords decided there were greater profits in clearing their lands for cattle grazing. Out went the tenants, women sobbing, men vowing vengeance, but they had no recourse in a legal sense and no way to fight the guns and clubs of men sent to evict them. Between 1838 and 1843, about 357,000 persons were turned out of their wretched but beloved cottages. Some were forced to move to poorhouses or workhouses established by the English. The man responsible for the system under the Poor Law, George Nichols, reported on the condition of the peasants in these words: "Their mode of living is unhappily so low that the establishment of one still lower is difficult."

If the Irishman could avoid the workhouse, he became a "spalpeen"—a migrant worker. He would walk barefoot to Dublin, pay his passage over to England, then tread through the countryside as far north as Scotland to help one farmer for a few days or a week before moving on to another job. His wife and children usually went begging for potatoes or whatever they could get while he was away. When the harvesting was done, he would return home with enough money to pay the rent. The potatoes they planted in the spring were dug and stored for the winter and the family hoped and prayed for good health and gave thanks that they had been able to get through another year.

Many families could not make their food and money stretch. In 1836, the Irish Poor Inquiry Commissioners counted those out of work and in need of relief for more than six months, and their dependents. The total was an appalling 2,385,000—more than one-quarter of the Irish people. Sir Thomas Larcom said: "It was the poor who supported the poor." One family was forever ready to share its meager store of potatoes with another, or even with a beggar passing by in the night. The farmer with a small plot of ground put aside one section to grow potatoes for the poor and the more prosperous farmer often helped his servants distribute bowls of mush to as many as fifty beggars every day in an especially tough season.

The Irish also banded together in mutual protection societies to fight injustice. Less than a century earlier, peasants had formed clandestine mobs called Whiteboys to strike against foreign oppressors. Now, the secret gang turned on greedy landlords. Some places they were called Ribbonmen and in other places Carders, Levellers, or Whitefeet. The leaders picked strangely descriptive and romantic names such as: Captain Moonlight, Captain Starlight, or Molly Maguire. Later on, the Molly Maguires were to be transplanted to America, a secret society in the anthracite coal fields of Pennsylvania in the 1850s.

Occasionally, a landlord would receive a notice such as this: "There did a man come to look for you one Day with what you might call a boney brace of Pistols to shoot you; and if you do not be lighter on your tenants than what you are, you shall surely be shot, so now we give you timely notice; and if you don't abide by this marke the Consequence."

What the Whiteboys sought was more land for tenants to plow or a halt to evictions. A landlord's reaction to these clandestine demands could mean his life or death. Some yielded to demands, gave a little and were not bothered further. Some resisted and were murdered. Gang vengeance sometimes was heaped upon a man who took over the land another had been evicted from on the ground that taking the property, even by lease, was the same as taking the bread from the mouths of women and children.

Sometimes the Whiteboys struck under cover of darkness, but many times a man marked for death was slain in his home or on the street in broad daylight. The gang would go to another town or even another county to get an assassin with the understanding that the favor would be returned at a later time. Using that system, the chances were slim that the killer would be recognized. When authorities attempted to question witnesses, a shrug would be the answer because no peasant would accuse the slayer of a cruel man.

Sir George Cornewall Lewis, the English Home Secretary under Lord Palmerston, saw the Whiteboy pack as a "vast trades' union for the protection of the Irish peasantry: the object being, not to regulate wages, or the hours of work, but to keep the actual occupant in possession of his land, and in general to regulate the relation of landlord and tenant for the benefit of the latter."

If the wronged tenant had been able to go to court to try to win his case, there would have been little need of secret protection societies, but no poor Irishman, especially a Catholic, expected English justice to be fair to him. In Dublin, sheriffs took oaths to enforce religious and political discrimination, and the English judge Lord Denman publicly said the courts in Ireland were "a mockery, a delusion and a snare." If two Protestants were on opposite sides in a case, or two Catholics were at odds, a judge most likely would base his decision on the evidence and legal arguments, but when a Catholic opposed a Protestant in court, justice was forgotten in a shocking display of religious antagonisms.

Of course, the courts had their troubles with the Irish, too. One magistrate said that any defendant needing an alibi could get one at any time from an array of friends or distant cousins. In small village courts, where the Irish settled differences among themselves, kissing the Bible or a crucifix was considered a guarantee that the witness would tell the truth, but in cases involving hated authority, a man often would kiss the thumb which held the Bible satisfying himself that he had not really taken an oath and could say what he damned pleased.

The Irish had an old saying that a "word in court is better than a pound in the purse." A magistrate might find himself showered with small gifts from the friends and relatives of a man on trial, or learn, after a jury had brought in its verdict, that a defendant had been freed because the panel was stacked with friends and distant relatives. Faced with courtroom prejudice for generations, the Irish put their fertile imaginations to work to overcome the legal odds against them. They regarded the law as a sort of test of wits and they welcomed the challenge. It was a talent which proved especially useful later in America.

We've already noted the Irish contribution to the Colonies and the new United States. In the early 1800s, about ten thousand persons a year left Ireland for America. In the 1820s, the English government began helping some immigrants to move to Canada, and that stirred more interest among the Irish in moving to the New World. Between 1825 and 1830, immigration to America from Ireland jumped to about twenty thousand per year and kept climbing in the 1830s.

Where did they get the twelve to twenty-five dollars for passage?

Sometimes a landlord, wanting to clear his property or taking real pity on a destitute family, paid to ship out scores of people. It was to the landlord's advantage to get the potato-digging paupers out of the way and put his farmland to better use. But he rarely paid more than their transatlantic fare, which meant that the immigrants arrived in the New World with only a few shillings in their pockets—if indeed they had any money at all. This angered local city governments on this side of the Atlantic which suddenly found themselves burdened by new charity cases.

In most cases, it was the poor working Irish man or girl already in America who paid much or all of the fare of those who followed. How they did it is an incredible story of the devotion of one human being to the cause of betterment of another. Irish laborers in America were earning from 75 cents to $1.25 per day —when they could find work—and servant girls received their room and board and as little as one dollar per week. Through backbreaking sacrifice, they were able to send home a few shillings or pounds at a time until a sister, a brother, a mother, father, daughter, aunt, uncle, cousin, or friend had enough money to buy the ship ticket. Five banks along the eastern seaboard reported sending to Ireland small drafts totalling nearly

[47]

$315,000 in 1836 and 1837. After the potato famine, the sum rose sharply, as we shall see.

Letters like this show the stuff that the Irish were made of. A husband in America wrote his wife: "I expect to go to newyork on the 17th of March to send you this Bill of Six Pounds which you will Get Cash for in the Provensil Bank of Ireland I will send it in the Revd Patrick ogara is care For you. dont answer this letter tull you Receive the next in which the money will Be for you. Keep your heart as God spared you, so long you will be shortly in the lands of Promise and live happy with me and our children."

That's the way they often did it. A father would be the first to go to America, or sometimes it was the mother, an intrepid parent preparing the way, reassuring the timid. A dozen back-breaking years might pass before the family was seated together around the same table in New York or Boston. The long separation made their hearts ache for their loved ones, but also drove them to work harder and longer for that bright day when they would all be one again.

In September 1845, the *Nation*, published in Dublin, believed it had good reason to be optimistic. It said: "The autumn is waning sunnily and cheerfully for the country. It is a busy and hopeful time. The husbandman is merry at his toil, because it has rich promise; and the beautiful giver of all good has, by a guarantee of abundance in the bad food of the poor, given assurance against famine."

A few weeks later, catastrophe struck without warning. Farmers sensed that something was wrong. The healthy potato plants gave off a peculiar odor, and the very next day, as one man said, "they were black as your shoe and burned to the clay."

The blight took one-third of the potato crop in 1845, and the full crop everywhere in Ireland the following year. In 1847, the disease seemed to be a little less severe, but in 1848, it hit with full, unmerciful force once again. The next year was somewhat better, with losses still heavy, and by 1850, the disease had run its course. Ireland was devastated by the five-year siege.

Reports of the suffering add a black page to the history of mankind. One Quaker, visiting Ireland in 1847, wrote: "I would greatly prefer being a donor to being a distributor of relief. It is much easier for a man to put his hand into his purse, than to labour from morning to night in filling out stirabout to crowds of half-clad, hungry people sinking with weakness and fever. Between today and yesterday, I saw the corpses of a girl, a man and old woman who died of hunger. This day I saw a woman sinking into a faint, while I was giving out relief at Pullathomas to some peculiarly wretched families. I saw thousands today of the most miserable people I have ever seen."

Father John O'Sullivan, a parish priest, wrote: "It is not long since I was called in to prepare a poor fellow, whose mother lay beside him dead two days, and he was burning with rage to think she should have come to such an end, as to die of starvation. I was called in a few days after to a miserable object, beside whom lay a child dead, for the twenty-four hours previous; two others lay beside her just expiring, and, horrible to relate, a famished cat got upon the bed, and was just about to gnaw the corpse of the deceased infant, until I prevented it. . . . Such is the mortality, that I do not think I exaggerate, when I give it as my opinion that a third of the population has been already carried away. Every morning four or five corpses are to be found on the street dead, the victims of famine and disease."

A landlord who tried to help, Lord Mountcashell, wrote these words of desperation: "This extensive district contains four parishes with a population of about 9800 souls. Some of this district belongs to me, but more than three-fourths to others. . . . I need not detail the sacrifices and exertions I have made, to assist the overwhelming mass of pauperism around me, during the last inclement winter. The poor know it, and are grateful; but my resources are at an end, and most of my tenants unable to pay me anything they owe me, so that I can do little more for them, although their situation daily becomes more critical. . . . There are at this moment over 7000 in the greatest state of misery and distress, out of which 5000 have not, unless given them, a single meal to provide for their wants tomorrow. . . . I am at this time giving food to a girl of twelve years old, the only remnant of a family, consisting of eight persons, all of whom were alive one fortnight ago."

Thousands died of typhus, typhoid, cholera, or "fever." There were no doctors or hospitals in some areas. Existing hospitals were packed to capacity, and doctors were so busy that patients died while waiting for them. Available medicines were all but useless, and country nurses resorted mostly to old-time remedies such as herb juice, cress and wild garlic, milk and water boiled with salt, and sheep's blood. In many cases, it might have been the cure that killed.

The smell of death hung over the land like a shroud. Graveyards were overcrowded and gravediggers scarce. Coffinmakers were overworked and wood hard to get. Men told of making as many as six coffins in one day, using the wood from dressers, tables, buildings, and boats—a few boards hammered together and tarred on the inside. Sometimes, the dead were wrapped in sheets, sometimes in sacks or straw mats. Occasionally, they made their last journey on the shoulders of a relative or friend, barely strong enough to carry them, or in a wheelbarrow. Community coffins finally became a necessity. They would transport one corpse to the grave, then be left there empty for the next user. There were coffins with hinged bottoms which were held over the burial place, the bottom opened, and the body dropped into a pit where several others lay sprinkled with lime.

Occasionally, sad to say, patients were condemned to death before their time by careless doctors or attendants who believed they were dead, and ordered them hauled away from hospitals or poorhouses to make room for the next barrage of victims. Sometimes, sepulchural groans would be heard from a wagon en route to the graveyard, but the driver was getting a fee for each body taken away, and probably moralized his ghoulishness with the premise that the poor souls were better off dead and buried.

There were special graveyards for children, for fever victims, for old people, and often Catholics were buried in Protestant graves for want of space elsewhere or the time to make it ready. There are stories of the old and the sick crawling along roads, hoping to reach consecrated ground before they died. Many did not have the strength to go more than a few yards. It's said about a certain part of Galway that there is no field in which people are not buried. The sites of many famine graves are still marked today. One stone bears the simple inscription: 1847. *Let None Meddle Here.*

An old Irish saying had it that God put the blight on the potatoes, but England put the hunger upon Ireland. The rot affected only the potato crop, not wheat, oats, or barley. Flour and oatmeal, butter and lard, beef, pork and bacon, all were loaded on outgoing ships and sent to England while Ireland starved. The money for these products was needed to pay the rent, and without the rent money, the hungry would not even have a roof over their heads. Had the Irish peasant been able to get work during those five terrible years, the famine would never have gripped the nation so desperately for so long.

Sir Robert Peel, a man of good sense and some imagination, was England's Prime Minister when the blight first appeared in 1845. He moved quickly to set up a relief program which sounds modern in its concept—he put men to work improving roads. The money for the projects was advanced by the government as a loan, not a gift, and the work was controlled locally and carried out by contractors. Local committees compiled lists of the neediest cases and gave the jobs to the heads of those families. Probably as many as 140,000 persons were at work at one time.

There were some problems. Payment for labor with money was not common and in some areas, there wasn't enough silver to go around. Special arrangements had to be made to round up more money on pay days. Sometimes workers had to do without their wages for a few weeks and this, of course, left them open to the scheming food dealers who charged exorbitant prices for food on credit. But, considering that the famine was not yet severe, the Peel public works program was a success. *The Freeman's Journal*, which certainly was not an ardent supporter, said: "The limited distress which Sir Robert Peel was called upon to meet, he provided for fairly and fully. No man died of famine during his administration, and it is a boast of which he might well be proud."

If Peel had continued in office—and history is filled with if's —other stronger measures might have been put into effect to ease Ireland's great suffering. But in 1846, the first year of deep crisis, Lord John Russell became Prime Minister, bringing with him to the office a profound devotion of "business as usual" and the belief that somehow the law of supply and demand would solve everything.

More jobs for the Irish had proved adequate to meet the situation the year before, and Lord Russell felt that the same plan would be sufficient in 1846. The Chancellor of the Exchequer told the House of Commons: "It was not the intention at all to import food for the use of the people of Ireland. In fact many merchants had declared that they would not import food at all if it were the intention of the government to do so."

Lord Russell agreed that private merchants ought to be in charge of providing food, saying: "We do not propose to interfere with the regular mode by which Indian corn and other kinds of grain may be brought into the country."

The Irish patriot Daniel O'Connell challenged the government's do-nothing attitude in these words: "Unhappily in the present state of the country, it will not be sufficient to procure employment for the people. The great difficulty is the procuring of sufficient food—food is already at a famine price and the leaving in the hands of the mercantile men the supplying of food as a commercial speculation will keep it at a famine price. The intervention of government is therefore absolutely necessary."

But the government was blindly stubborn. It agreed to establish government food depots only on Ireland's west coast where wholesalers and retailers were practically nonexistent, and to leave the east coast's private interests to provide food for that section. Sir Randolph Routh protested: "In a great calamity, we cannot be found wanting. The relief must be forthcoming."

Routh was told: "The Chancellor of the Exchequer will on no account permit you to undertake to provide food for any portion of the eastern district of Ireland. . . . No exigency, however pressing, is to induce you to furnish supplies of food for any districts except those for which we have already undertaken."

Even in the west, the depots were not permitted to open as long as any food was available in the neighborhood. In the town of Skibbereen, people died of starvation in the fall of 1846, but the local government provision house did not open until December, and the treasury did not get around to granting permission for sales to begin in all government stores until after Christmas. Prices were an issue. At first, London wanted to add 30 per cent to the cost price to make certain that local food dealers would not be undercut. Finally, the mark-up was set at 15 per cent because it was felt that a quick turnover cash business would provide sufficient profit. On each ton of Indian meal sold in the hunger depots, the government made more than twenty dollars.

The sick were expected to buy their food just as everyone else when the original relief committee rules were drawn up, but later, the restrictions were relaxed. Free food then could be given

[53]

to the sick and to those unable to work for other reasons, but *only* if the local workhouse was filled and unable to accept any new clients.

England's shortsighted policies only added to the growing death list, and to the distress of local officials, coroner's juries began handing down verdicts at inquests of "death by starvation." One jury in Galway vehemently declared that Lord John Russell and Sir Randolph Routh had combined to starve the Irish people and therefore were both guilty of willful murder.

The road-building program was proving to be too expensive to landowners while not providing enough food money to workers. A treasury official wondered whether the time had not come to approach the food problem directly instead of indirectly, and "provide for the outdoor relief of every destitute person."

In the winter of 1846, relief organizations were founded in Ireland to collect funds from every part of the world. One of the first in action was the Society of Friends (the Quakers) and this organization took the most direct approach possible to hunger— the establishment of soup kitchens.

It seems incredible now that anyone would oppose such a move to alleviate starvation, but Sir Randolph was concerned that the handing out of cooked food would increase the dependence of the poor, and he suggested that it might be better to give them the ingredients—and teach them to cook their own food!

Finally, the Soup Kitchen Act established committees to administer this badly needed relief, and to enforce the restrictions placed upon the free food. Ration cards were issued stating the amount to which each person was entitled. If one person in a family happened to be working, free food was denied to *all* the others, and to make certain that this rule was not violated, all able-bodied members of a family—men, women, and children —were required to be present at the soup kitchen before any food was handed out. Personal cleanliness was another condition imposed upon relief cases and if any member of a ragged, destitute family showed up at a relief station with smudged hands or face or dirty clothing, those with him might be denied food that day.

In some areas, a man who owned more than one-quarter acre of land, a horse or cow, or a donkey would be denied relief. Some penny-pinching relief committees dropped persons from the free food list if they looked less than starving or seemed to be gaining weight. A woman was denied rations when she admitted that she had given some of her food to the children of her dead brother. A magistrate had to intervene to keep the poor, loyal woman from starving.

To stay alive, the peasants developed many ingenious methods. One woman collected three rations by having three different disguises. A man registered for rations for himself and the only other member of his family, Sean, who later turned out to be a big gray cat. Some families buried their dead secretly at night to avoid losing their food portions.]

The memories of soup kitchens and road projects have been preserved in place names such as *Páirc an tSúip* (Soup Park) in West Kerry, Stirabout Lane, Porridge Way, Meal Road, Kelly's Big Road (named for the engineer in charge), and Father Donal's Road (named after the priest who sponsored it).

The starvation, the humiliation of poverty in the beloved former homeland, caused great pain among the Irish in America. Less than two months after the rot first struck the potatoes in 1845, Boston Irish formed the Charitable Relief Fund. Hundreds of dollars were collected in a few weeks and that was before the famine had reached its most desperate stage. In 1846, when hopes for a better potato harvest were wiped out by total blight, Americans for Irish Relief met in Washington, and similar groups got together in New York, Philadelphia, Baltimore, St. Louis, and Dubuque, Iowa. A few months later, in early 1847, American relief measures took a great leap forward. Church officials in Boston sent $20,000 as a first installment to help the Irish. Captain Robert Forbes of Boston, former skipper of a China clipper, suggested that a man o'war be converted into a mercy ship to deliver provisions to Ireland. Congress agreed, despite the fact that the Mexican War was being fought, and the *Jamestown* was turned over to the Boston relief committee. Forbes and some of his former seamates took on a voluntary crew; wheat, flour, and potatoes were loaded aboard, and the ship sailed March 28, 1847. Forbes arrived in Cork fifteen days later—a fast voyage for the time.

Businessmen in New York got behind the relief program, and a rally at the Broadway Tabernacle pledged contributions of $22,000 in one night.

In that same month of February 1847, Senator John J. Crittenden of Kentucky and Representative Washington Hunt of New York introduced bills asking Congress to appropriate $500,000. The money would be used to buy provisions to be turned over to England for distribution in Ireland and Scotland—a nineteenth-century version of CARE packages. The Senate approved, but the House held up the measure in committee, probably because the money was needed to fight the Mexican War.

However, members of the House and Senate chipped in $1300, and reporters covering Congress contributed $100 to Irish Relief. Choctaw Indians voted to send a gift of food, and West Point cadets pooled their allowances for a total of $300. The city of Cincinnati donated 5000 barrels of foodstuffs. These American contributions probably totaled more than a million dollars before the famine ended, with another $9,000,000 going to relatives and friends directly from the Irish fortunate enough to be in America.

An official of the Provincial Bank of Ireland wrote in 1847 that during the previous year about $725,000 had been sent from America to Ireland. Other estimates place the figure above one million dollars. The British Colonial Land and Emigration Commissioners reported that the money flow reached a high mark in 1854 with $8,650,000 going to Ireland from thrifty countrymen in America.

The cost of the hunger in human terms was staggering. The world has known famine time and again. The *Encyclopaedia Britannica* lists thirty-two major famines from 436 B.C. to 1943 A.D. India and China have seen as many as 1,000,000 persons perish from hunger in a single year. As late as 1921, starving Russians dug the newly dead from graves for food, and ate grass and animal filth. In all such cases of famine, whether they occurred in China, India or Russia, there was no escape. Starving peasants could only stay and await slow death.

In 1851, the census put Ireland's population at 6,552,385—a severe drop from the 9,000,000 it should have been had the rate of normal growth continued in the famine years. It is estimated that more than a million died and more than a million left Ireland for other countries.

If any good came out of the awful suffering in Ireland it was this: the famine drove hundreds of thousands of Irish to America in one of history's greatest migrations.

IRISH EMIGRATION TO AMERICA DURING THE FAMINE YEARS

1845—50,000
1846—68,000
1847—117,000
1848—154,000
1849—177,000
1850—181,000
1851—216,000
1852—193,000
1853—157,000
1854—111,000
1855—57,000

The Irishman headed for America was always cautioned to avoid a fall or winter voyage and to leave instead in the spring when the winds grew warmer and the sunlight brighter. To arrive in New York or Boston in May or June was considered ideal because outdoor work would be easier to get and he could sleep outside if necessary, and both considerations were important to a man in a new land without home or job.

But when the full effect of the potato blight was felt across Ireland in the late summer of 1846, thousands decided to risk their lives on a winter crossing, ready to undergo any misery "save that of remaining in Ireland." In January 1847, six thousand Irish sailed from Liverpool. Most of them were the poorest of the poor with no land or cottage to call their own. They could not delay for even a few more weeks with both starvation and the landlord confronting them. A few months later, the very poor were followed by those a step higher on the ladder—small landowners. Local newspapers in the south and west of Ireland carried thousands of ads putting small farms up for sale. Often, families who had vowed never to leave Ireland decided overnight to escape and a few weeks later were aboard ships. Some villages in Galway saw one-third of their people pack their few belongings and go during March and April of 1847. That year, almost twice as many persons left Ireland as in 1846.

It soon became an accepted risk to leave for America in the autumn—not because the farmer hoped the new potato harvest would be better than the last, but because he hoped it would bring in enough money to enable him to pay his ship passage and have a little money left over. Sometimes, the landlord was deserted by "rent jumpers." One letter described the practice this way: "They cut the corn on Sunday, sell it on Monday morning, and are off to America in the evening, leaving the waste lands behind them and the landlords without rent."

In port, lively fights broke out aboard immigrant ships if

sheriffs or bailiffs caught up with former tenants trying to make quick getaways.

Many big landowners were even more interested in helping their tenants to migrate after the famine struck than they had been a decade or two before. In 1847, there were reports that a Dublin shipping agent was booking over 8000 passages on orders of landlords. Many peasants resisted, muttering that it was no more than eviction and deportation, but the landowners believed they were doing the poor a favor.

A Maj. Mahon, who owned a large estate in Roscommon, had 2400 people living on his 2100 acres and he said they produced only one-third of the food they needed to stay alive. They were three years behind in their rents with no prospect, in the disastrous year of 1848, of being able to pay current bills, much less catch up. Mahon decided that the total cost of sending the "surplus" to America was considerably less than the expense of supporting them for a year as paupers, so he offered them the choice of emigration or eviction. The tenant would be given free passage and provisions, with permission to sell or carry away farm stock and belongings. They were promised a good sea diet —better than most immigrants were getting. The deal was so attractive for the time that most of the tenants accepted, believing that any move would be an improvement. Mahon was quite proud of his effort, boasting that it had cost him more than $30,000, but the venture ended in a double tragedy. The voyage was long, and a combination of hunger, thirst, and disease took the lives of one-fourth of Mahon's tenants. The medical officer at Quebec declared the survivors were the most wretched and diseased he had ever seen. A few months later, Mahon was murdered, victim of peasants outraged by accounts they had heard of the voyage.

The English port of Liverpool had a near monopoly of Irish emigrant traffic to America because it was an important terminal on the cargo trade route. About nine-tenths of the travelers who boarded ships at Liverpool were Catholic Irish, and most of them sailed on American ships. The Irish preferred Liverpool because the emigrant ships in Irish ports were the worst on the seas—rickety, overcrowded, dirty vessels alive with vermin.

American ships were the best—cleaner and roomier than the British, and many New York or Boston shipowners were building or redesigning their vessels with an eye to capturing the emigrant business. They installed permanent berths on cargo ships, added extra decks and closed off exposed areas.

Liverpool's bustling activity attracted every known form of racketeer—loan sharks, fast-talking liars, confidence men, gamblers, and just plain thieves. Sir George Stephen of the Colonial Office said most of the wide-eyed peasants were "of the most simple and ignorant character; they will believe anything; they will find themselves in a strange place, and they are disposed to attend to every word that is said, and to give up to it; consequently, there could not be a more convenient prey, as it were, to those who are disposed to defraud them."

The whole system operated against the trusting emigrant, because English and American shipowners tried to avoid direct dealings with the travelers, and instead, sold space to Liverpool brokers. The reputation of these middlemen was such that one admitted: "A respectable man hardly likes to say he is a passenger broker."

A man from Galway might arrive with a ticket he'd paid for in his town, or a ticket sent from America, and find himself assigned to a smaller, less desirable ship than the one his passage called for and with a longer wait than he had planned on. Or, he might be told that prices had been increased and he would have to accept transportation to Quebec rather than New York, or make up the difference in price. Occasionally, an Irish family, unable to read, would purchase tickets to "St. John" only to find out later that they were valid only as far as St. John,

Newfoundland, and not the town of the same name in New Brunswick. Emigrants bound for Charleston or New Orleans were convinced by unscrupulous agents that Boston was the nearest port—only a "short walk away."

The Irish, trusting as they were, were not inclined to accept fraud once they discovered it, and several passenger agents and shipowners were forced out of business or ordered by law to make good on paper promises.

While emigrants waited in Liverpool, they were prey to boardinghouse keepers and their runners—dubbed "man-catchers" by the Irish. This breed of scoundrel often was Irish and employed a well-cultivated brogue to strike up friendships with emigrating countrymen. The newly arrived peasant would be led to a small, dingy lodginghouse which had been given an Irish name and equipped with absurdly high rates. Then the "catcher," still pretending to be the traveler's best friend, would take him on a tour of passenger agents and pretend to bargain for the lowest-priced passage, when actually the "thief" was seeking the highest commission for himself. The emigrant would be taken to provision shops and sold large quantities of inferior food, and then to stores to buy other "essentials" he didn't need, including cooking utensils, water jugs of various sizes, and even chamber pots. Usually, he was told that the little money he had was worthless in America, and his friend, the "catcher," would be glad to take it off his hands and do him the favor of providing a little American money. Naturally, the exchange rates were rigged to give the confidence man a handsome commission. These tricks usually worked because the Irish had never been exposed to such slick operators in their villages or on their little farms, and besides, no price was too great to pay for the privilege of sailing to America.

The trip from Liverpool to New York usually took about five weeks, but in midsummer, prevailing southwest winds often extended the time required. If ships ran into rough storms, or were becalmed, the journey took longer, giving rise to fears among both passengers and crew that the food or water would run out.

Fares actually were lower in the 1840s than they were in the 1800s. At the beginning of the century, an emigrant paid from $50 to $60 to go from Londonderry to New York. A few decades later, fares ranged from $12.50 to $20. With demand high in 1847, passage from Liverpool and New York was often as much as $35, but the average fare paid in 1851 was $17.50.

A well-organized routine preceded the sailing. First, the cargo was hauled aboard and then the emigrants were allowed to scramble up the gangplank with their luggage. When the tides and winds were right, off went the ropes and up went the anchor. Sometimes a dozen ships left at the same moment, and hundreds lined the shores to wave hats and handkerchiefs and to be waved at from the ships' railings. Many wept, but the travelers often sang and danced as the ships left the harbor. After all, they had already said their sad farewells to their farms and villages, and leaving Liverpool or another large port was not a time for crying but for rejoicing. At last, they were on their way to America.

When a ship reached open water, the emigrants were called to stand before the captain, who compared their names with the passenger list, and tried to match up names and ages. Sometimes "Baby Mary" turned out to be rather tall for her age of nine or ten, and the half-price fare meant to cover a boy of twelve or under was paid for a strapping young farmer of seventeen. While the captain and his agents attempted to straighten out these minor matters, the crew searched the cargo and luggage for stowaways. It was a rare voyage which did not turn up more than one illegal traveler within an hour after sailing. Often, he or she would be returned aboard the pilot's boat, but sometimes a young man would be allowed to work his way over as a crew member, or some friend or relative aboard would hand over a down payment on the stowaway's fare along with goods to be held as security until the full fare was paid. There were times, of course, when stowaways escaped notice by mingling with the passengers or crew throughout the voyage, or by staying hidden among the trunks and casks. Some became desperately ill and died rather than give themselves up and risk being sent back to Ireland.

Even the best ships were cramped for adequate passenger space. On many vessels, only five-and-a-half to six feet separated the decks, and double tiers of berths were run along the sides of the ship with each berth meant to hold four adults. The law generously required that each adult be given eighteen inches shoulder width and six feet in length, so four persons slept in a space six feet by six feet. The clerk in charge of assigning berths usually tried to keep families together, but there was no guarantee that one couple would not share a berth with another, or with two young men or young women. One ship's clerk said he was accustomed to men and women of different names asking to be put next to each other, but among the Catholic Irish, morality was not taken lightly. In most cases, the man had assumed the role of protector, assuring the girl and her parents at home that she would be guarded from any annoyance during the long voyage.

Cooking was always a major problem. Facilities were primitive—sometimes a grill, a stove, or an open fireplace of brick and stone on deck. At the start of the journey, a score or more of women would cluster around the fire trying to prepare food for their own families. Coffee, soup, stew, and a variety of other dishes might be in preparation at one time with salt spray adding its distinctive flavor to the pots. Others would be waiting for their turn to cook, elbowing one another aside, and sometimes heated arguments or fights broke out over which family was next to use the fire. Some people waited hours for breakfast and dinner. Later on, a few women would be appointed to cook simple, hot meals for large groups, which turned out to be a better arrangement. On many ships, as food began to run out, hot meals became a luxury and weary passengers had to turn to cold meal, hard bread, and water to stay alive. It was almost a miracle if the water was fit to drink after weeks at sea, because the casks which held the water probably had held other fluids previously—vinegar, molasses, or turpentine—and some water kegs were sprinkled with gunpowder as a preservative, which blackened the water and made it fouler with each passing day.

The hunger which haunted the Irish at home often rode with them on the emigrant ships. Accounts such as the following were not unusual:

" . . . After fourteen days had elapsed, the captain informed them that they would get nothing to eat except bread and meat. After this each person received two biscuits, one pint of water, and the eighth part of a pound of meat per day. This regulation continued for two or three weeks, when they one and all declared they could not any longer exist on the small allowance they received; that they must, without doubt, perish. The hunger and thirst being at this time so great, and the children continually crying out for bread and drink, some of the men, resolved, at all events to procure bread, broke open the apartment wherein it was kept, and took some. This was discovered by the captain, as were also those who did the same, when each of them was ordered to, and actually did, receive, after being first tied, a number of lashes on their bare backs well laid on. The whole of the passengers were also punished for this offence. The men received no bread, the women but one biscuit.

"This continued for nine days, when the men were again allowed one biscuit per day. In this situation their condition became dreadful, so much so that five and twenty men, women and children actually perished for want of the common necessities of life, in short, for want of bread. . . . The hunger was so great on board that all the bones about the ship were hunted

[64]

up by them, pounded with a hammer and eaten; and what is more lamentable, some of the deceased persons, not many hours before their death, crawled on their hands and feet to the captain and begged him, for God's sake, to give them a mouthful of bread or a drop of water to keep them from perishing. But their supplications were in vain; he most obstinately refused, and thus did they perish."

A variety of diseases including cholera, typhus, and intestinal flu swept the emigrant ships, and the wails and groans of the sick and dying below decks were terrible even on bright days when most people were on the top deck. When rough weather hit and the hatches had to be closed, the moaning was almost unbearable, and the stench reminded some of a cesspool. But in spite of the sickness, bad food and polluted water, the death toll on the so-called "coffin ships" of the famine years was surprisingly low. In George W. Potter's *To the Golden Door*, it's said that the mortality of the 1847 emigration to Canada is the worst on record. Of 86,812 who made the trip, 6116 died at sea, 4149 in quarantine, and 7180 in shore hospitals—or about 20 per cent of the total emigrants.

Passengers fortunate enough to remain in fair health often sang and danced, told stories and marked off a calendar to help pass the days and weeks of the long journey. Then would come the sea gulls, bits of floating trees or shrubs, and finally, the first sight of an American lighthouse, beckoning with its blinking beacon. The next morning, the low, green shore line told the long-suffering emigrants that they had, indeed, reached America, and that a new world of wonders and challenges awaited them. Dangers and disappointments also lurked around this new corner of opportunity, but they would face them as had the others who had gone before, certain that they were making the right choice.

This was America, "where every day is like Christmas."

[65]

5 URBAN IRISH:

Settling in America

The Irishman setting foot in New York for the first time in the early 1800s found himself in a bustling port which looked like a country town. Behind the tough and dirty waterfront sat the factories and shops, and behind them, houses of dark, weather-beaten wood or bright red brick. Not too far away, the city opened into fields and meadows. Sheep grazed on what is now Central Park. He could hear the baas of lambs being led to the slaughterhouses, the clopping of horses' hoofs on the cobblestones, the creaking of carriages and the rumbling of heavy wagons. The raucous voices of sailors mingled with the shouts of street vendors and the cries and laughter of children.

All this was so bewildering to the new immigrant that he was eager to accept the first words of advice and encouragement offered. Much of the time, this was unfortunate because the words came from the New York version of the Liverpool "runner"— the "shoulder-hitter." He sported a green hat, a well-maintained brogue, and a line stretching all the way back to Cork, Limerick, Galway, or wherever he said he was from. He was quick to help with the bundles or the babies and steer the trusting immigrant family to a "friendly Irish boardinghouse." Usually, these were dilapidated three-story buildings near the waterfront, with a grog shop on the ground floor. The man was invited in for a sip to celebrate the arrival, and the family led to its cramped room upstairs. No mention was made of rent for the first day or two and by the time the family got around to asking timidly what the charges were, the bill for the room and the one or more celebrations at the grog shop often was more money than they had brought with them to America. The "friendly" Irish hotelkeeper generously offered to extend credit while the head of the family found work, but often the bills piled up faster than the wages, and the Irishman once again found himself at the mercy of a landlord every bit as unscrupulous as the one from whom he had escaped.

If the immigrant planned to stay in New York only a few days before heading into the back country for a job, he needed travel information and tickets, and the "shoulder-hitter," or a cohort working as a passenger agent, practiced additional trickery. The unschooled Irishman might be sold worthless coupons with pictures of trains or boats on them and told they were good for travel to Philadelphia or a ride up the Hudson to Albany. Or, the victim might be put aboard a steamer for Albany with additional tickets enabling him to continue his journey from there by rail. Many times, he found he had been overcharged on train fare, or had underpaid and must make up the difference, or, worse yet, that no such train ran to the place he wanted to go.

Groups were formed to counter these gyp artists. In 1790, Philadelphia Irish founded a Hibernian Society for the Relief of Emigrants. In 1817, the Shamrock Society issued printed advice to newcomers. The Friendly Sons of St. Patrick, and the Irish Emigrant Association also were among the early aid organizations. One of the most effective was the Irish Emigrant

Society created in 1841 with the help of Bishop John Joseph Hughes, later the first archbishop of New York. Public officials paid little attention to these groups at first because they considered it the duty of the Catholic clergy to watch over and shepherd the new arrivals from Ireland, and the Church did try. But the flood of immigrants was too great. The Society of St. Vincent de Paul was formed in 1846 to combat misery and help make life a little easier for the Irish poor in New York. That same year, Bishop Hughes requested and received several Sisters of Mercy from Ireland to open a home for the care of destitute immigrant girls.

Finally, in 1847, the state decided to take an active interest in the newcomers. With the famine driving thousands more Irish across the sea, the New York Legislature set up the Board of Commissioners of Emigration, which had among its ten members, the presidents of the Irish and German immigrant societies. The board levied a tax of $1.50 on each passenger to arrive for the support of a quarantine hospital, an immigration staff, and a travel and employment aid center. The hard-working commissioners drove many dishonest runners and travel agents out of business, but the landing place of the immigrants had to be changed occasionally to keep the agents as far away as possible. The commissioners complained: "The work never ceases, new schemes of fraud spring up whenever the occasion offers."

The health of immigrants also presented officials with a major headache. The Irish were so run down by inadequate food even before the big famine that they were the easy targets of disease, and the horrid holds of the "coffin ships" were excellent breeding places for the germs. In 1847, emergency hospitals had to be set up on Staten Island and Long Island to care for the hundreds of sick. Several towns along the Hudson River, including Albany, refused to allow immigrants to leave the steamers, even for an hour, on their way to jobs in the West. In 1849, a severe cholera epidemic, a rugged winter, and a business recession forced the

[68]

New York commissioners to spend more than $380,000 on the health and relief of immigrants. One of the board members wrote: "We are obliged to keep supplies of provision in our office in the city to give to those who come in famishing. . . . The women and children we cannot thrust aside." In 1851, and again in the winter of 1854, epidemics raged in New York, and little wonder when we realize that less than one-third of the city was equipped with a sewer system.

When the Irish moved out of the temporary hotels and boardinghouses, they moved into tenements or old warehouses, or trudged farther out to become squatters in a shanty town. It's difficult to say which was worse, but certainly the slums they lived in were as squalid and disgraceful as any this country will ever know.

Houses that once sheltered a single family in middle-class comfort became the depressing quarters of a dozen families with six or seven persons crowded into each room. Cellars and attics held not one family but two or three or more, separated by thin partitions which often did not even reach the ceiling. Every word, every move could be heard throughout the floor, and the precious or dreariest moments of family life were public knowledge. All tenants would use the same kitchen, or try to cook in their part of a room, but in either case the result would be the same—a devastating mixture of odors which lasted through day and night and hung on for weeks. Ventilation was poor because most houses had precious few windows at the front and rear, with none in the basements or attics, and windows were kept closed through the long winters for fear that fuel might be wasted. Ten or twenty families might depend upon one or two standpipes for their entire water supply, and many times the pipes were clogged and the water unfit to drink or hardly to wash in. Privies were not far away—not far enough from the water supply—and they contributed to the disease rate by clogging up, overflowing, and seeping into the cellars where people were trying to live.

Not a foot of space went to waste if a slum landlord could help it. Tiny shacks were slapped together in back yards, gardens, and alleyways, and the poor huddled inside their drafty walls and under leaky roofs. They were seldom vacant as the tide of immigration rose.

The Irish clustered in the notorious Five Points section of New York—a depressed and crime-ridden area on a filled-in swamp in the old 6th Ward. One of the worst examples of slum housing was the Old Brewery, first built in 1792, and halfway converted into living space in 1837. Several hundred men, women, and children called that dank, vermin-infested hole home, and it was shared almost equally by the Irish and Negroes. The Irish were blamed for the rising crime rate in Five Points and attacked in nativist, anti-Catholic newspapers as "assassins and robbers," "the filthy off-casts of Europe." Law-breakers multiplied like germs in that primitive environment, and there were nights when police could not cope with all the brawls and petty thefts. The next day, the newspapers would be filled with the names of Irish charged with disturbing the peace, or worse.

But every immigrant group that arrived in this country ragged and rejected, having to fight its way up, has clashed with authority and offended "law-abiding citizens." Once members of the group have been able to break out of their social trap and join the mainstream of American life, most of them have become as decent and law-abiding as other citizens. The Irish, as we have already noted, had an innate respect for the law, and in time it gave them a special place in New York and other cities.

In the 1820s, there were an estimated 100,000 Catholic Irish in the State of New York, and half of them lived in towns along the Erie Canal. They took their muscles, customs, and religion into Albany, Troy, Utica, Rome, Rochester, and Buffalo.

By 1867, more than 200,000 people of Irish origin lived in the City of New York alone, and one day New York would be "more Irish than Dublin."

New York was the Irishman's capital in this country, affording protection to exiles, a base for the Irish resistance movement, a center of Catholic Church activity, and symbolizing wealth and opportunity for the poverty-stricken.

This "bustling country town" known as New York and the Irish grew up together.

A decision made in London sent thousands of Irish to Boston. The British government subsidized the Cunard Steamship Line to assure fast and direct contact with its colonies. In 1841, Post Office investigators decided that the best way to send mail from England to Canada was by way of Boston, so Cunard was advised to direct its ships there, and a few years later, other lines were doing the same, just in time to carry more famine victims away from Ireland to Boston, a port growing in importance.

Immigration began to burgeon in 1840. Five years later, so many newcomers had arrived that one expert said flatly that Boston simply could not house any more people. Yet, in the next ten years, the years of the hunger, more than 230,000 persons converged on Boston, not only from Ireland, but from other lands as well, and enough of them stayed on to raise the city's population by one third, and make an already congested city uncomfortably crowded.

The Swedes and Germans might arrive and depart as a group, eager to work the cheap farmland available in Minnesota and Wisconsin. But the Irish, for the most part, came to Boston to stay because they were too poor to go on and because there were other Irish there to give them that important sense of belonging and the feeling of togetherness.

They tended to stay in the older sections along the waterfront and to try to work nearby. To avoid travel in water-locked Boston was to save the twenty cents or more per day eaten up by tolls or fares while traveling to the quiet suburbs or other desirable sections within the city itself. Even in the 1850s, when the horse-railroad, and larger ferryboats made lower fares possible, most of the Irish chose to remain in the old neighborhoods.

The slums grew according to the old New York pattern. Once exclusive mansions and huge unused warehouses passed through a series of owners until, finally, they were converted into the depressing monstrosities the very poor could barely afford. It was bad enough dealing with some unscrupulous landlords, but even worse when the Irish found themselves victimized, once again, by a rental agent or middleman leaseholder. Sometimes, a contractor, who might be Irish himself, would rent an old building at an annual rate, cut it up into tiny flats, and then take in immigrant families on a weekly basis at high rates. These sub-landlords cared little for building or tenant as long as they got their money, and because of this, both building and tenant suffered with the poverty-trapped renter suffering most.

In *Boston's Immigrants*, Oscar Handlin, professor of history at Harvard, tells of the landlord who erected two four-story wooden structures, which contained 32 one-room apartments never brightened by sunlight. A narrow alleyway half blocked by privies and water hydrants separated the buildings. In another place, the walk separating two tenements was only ten feet. Every last inch of space was put to use by profit-minded builders in these areas and sheds took the place of yards and gardens. The makers of the first Boston atlas threw up their hands at trying to map the alleyways and walks, and noted simply that the area was "full of sheds and shanties."

One of the worst examples was the haven's Half-Moon Place. In 1849, the Cholera Committee described it in these words: "A large part of the area is occupied by . . . twelve or fourteen privies, constantly overflowing, and by ill constructed and worn out sinks and drains, into which are hourly thrown solid substances, of all sorts, which choke them up and cause the liquid . . . to run over. A steep staircase affords a passage to Humphrey place, some fifty feet above. Side by side with the staircase, and fully exposed, a large, square wood drain makes a precipitous descent, conducting, half hidden, half revealed, not only the waste waters of the houses in Humphrey place, but also, the contents of its privies below; which, as may be supposed, is redolent of the fact."

Living costs were high for the time and for the dreary rooms the immigrants took out of desperation. Even the grimmest room cost about $1.50 per week, and that figure was the minimum for an attic. The rent for a cellar was at least $2.00 per week. Each room contained several persons, and many times two or more families lived together. Attic rooms only three feet high were rented out, and basements were even more popular. A census disclosed that from five to fifteen persons were sleeping in each Boston slum basement every night in 1850, and one basement packed in 39 persons. Basements held some advantages, such as warmth in the winter and coolness in the summer, but they were often without ventilation, infested with vermin, and flooded after heavy rains.

The rooms the Irish lived in were plain and unpainted. There would be a narrow bed or two, a few chairs and a table, a washtub and a few pegs to hang their clothes on. Windows often were broken, roofs were leaky, and the stairs rickety.

The Committee on Internal Health complained: "In such a state of things, there can be no cleanliness, privacy, or proper ventilation . . . and, with the ignorance, carelessness, and generally loose and dirty habits which prevail among the occupants, the necessary evils are greatly increased both in amount and intensity. In Broad Street and all the surrounding neighborhood the situation of the Irish is particularly wretched. . . . This

whole district is a perfect hive of human beings, without comforts and mostly without common necessaries; in many cases,
huddled together like brutes, without regard to sex, or age, or
sense of decency; grown men and women sleeping together in the
same apartment, and sometimes wife and husband, brothers and
sisters in the same bed. Under such circumstances, self-respect,
forethought, all high and noble virtues, soon die out, and sullen
indifference and despair, or disorder, intemperance and utter
degradation reign supreme."

Whatever effect these squalid cells had on Irish morals and
morale, their effect on the health of the newcomer was devastating. During the Boston cholera epidemic in 1849, the worst out-
breaks occurred in the Irish districts. Burgess Alley alone had
200 cases. In the city, 700 persons died, and 500 of them were
Irish.

Tuberculosis was another killer, reaching its peak in 1855.
Pneumonia, bronchitis, and intestinal diseases took their tolls.
So many died so young that it was said that the Irish lived an
average of only fourteen years after arriving in Boston. Authorities decided that one out of every seventeen immigrant Irishmen died in the year 1850.

Poverty was a major drain on the city of Boston. In 1850, the
cost of poor relief went above $100,000 for the first time, and
a decade later reached a peak of $168,389 in one year. Massa-
chusetts had tried to meet the problem by setting up four workhouses, where inmates could earn some of their keep, and it
also imposed a tax requiring immigrants to help support their
countrymen who became charity cases. But the cost of relief
kept rising, and no workhouses or special taxes could hold back
the tidal wave of Irish during the famine years.

Between 1845 and 1860, more immigrants came to this country from Ireland than all the rest of the world had sent us since
1776. The number of Irish who arrived in Boston during those
15 years topped 150,000. Not all of them stayed there, of course,

but a Massachusetts survey in 1850 reported 35,287 Irish-born in Boston, and five years later, the number had climbed to 68,100.

This early "population explosion" and the prolific nature of the Irish were to have a deep effect on Boston—on its business, social, educational, and religious life.

The Irish would change the city, and the city would change them.

Philadelphia was a favorite haven of immigrants from Ireland from early Colonial days. It offered some religious tolerance to Protestants and Catholics alike, and the city's part in this country's struggle for independence made it a symbol for Ireland's freedom fighters.

One of these political exiles was Mathew Carey, who arrived in 1784. He had been a hunted man in Dublin, and probably would not have escaped alive if the police had been a little smarter. He left surreptitiously and sailed to America disguised as a woman. Carey had worked in Ben Franklin's little printing shop near Paris and won the friendship of many prominent Frenchmen, including the Marquis de Lafayette. During a visit to Mount Vernon, Lafayette asked the young exile to meet with him there, and presented him with $400 to help the twenty-four-year-old Irishman get started in this country. Carey had been an editor in Dublin of the *Freemen's Journal*. He used the money to start the *Pennsylvania Herald* in 1785 and by the early 1800s, he had the biggest publishing and book-distributing business in the United States. His son, Henry Charles Carey, became a leading writer and thinker in the American school of economics. The Careys certainly would be on almost anyone's list of leading immigrants from Ireland.

Many of the Irish who landed in the city during the famine years stayed, but thousands in desperate need of jobs found them on canals and in the coal mines, and settled in all parts of Pennsylvania.

There had been Carrolls in Maryland since 1688, when Charles Carroll stepped ashore to become Lord Baltimore's Attorney General. His descendants, as we've already noted, included a signer of the Declaration of Independence, a delegate to the Constitutional Convention, and the first Roman Catholic Bishop in this country. The Signer's father, also named Charles Carroll, was considered the wealthiest man in the colonies, but could not hold office or vote, attend church services or teach children because of his religion, and for a time he paid double taxes. But when a friend suggested that it might be easier to drop his religion, Carroll said: "Do you advise me to quit a "false" religion and adopt one equally false . . . to humour the prejudices of fools or to be on a footing with knaves? I have too much sincerity and too much pride to do either."

Irish immigrants flowed into Baltimore to work on the canals and railroads, and join those who had moved into western Maryland earlier to build roads.

In the Ohio towns of Youngstown, Defiance, Dayton, and Toledo, the Irish were second only to the Germans among the foreign-born. Cincinnati attracted the state's largest group of Irish. In 1831, there were enough to support the *Catholic Telegraph*, founded by Bishop John Purcell. In 1842, Charles Dickens visited the city during an American tour, and reported seeing lines of green-scarved Irishmen marching in a Temperance Parade. He found them "as jolly and good-humored as ever, and working the hardest for their living."

The Irish who could save a few pennies trekked to Indiana, Ohio, Michigan, Wisconsin, and Illinois. They arrived with less on their backs and in their pockets than the more fortunate immigrants from other countries, but they reached the frontier.

There were nearly 200 Catholic Irish in Dubuque, Iowa, in 1835, according to the nose count of a mission priest. Galena,

Illinois, not far away, had a lively sprinkling of Foleys, Finleys, Rileys, and Murphys in the 1820s. At that time, Galena was larger than Chicago.

Dr. William Egan, a man of many talents, helped put Chicago on the map. He listed his occupations as "physician, lawyer, real estate operator and politician," but still found time to tout his adopted town as a place worthy of everyone's attention. He was the leading speaker at the breaking of ground for the Illinois and Michigan Canal in 1836, a project that provided work for thousands of willing Irish backs.

The frontier town of St. Louis had an Erin Benevolent Society in the early 1800s, and staged a day-long celebration in honor of St. Patrick in 1827. The title of "richest man west of the Mississippi" was the property of one John Mullanphy. He made most of his money in cotton. During the War of 1812, Andrew Jackson seized Mullanphy's cotton to stack for barricades against a British attack on New Orleans. According to the story, when the Irishman protested, Jackson handed him a gun and told him to get up there and defend his cotton. Mullanphy was especially quick on the draw in business. When he heard that peace was near, he went to New Orleans as quickly as possible, and bought up all the cotton he could find at four cents a bale, chartered a ship, and sent it to England, where he sold it at thirty cents a pound.

At the opening of the Civil War, the Irish were the largest foreign-born group in the South, despite the fact that there was little to draw any poor immigrant to that section of the country. He could not compete with slave labor in the cotton fields, and in the cities he was forced to compete with free Negroes for the lowest-paying jobs.

New Orleans had the largest number of Irish immigrants in the South, because it was the second largest receiver of new arrivals from overseas, next to New York. The city is known for its French and Spanish characteristics, but one writer noted:

[77]

"In 1830 with 49,826 inhabitants and in 1840 with 102,193, New Orleans had a population that was almost half foreign; of these foreigners, the Irish were, by far, the largest immigrant group."

Health problems plagued immigrants there, too. One epidemic of yellow fever struck down 7000 persons and half of them were Irish. According to one source: "If it had not been for the constantly recurring epidemics, New Orleans might have been as much an American Dublin as Boston and New York."

Some Catholics from Ireland believed that the states of Coahuila and Texas in Catholic Mexico might be good places to settle. Two of them, John McMullen and James McGloin, received a land grant from Mexico on condition that they bring colonists to develop it, and they were able to round up three boatloads of immigrants to settle the community of San Patricio between 1829 and 1833. James Power helped form another Irish colony of Refugio, near the Gulf of Mexico. When Texas moved toward independence, the Irish, always independence-minded, joined the Americans rather than the Mexicans. Forty-two Irish colonists signed the Goliad Declaration of Independence, and James Power signed the Texas constitution.

So much for the myth that nearly all the Irish walked down the gangplanks of ships in New York and Boston, built shanties and stayed there. Not only did they spread out to cities in the South and Midwest, but some of them, probably about 10 per cent, took up farming. There was no good reason why the Irishman should have done so, considering his disastrous experience on the land of the old country. Farming there gave him nothing more than a bowl of potatoes, even in the better years. In addition, most Irishmen were not all-around farmers with the kind of knowledge needed to run a large plot of ground in America with an assortment of fowl, livestock, and crops. Also, an operation of that kind requires a considerable amount of cash, which the immigrant Irishman did not have.

Still, Irish aid societies, guidebooks, and group newspapers advised the Irish to go west, leave the cities, and work for their forty acres in the wilderness. There were several schemes for Irish settlement in rural areas. In the 1860s, a hundred families came to farm in the Niagara River Valley, and a few years earlier, smaller groups of Irish immigrants founded farm neighborhoods in Pennsylvania. By 1870, there were Irish farmers in every rural county in Illinois. Fellow countrymen in Iowa were reading the *Boston Pilot*. Just before the Civil War, Minnesota counted nearly 13,000 Irish and many of them tilled the soil. Wisconsin reported practically the same figure.

Apparently, they did reasonably well. Joseph Schafer, an expert on the history of American farming, said of the Irish: "While there is a considerable vestige of permanently unprosperous Irish through the countryside, the proportion of successful farmers among them is as high as among the native and English stock.

The Irish journalist and orator, Thomas D'Arcy McGee, wanted to get the citified Irish out of their cellars and attics and their children out of the dirty streets of the slums. In one poem, he contrasted the life of the immigrant in New York with the joys of farm life, and wrote:

> The Irish homes of Illinois
> The happy homes of Illinois
> No landlord there
> Can cause despair
> Nor blight our fields in Illinois.

The colonization schemes of McGee and others collapsed under some important and determined opposition. Bishop Hughes of New York said most Irishmen would not know how to chop down a tree to clear their land, and would find the hardships and hazards too great to fight. He said he was opposed to all separate Irish settlements, and influential newspapers such as the *Irish News* and the *Freemen's Journal* supported his point of view. As late as 1881, the *Journal's* editor wrote: "If the Irishmen in New York are agricultural-minded they have plenty of unoccupied land in Long Island."

Plans for Irish farming communities were proposed in 1904 and again as recently as 1917, but by that time, most of the O'Learys, Finnegans, and O'Malleys were very much at home in the cities and the towns and not really interested in what remained of the frontier out west.

They loved people, wanted to be near their neighbors, their schools, and their Church. They had put aside their shovels and were through digging ditches and canals.

The Quinns, O'Connors, and O'Callahans had found the jobs they needed to help them crawl out of the hellholes of Five Points and Half-Moon Alley.

6 LABORING IRISH:

The Jump between Farming and Industry

An old Irish proverb says, "God never shuts one door but what he opens another." When, with homelessness and hunger, he closed the door marked "Ireland," he swung open another —marked "America."

Like the original colonists before them, the Irish migrated for many reasons—for greater freedom of worship, for an escape from the punishment meted out to revolutionaries, for sheer adventure. But one single reason was behind the overwhelming majority of emigrations—to get a job that would fend off starvation. At home was famine. Here—for the man willing to work for it—plenty. For the first time in modern history, a starving people was able to escape death—by changing countries.

The Irish were lucky in another respect too. Had they been able to choose from the span of centuries, they couldn't have picked a better period in which to migrate. The Western world was just entering that great era of change historians call the Industrial Revolution—the gradual switch from a farm to a factory economy. And the emigrating Irishman, in a single jump, made the switch with it. One day he was digging the depleted fields of an absentee landlord with implements long outdated, in a country that had not caught up with its times. A month later, he was unreeling the steel rails that were to lace together the greatest industrial empire of all time, in a country ahead of its day. In a sense, he leaped straight from the eighteenth to the twentieth century.

He had to adjust, not only to a new nation, but to a new kind of nation. The adjustment wasn't always easy. During this difficult time of change, he found it necessary on occasion to vent pent-up emotions in a brawl or two, or dose himself liberally.

Yes, the Irishman hit it right. Just as his way of life was going out of fashion at home, a new one was coming into style in America. The U.S.A., busily building a new world, needed all the strong backs it could find. It beckoned wildly to the people of Europe—and, because transatlantic passage was cheap, they poured across the sea. Between 1820 and 1860, better than five million passengers arrived from more than twenty countries. The United Kingdom furnished the largest number of all, two and three-quarter millions, of which nearly a million were from Ireland.

The Irishman was lucky in another way, too. He got in under the wire before the frontier closed. Once the United States had the Civil War out of the way, it started opening up the West. It pushed rail lines clear across the country, then passed the Homestead Act, freeing the West for colonization. Millions of immigrants, including the Irish, spread into this rich new land. By 1900, the frontier hardly existed any longer. During this period of frontier expansion, Western Europe, including Ireland, sent two million immigrants to America to join those already here—Eastern and Southern Europe sent only 180,000.

Then, during the first decade of the twentieth century, the trickle from Eastern and Southern Europe swelled into a six-million-man torrent. However, by this time, the best farming

[82]

Ireland's scholars kept the flame of knowledge burning throughout the so-called "Dark Ages." Early in the ninth century, monks began work on the "Book of Kells" which has been called "the most beautiful book in the world." This illuminated volume with its highly colored letters and designs, is a Latin translation of the Four Gospels. The masterpiece is now at Trinity College, Dublin. One page is turned each day to preserve its brilliant colors.

Ireland's beginnings are shrouded in the misty past. This dolmen or cromlech is in County Longford. No one knows who put the rocks together in this fashion— or why. Dolmens are to be found today in many sections of Ireland.

NORTH CHANNEL

Giant's Causeway   RATHLIN I.

Cushendun
Cushendall
ANTRIM
Larne
Londonderry
LONDON-
DERRY
Antrim   Carrickfergus
NORTHERN
IRELAND   Belfast
Ballyshannon   TYRONE
DOWN
FERMANAGH   ARMAGH
MONAGHAN

DONEGAL

ATLANTIC OCEAN

MAYO   SLIGO
Castlebar   LEITRIM   CAVAN   Dundalk
LOUTH
ROSCOMMON   Drogheda
LONGFORD   MEATH   Balbriggan
WEST
MEATH
Clifden   GALWAY   Athlone   Dublin
Galway   EIRE   OFFALY   Bray
GALWAY BAY   KILDARE
ARAN IS.   WICKLOW   Wicklow
CLARE   LEIX
Ennis   TIPPERARY   CAR-
Labasheeda   Limerick   LOW
SHANNON   LIMERICK   KILKENNY   WEXFORD
KERRY   Buttevant   Tipperary   Wexford
Waterford
Killarney   CORK   WATERFORD
DINGLE BAY   Cork   Youghal
Knight's Town   Kenmare   Blarney   Cobh (Queenstown)
ST. GEORGE'S CHANNEL
BANTRY BAY

IRISH SEA

SCALE OF MILES   0   50   100

While the rest of the world was preoccupied with history's first global war, Ireland was fighting a private war of its own—for freedom from the British. In this 1916 photograph, British soldiers open fire on Irish patriots sniping from houses 200 yards away.

Oliver Cromwell was one of Ireland's most brutal conquerors and his name is still reviled in town and country. In the 1650s, Cromwell's men slaughtered hundreds in the Massacre at Drogheda. Defenseless women and children were killed along with priests and town leaders.

In all the catalogues of Irish patriots, none is revered above Theobold Wolfe Tone, ironically a Presbyterian and the descendant of a Cromwellian planter. This is his bust, which stands in Trinity College, Dublin.

So numerous are Ireland's political heroes that it would be difficult to single out one man as the "George Washington of his country." Perhaps the best choice would be Charles Stewart Parnell, to whom Dublin erected this monument.

lands were virtually gone. Thus, the Irish not only were lucky in immigrating during the right century, but also during the right decades of that century.

The Irishman, in accepting the famineproof way of life America offered, also had to accept the strange jobs that went with it. He knew nothing of industrial work—even today only one-fifth of the breadwinning population of Ireland is employed in factories. Yet, that was the kind of work America offered: tending machines, laying rails, and digging canals.

The women had it easier. By and large, they went into domestic service—from keeping house for a family in Ireland to keeping house for a family in America. It was a far bigger and more luxurious house—and someone else's family.

Back home in Ireland, where the incentive was small, the Irish bore a reputation of apathy about work. "The Indolent Irish," their English landlords had called them, and the appellation was current in America. But not for long.

The Irishman made it clear that he would perform any job offered, so long as it paid a wage and did not conflict with his faith. Ralph Waldo Emerson wrote Henry Thoreau: "The humanity of the town suffers with the poor Irish, who receive but sixty, or even fifty cents, for working from dark till dark . . . Peter Hutchinson told me he had never seen men perform so much." Soon, an expression became current in America, "He [a good workman] does as much work as an Irishman."

The Irish had good reason to work hard. A laborer's wages in Ireland averaged around a dime a day. Here, they were a fabulous fifty cents, or even a dollar.

The first Irish over sent back letters filled with glowing words about America. "We eat like 'twas Christmas every day," said one. An old lady wrote home that this country had the best almshouses anywhere. In 1848, an Irish laborer in the Hudson River town of Peekskill (he spelled it "Beekskill") wrote his wife: "I work on a Railway at 8 shillings per day and pays 18 shillings per week for my Boarding this is a good country for them that is able to work. So I will be able to pay yours passage withe the help of God on the First of August next."

His letter, like millions of others, contained not only glowing words but also money.

The British Colonial Land and Immigration Commissioners kept a "confessedly very imperfect" account of Irish remittances back home. Their figures show that from 1848 to 1861, inclusive, Irish immigrants, earning the lowest salaries paid in America, sent home just short of $60,000,000. And this in a day when a dollar was worth no less than a dollar and twelve to twenty-five of them would buy a passage from Ireland to the United States.

There were other spurs to immigration beside money and letters home. Leading Irish refugees who had escaped to America published, in 1816, a pamphlet entitled "Hints to Irishmen Who Intend with Their Families to Make a Permanent Residence in America." It described with enthusiasm the demand for laborers and artisans and the wages an Irishman might expect to receive.

A popular song of the day said of America:

They say there's bread and work for all
And the sun shines always there.

The Irish responded to these enticements with enthusiasm. In the 1830s three-quarters of a million came to America, some 70 per cent of them laborers, but including a fair dusting of artisans and farmers with sufficient cash and skills to tide them over. However, after the potato crops began to fail, the type of immigrant changed. These were men and women who had felt the hot breath of death, who could not remember when they had not been hungry, who may even have stolen money to escape slow starvation. They came to America with little more than the clothes they wore and no more qualification for a job than a willingness to work and a back strongly sinewed by pushing a plow across barren land.

Statistics on precisely how early immigrants earned a living aren't easy to come by. But Professor Handlin, in his classic *Boston's Immigrants*, has come as close as any man can.

The first U.S. census was in 1790. However, it wasn't until 1850 that our decennial census asked such questions as "occupation" and "place of birth."

It would seem an easy task to go back to that census and find out just what jobs the early Irish held. Not so! The census completely failed to set up clear categories of occupations, so it was all but worthless in determining who did what for a living. For instance, it lumped together in one category "commerce, trade, manufactures, mechanic arts, and mining." As Handlin remarks, almost anyone in Boston could come under that tent. Some other groupings were "agriculture," "labor, not agriculture," "law, medicine and divinity," and "other pursuits requiring education."

Understandably, Professor Handlin found these categories all but worthless when he set out to write his book about Boston's immigrant. But he knew that the census had been taken by federal marshals. And he discovered their original records stored in Washington. The enumerators were considerably more specific in listing occupations than the men who wrote the final census report, and Professor Handlin was able to discover just what Boston's immigrants—largely Irish—did for a living.

They, in a word, labored. Forty-eight per cent of the city's Irish-born—7007 out of 14,595—were laborers. By contrast, only 20 per cent of the city's Negroes were laborers, 12 per cent of the German-born, and 8 per cent of those born in the British Isles other than Ireland.

In the second largest category, 2292 or 15 per cent were domestic servants. By contrast, 8 per cent of the city's Negroes were domestic servants, 3 per cent of the Germans, and 7 per cent of those born in the British Isles other than Ireland.

Among the remaining Irish-born there were 1145 tailors, 356 carpenters, 307 smiths, 247 workers in heavy industry, 222 waiters, 211 peddlers and other traders, 206 shoemakers, 203 masons, 190 seamen, 184 food dealers, 169 cabmen and truckmen, 132 clerks, 119 painters, and so on, including 32 physicians, 4 teachers, 24 actors and musicians, one lone financier and 177 with no known occupation. Oddly enough the list includes only 12 policemen.

The story is the same in other cities besides Boston. For the most part, the immigrant Irishman, because he brought no useful skill with him to the cities of America, had to start at the lowest rung of every occupational ladder—as hodcarrier or helper, street cleaner or porter, waiter or bartender, boatman, stevedore, or longshoreman.

As for the women, they became laundresses, charwomen, chambermaids, and waitresses. In Boston and New York, nearly every well-to-do household had its Irish maid. By 1860, the number of Irish girls employed as domestic servants was estimated to be 70,000 in New York alone. And the figure might well have been twice that in Boston.

When the garment trades began to center in New York around the middle of the century, Irishwomen operated the new sewing machines. Later, Jewish women sat behind those same machines. Now they're run by Puerto Ricans.

Many of the men went into transportation—as carters, cabmen, and carmen, or livery-stable workers. Often the Irishman took his first job caring for animals, because that was work he knew. Sometimes he went on to become a driver, then perhaps set up his own business, hauling freight or passengers or simply stabling horses.

And penny by penny, many of the Irish managed to save enough to open their own businesses. By all odds, the most numerous of these private endeavors were saloons. Not only the cheaper but also the better bars in the finest hotels were staffed by the Irish. Again, it was work they knew.

On the whole, the Irish willingly went into any field open to them except one—farming. Bishop Hughes notwithstanding, many of their priests and most of their lay leaders urged them to move out of the Eastern seaboard's crowded cities onto farms in the Middle West and West.

But most of them stuck to the cities. The reasons for this attitude were many. First, the Irishman didn't have the eight or nine dollars it took to move to the Middle West, and the additional money to establish himself once there. Second, he'd had enough of farming. All his memories of the agricultural life were bitter ones. He'd left Ireland because he couldn't support himself there as a farmer, and he wasn't going to try farming again. Besides, America represented to him, not only a new country, but also an exciting new kind of life. Plowing fields wasn't it.

Besides, rural America abounded with anti-Irish, anti-Catholic feeling. The Irishman felt he'd be better off amid people of his own kind, not isolated on a lonely farm.

Nonetheless, Irish leaders in the East persisted in trying to drain off into the empty countryside some of the Irish accumulating in the seaboard's swollen cities. In 1811, the New York *Shamrock* offered a booklet of advice to Irishmen who wanted to buy land. The aforementioned Thomas D'Arcy McGee wrote:

> In the villages of New England
> Are you happy, we would know:
> Are you welcome, are you trusted?
> Are you not? Then rise and go!

The Irish Emigrant Society of New York petitioned Congress to set aside public lands in Illinois for the Irish before temptation "presents to their lips the cup that turns man to brute, and the very energies that would have made the fields to blossom make the city groan." The House of Representatives turned the request down, 83 to 71.

There were wild-eyed schemes aplenty for the establishment of a "New Ireland" somewhere in the Far West, in Canada, or in Mexico.

The most ambitious of these led to the calling of the Irish Emigrant Aid Convention in Buffalo in 1856. The meeting, attended by about eighty lay and ecclesiastical leaders of the United States and Canada, proposed to establish a joint stock company which would buy land for sale on the installment plan to Irish settlers. The project managed to raise some $15,000 in three months, but eventually collapsed because of the opposition of Bishop Hughes and other clergy in the East.

Many Irish fled from the overcrowded cities to the countryside—but not to the farm. Some of them worked on road projects. In 1806, Congress finally got around to giving its blessing to a pet project of George Washington—the National Road. Thousands of Irishmen, recruited right from the docks, built the $7,000,000 turnpike, stretching 800 miles from Cumberland, Maryland, to Indianapolis. Many of them, liking the land, dropped off the work gangs to settle down in Pennsylvania, Ohio, and Indiana. But most, when the project was finished, returned to the tenements of the big cities.

However, it was in the construction of another form of transportation that the Irishman was most prominent. He arrived at a time when the United States was trying to solve the shipping problem inherent in its immensity by cutting great canals across the land, and he took on the job of building them.

George Washington headed the first company formed to build the Chesapeake and Ohio Canal, which finally was finished in 1840—by Irish workmen. The first canal in this country was dug at South Hadley, Massachusetts, between 1792 and 1796. But the great era of canal-building didn't come until the second decade of the succeeding century.

Settlers who opened new land in western New York, Pennsylvania, and Ohio had a difficult shipping problem on their hands. They needed to buy manufactured goods from the big cities in the East—and to ship their farm products to those cities for sale. Wagon haulage was sky high. It cost a hundred dollars to send a ton of freight from Buffalo to New York City, and the trip took twenty days. River freight was cheap and fast—especially if one used the new flat-bottomed steamers. But there were no through water routes between the new western farmland and the big cities in the East. One answer, of course, was to dig them. But most people thought that solution too costly.

A man who held a different opinion was DeWitt Clinton, Governor of New York. He proposed cutting a canal from the Hudson River at Albany 350 miles westward to Lake Erie at Buffalo.

Impossible! said the cynics, and the federal government agreed. It would have no part of such a harebrained project. So Clinton talked New York State into going it alone.

When the first spadeful of dirt was turned in 1817, the Irish had not arrived in any numbers. But as the great scar inched its way across the map of New York, more and more Irish—anxious to get out of the cities where jobs were scarce—entered the ranks of laborers. By 1818, three thousand of them were working on the project.

Early in the game, the Erie Commissioners hit on a system that was to be adopted by later canal and railroad builders. They accepted competitive bids for short sections of the waterway, varying up to three miles, then loaned money to the would-be entrepreneurs to hire laborers and buy equipment.

The more ambitious Irish diggers soon set themselves up as contractors. After the Erie Canal was finished in 1825, many of them moved on to other canals or to railroad or building construction. Thus was born the Irish contractor, who still flour-ishes in our big cities.

The Erie Canal not only gave employment to thousands of Irish, it also channeled them out of the big cities into the hinter-land. The Erie and the thousand miles of branch canals that were constructed after 1825 needed numbers of men for mainte-nance and operation. And many of the laborers, digging their way west from Albany to Buffalo, dropped out to help run the canal.

Others turned away from its banks to find different employ-ment—as hands on the rich farms of upstate New York, as chop-pers in its thick forests, as stonecutters in the quarries, as salt-makers, lake sailors, Buffalo longshoremen, or as merchants and businessmen.

The Erie Canal that the Irish had dug added to the prosperity of the upstate cities—Albany, Utica, Troy, Rome, Syracuse, Lock-port, Rochester, and Buffalo. And the Irish themselves added to the population of those cities. The canal, which carried goods from the Great Lakes to Manhattan in eight days, helped to double New York City's population in the space of twenty years. And the Irish, whose ten-dollars-a-month labor had created the canal, rose with the general prosperity.

The success of "Clinton's Ditch" inspired other canals, and more Irish were coming ashore to water this inspiration into life with their perspiration. In 1826, more than a hundred canals were finished, in the making, or projected.

An army of Irishmen labored on Pennsylvania's combined canal and portage railroad, which was started in 1831 as a direct result of the Erie's success. This project, regarded as the engi-neering wonder of its age, linked Pittsburgh and Philadelphia. The Pennsylvania Main Line Canal carried boats from Philadel-phia to Hollidaysburg, where the portage railroad picked them up for the trip over the crest of the Allegheny Mountains to

Johnstown. There, the canal took over again for the run to Pittsburgh.

Thousands of men, mostly Irish, dug the Ohio and Erie Canal. Others, farther west, cut the Wabash and Erie, linking Lake Erie and the Ohio River at Evansville, Indiana. Still farther west, other Irishmen swarmed into the muddy little town of Chicago where the Illinois and Michigan Canal was sprouting. When cash was tight, the Illinois and Michigan laborers were paid in scrip convertible into land holdings. Most of the needy Irish were forced to sell their paper at a discount, a step their ancestors were to regret.

Agents for contractors waited on the docks of Boston and New York to persuade Irishmen used to digging for potatoes to dig for a paycheck instead. Ads asking for diggers appeared in Irish newspapers. Sharp contractors often advertised for two thousand men when they only wanted a thousand, in order to beat down the wages.

The practice of letting out contracts for small segments of a canal also led to another labor abuse. The subcontractor, operating on a shoestring, sometimes ran into financial difficulties which he solved by making off with the payroll. Such incidents, more often than not, touched off one of the riots whose frequency made the Irish canal worker infamous for brawling.

Such riots might not have been so frequent and so violent had it not been for the whisky that was a standard part of the canal digger's ration. Just as the modern office worker has his coffee break, so the canal digger had his whisky break. Some contractors offered as many as five or more such alcoholic breathers a day, the first at sunrise, when work started. The contractor believed that he more than made up for the cost of the stimulant by the increased surge of work it brought on.

The digger needed all the strength he could muster to get through a day. His backbreaking labors started the moment the sun peeped over the horizon, and lasted until it was too dark to dig, with time out only for food and drink. He lived in a crudely built hut, scant protection against wind, rain, and swarms of insects. Understandably, no women were permitted in these shanty towns, so he was separated from his family. He was prey to injury and disease, with no physician to treat him. Little wonder he rioted when a crook made off with the few dollars he'd worked a month to earn.

The Chesapeake and Ohio Canal Company, for instance, building a waterway from the Potomac to the Maryland coal mines and thence, it hoped, to the Ohio, often was in financial difficulties, and the men sometimes waited many months for their pay. It was little enough—eight to nine dollars a month in winter, with deductions for board and time lost because of bad weather, and ten to twelve dollars a month in summer, with food included. But what food! Contemporary accounts say many of the men literally died of malnutrition and the ailments it brought on. In time, illness became so frequent that the company was forced to hire a doctor to care for the ailing.

But even he was not proof against disease. When cholera struck the Chesapeake and Ohio operation in 1833, hundreds of men died. The late George W. Potter, whose *To the Golden Door* gives a vivid account of the disaster, quotes a contemporary source as saying:

"The poor creatures, after seeing a few sudden and awful deaths among friends, straggled off in all directions through the country; but for many of them, the panic came too late. They were dying in all parts of Washington County at a distance of five to 15 miles from the river. I myself saw numbers of them in carts and on foot making their way toward Pennsylvania."

Men left their friends dying in fields or on roads. Often, if one of a group in a shanty fell ill, the others forced him outside to die, so as to lessen the chance of contamination.

The company set up an emergency hospital at Harpers Ferry, "with as few and as cheap articles . . . as possible," as directed by its president. Even so, the laborers were assessed twenty-five cents a month for their share of the hospital's upkeep. But the deaths continued.

The authorities at Hagerstown, Maryland would not permit the burial of cholera victims in St. Mary's Catholic cemetery. The company itself refused to provide plots for the dead. Finally, however, the board of directors authorized the engineers "to use any waste ground owned by the company for the interment of persons dying upon the works of the company."

Labor unions were unheard of in those days, but the Irish canal diggers formed a rough substitute for them anyway. As they had fought villainous landlords in the Old Country, so they fought crooked and grasping contractors in the New Country— with secret societies. The first Irish secret society is believed to have been formed on the Delaware and Hudson Canal around 1827, and soon the groups had sprung up on other public works.

Often a society would send an anonymous note warning a contractor that he'd better fire a certain offending foreman. If he laughed off the threats, the foreman might be found the following night with his throat cut. Occasionally, a contractor out of favor with a secret society was ordered to give up a job entirely. If he didn't his equipment might be smashed.

Sometimes a secret society enforced a boycott on an offending contractor by beating up his laborers until no one would work for him. Witnesses dared not testify against a known member of a secret society in a court of law. Its vengeance was swift and complete—often death.

In such cases, the executioner usually came from some distance—possibly the next section. Thus, the men who normally would fall under suspicion were able to provide themselves with iron-clad alibis. Later, perhaps, one of their number would be called on to return the favor by serving as enforcer in another section.

The secret societies sometimes turned, not on outsiders, but on one another. A classic example was the fight between a group of South Irishmen called the Corkonians and a band of County Longford men from the North of Ireland. The battle took place in 1834, on the Chesapeake and Ohio Canal.

The Corkonians watched Longford men take jobs they thought should be theirs, and decided to enforce a closed shop. Guerrilla warfare between the two groups dragged on for some months, but finally broke out into the open when a Longford man was beaten up by a group of Corkonians. The Longfords and Corkonians met in open battle near the town of Williamsport, Pennsylvania. Some 300 Corkonians, outnumbered two to one, were put to rout by the Longford men. Five persons were killed, dozens brutally mauled.

The outraged citizenry called out the militia, but instead of sending the two groups packing, it was decided to negotiate a peace. Fourteen leaders from each faction were called together at Lyle's Tavern in Williamsport. There, with the leading citizens of the village looking on, they drew up a peace treaty. The document that proclaimed the hoped-for end of bloody brawling read in part:

"Whereas great commotions and divers riotous acts have resulted from certain misunderstandings and alleged grievances, mutually urged by two parties of laborers and mechanics, engaged on the line of the Chesapeake and Ohio Canal, and natives of Ireland; the one commonly known as the Longford men, the other as the Corkonians; and whereas it has been found that these riotous acts are calculated to disturb the public peace, without being in the least degree beneficial to the parties opposed to each other, but on the contrary are productive of great injury and distress to the workingmen and their families—

"Therefore, we, the undersigned, representatives of each party, have agreed to, and do pledge ourselves to support and carry into effect the following terms of the agreement:

"We agree, for ourselves, that we will not, either individually or collectively, interrupt, or suffer to be interrupted in our presence, any person engaged on the line of the canal, for or on account of a local difference of national prejudice and that we will use our influence to destroy all these matters of difference growing out of this distinction of parties, known as Corkonians and Longfords."

Many times, secret societies enforced strikes, or "turnouts," as they then were called, to protest abuses or enforce demands for higher wages. As often as not, the local militia broke up the "turnout."

The Irish had no sooner dug the nation's canals than they were called upon to supplant—or at least supplement—them with another form of transportation, the railroad.

The nation had been tinkering with railroads for some time, with only so-so results. The Baltimore and Ohio started general operation in 1830, but offered little competition to the canals. However, the business panic of 1837 put an end to almost all canal building, and by the time it was over, the railroads were here to stay.

First, the railroads were built as feeders to the canals and rivers, but they soon tired of this supplementary role, and the long main lines began going into operation, sometimes only cinder-throwing distance from the rival canal.

By 1840, there were 1076 miles of canals in the United States and 2818 miles of railroads. By 1850, rail lines had stretched to 9021 miles and canal mileage had shrunk, as banks caved in here and there. In another ten years, railroad mileage had tripled and the canals were all but empty.

The workmen who had built the canals built the railroads. Irish laborers dropped their shovels and picked up spiking mauls and rail tongs. The wages were the same—a dollar or less a day. There were the same shanties, the same backbreaking labor —up to 16 hours under a broiling sun. The physical perils were the same—the average working life of a railroader, it was estimated at the time, ran no more than seven years. The contractors and subcontractors were the same—and their morals were as mixed as ever.

Time and again, bosses made off with payrolls. Not only that, contractors often forced the laborers to trade at the stores they'd established, by paying them on paper only redeemable there. The prices, of course, were highly inflated. One contractor on the New York and Erie Railroad opened a drygoods store nearby, and forced the workers to accept their pay in clothing, which they had to sell at a loss to buy food.

Often, contractors paid their men in shinplaster, bills of distant, perhaps nonexistent, banks, which they'd purchased at a discount, and which were not negotiable in most nearby stores.

A contractor learned to capitalize on his laborers' weakness for drink. Sometimes he opened a grog shop, with inflated prices but liberal credit, so he could get the men in his debt.

Again, finding himself unable to meet a payroll, he would treat his workers to a barrel of free whisky. Before they had reached the bottom, likely as not, men of one county were fighting men of another. When the law was summoned, the drunken diggers fled. They were too fearful of arrest to return to their jobs, so the contractor pocketed the payroll and hired another crew. Meanwhile, another black eye for Irish labor.

But just as the Irish laborers found the same poor working conditions and the same cheating contractors on the railroads as on the canals, so they met those conditions in the same way—with the secret society. And, as they had on the canals, the secret societies sometimes went too far.

In November 1834, for instance, members of a secret society on the Baltimore and Ohio Railroad killed two men, beat up several others, then looted a store and a tavern. Anne Arundel County in Maryland called out the militia, surrounded two sections of the railroad, and clamped 300 men in jail. They were kept there until detectives had tracked down the murderers. One of them was hanged, two others given long jail terms.

The inhabitants of Anne Arundel and Prince Georges Counties, at a protest meeting, blamed the whole incident on the railroad for hiring "the present class of Irish laborers" whom they called "a gang of ruffians and murderers." They sent a letter to the president of the B&O warning that if it didn't take measures to protect the citizenry, they would "drive every Irishman off the road from the Patapsco to the Big Patuxent." The Irish, taking their cue, fled in all directions. Local authorities, to make sure they did not return, knocked apart their miserable shanties.

Labor contractors were not content to sign up Irishmen as they pushed their heads up out of the reeking holds of the immigrant ships—they sent to Ireland to fetch them. Advertisements in Irish newspapers told of high wages, good food, and plenty of liquor on the gangs constructing American canals and railroads. Thousands of Irishmen, looking around at their miserable homes, decided to go.

Those who could not raise the fare frequently were advanced it by the labor contractor. Once here, they found themselves in virtual bondage, working without pay until the loan could be satisfied. "Working off the dead horse," the Irish called it.

There was one thing the Irishman got out of it all, besides a start in America. Forced to build, he learned how to be a good builder. Irish names adorn many—perhaps most—of the big multi-city construction companies in America: names such as McShane, Tulley, Farley, Foley, Kelly, Walsh, Driscoll, McDonald, and Crimmins. When subway builder John McDonald died in 1911, all power on the New York subways was shut off for two minutes. Daniel Crimmins, looking up instead of down, built many of New York's now-demolished Els. He also paved Broadway and erected some 400 big buildings in New York City.

The early Irish worked at other hard and dangerous jobs besides building the nation's transportation systems. They also worked to obtain the fuel for those systems. Between the Civil War and World War I, coal mining became one of the fastest-growing industries in America. Production doubled every eight or nine years.

Most of it still comes from fields in Pennsylvania and West Virginia. And it was in those fields that the Irishman, with no experience in mining, first went down into the pits.

In the 1860s and 1870s, the miners were about half Irish, and the rest English, Scottish, and Welsh—Modocs, they were called. Ireland has no coal mines. Even today it gets its power from hydroelectric projects or from peat-fuel generators. What coal is needed must be imported from England.

But it was different elsewhere in the British Isles. England's whole industrial economy is based on coal, which it has mined for centuries. Scotland has its great Lanarkshire mines and the pits around the Firth of Forth. The rich fields of Wales, which provide the best grade of steam coal, are an important factor in Britain's industrial greatness.

Thus the Modocs—experienced miners all—got the better jobs; the Irish were the laborers. This only tended to increase the natural animosity of the two groups.

To say that conditions in the mines were bad would be one of the more colossal understatements. Men crouched in narrow seams, hacking the coal off the walls with hand picks. Women and boys dragged it in baskets to the surface. There, children and old men sorted out the slate. A child, glancing at the bent gnarled old man working beside him, could read the pages of his own future: from sorting coal, to digging it, to sorting it again, with poverty and pain all the way.

For his work, the miner made around thirty dollars a month, oftentimes less. Some mines paid in scrip, redeemable only in company stores. In many cases, the miner was compensated by the ton of coal shoveled. At the end of the day, a checkman looked over the coal each man had produced to estimate how much of it was slate. He decided, in effect, how much the miner made for his work, and his word was law. Since his sinecure depended on the good will of management, the checkman tended to find a high percentage of slate in all coal. If times were hard, the word went out, and the amount of slate "discovered" by the checkman rose spectacularly.

Sometimes the miner was paid by the carload. Here, too, he often was cheated. Management frequently increased the size of a car without telling him.

The miner usually lived in a company house and bought his food at a company store. The house was a dirty hovel, and although he paid only six or seven dollars a month for it, the rent fell due whether he was working or not. In slack times, the mines closed down, and the men went heavily into the red. Many, for all their lives, were never free of a cloud of debt over their heads.

Even after working a month of hard six-day weeks composed of 15-hour days, a man sometimes found himself in debt to the company—or, at best, breaking even—because of its charges for supplies, rent and groceries. Leonard Wibberley gives, in his *Coming of the Green*, an actual sample of such a "bobtail check" as it was called.

A man had mined 49 tons of coal at seven and one-half cents a ton, for which he was credited with 35 dollars and three cents. Against this, he was charged eight dollars and 25 cents for supplies, 30 cents for the services of a blacksmith, 30 cents for fixing two drills, six dollars rent, and 20 dollars and 18 cents for groceries—which added up to exactly 35 dollars and three cents.

Thus, in many cases, the men were simply provided with a livelihood for their labor, and in this they were no different from Southern slaves, except the slaves didn't perform such dangerous work.

Of course, the miners were free to live in other than company houses and to buy at other than company stores. But it was a well-known fact that the tenure of such miners was short. They were the first fired. Not only that, the mines often were located in isolated places where there were no other stores to trade in or houses to rent.

To earn his dubious living, the miner labored in an unventilated shaft where the air was hot as a stove and thick with coal dust. Often he worked thigh-deep in water. A furnace roared at the bottom of the entrance shaft, its purpose to provide some air circulation and thus prevent the accumulation of an explosive methane mixture called firedamp. But the furnace itself sometimes set off the explosion—barring all exit from the mine and cooking the trapped miners alive.

Death sometimes came in other ways—through slow suffocation in an airless chamber deep in the earth, for instance, or under a ton of rock crashing through weak supports.

In the Avondale pit at Plymouth, Pennsylvania, 179 died in 1869 when the furnace set off an explosion. One hundred and twelve died in 1884 at Pocahontas, Virginia. Seven years later, the toll was 109 at Mount Pleasant, Pennsylvania. In 1900, at Scofield, Utah, 200 were killed in a mine disaster. There were two major mine tragedies in 1902—one of which killed 184 in Coal Creek, Tennessee, another taking 112 lives at Johnstown, Pennsylvania. Besides these, there were scores of small disasters, killing ten or 15 men.

The states and the federal government passed laws, of course. But they were not strictly enforced. The mine owners, it must be remembered, were men of influence, backed by money and friends in high places.

During this period, there were no workmen's compensation laws; no pensions for the maimed, the ill, and the aged; no benefits for widows whose husbands would lay forever in the coal seams of Pennsylvania. If a man became too old or too ill to work, he sent his children into the sorting room or his wife to scrub floors.

As soon as a boy was old enough, he joined his father in the mines to help support the family—and thus the vicious circle would start all over again. For another generation, the family would be chained to the coal fields.

The mine company owned the mine town, lock, stock, and barrel. The police were in its pay, as were town officials. The miner was completely at the mercy of the owners. Starting in 1861 and continuing until 1875, there were several attempts to form miners' unions. Every one collapsed. In some instances, the organizers sold out to the company. In others, the infant union resorted to a strike which hurt the miners more than the company. Management police saw to it that there were no picket lines. In the end, cracked heads and starved bellies sent the men back into the pits for the same miserable wages they'd received before.

Here—as on the canals and railroads—the beleaguered Irishman resorted to his ancient weapon: the secret society. The Molly Maguires, or something like them, became active in the Pennsylvania coal fields after the collapse of the Mineworkers Benevolent Association in 1875.

Of course, no one ever proved that the long chain of assassinations, burnings, and beatings in the Pennsylvania coal fields were hatched by a single terrorist organization—much less that it was named the Molly Maguires. The reader will recall that a secret society was active in Ireland at the time whose members were called Molly Maguires because they set out on their midnight forays dressed as women. For some reason, it was assumed that the Mollys had crossed the Atlantic to America, and that they were active in Pennsylvania.

The Ancient Order of Hibernians, in most states dedicated

to charity, sociability, and bigger and better St. Patrick's Day parades, was in Pennsylvania somewhat more militant. In fact, many men suspected of being Mollys also were members of the Hibernians, and some persons thought the two identical. Here again, nothing was ever proved.

In 1862, mine foreman F. W. S. Langdon of Carbon County was murdered after he'd accused a man suspected of being a Molly Maguire of disrespect to the American flag. In 1863, mine boss James Bergan of Schuylkill County was killed by five strangers who invaded his home late at night. A month later, a Heckscherville mine owner was attacked by a band of men but escaped when he pulled a gun. In 1865, superintendent David Muir of a Schuylkill colliery was murdered. A year later, the same thing happened to another colliery superintendent, and in 1874 to a third.

After the final effort at unionization was crushed in 1875, the terrorism increased. A mine foreman was murdered on his way to work. Two days later, another was shot down in a railroad station. And so it went.

The mine owners, whose police departments were powerless against the Molly Maguires, decided to get outside help. They turned to a man whose fame was growing by leaps and bounds in the United States—Allan Pinkerton. Pinkerton had emigrated from Glasgow to the United States in 1842 and had opened a cooper's shop in West Dundee, Illinois. He was an ardent abolitionist, and his shop became a way station on the so-called Underground Railroad, which fugitive slaves followed out of the South.

After he had discovered and broken up a gang of counterfeiters, Pinkerton was elected county sheriff in 1846, and four years later became the first detective in the Chicago police force. In the same year, he established his own detective agency —thus becoming America's first "private eye," the prototype of a band perhaps more numerous in fiction than in fact. Pinkerton solved a number of train and express company robberies and his agency flourished.

In 1861, he foiled a plot to assassinate Abraham Lincoln en route to Washington for his inauguration, and during the Civil War he organized an espionage system behind Confederate lines. The mine owners understandably decided that if anyone could bring the Molly Maguires to heel, Allan Pinkerton was the man.

Pinkerton picked one of his best operatives to handle the job. He was an Irish-born detective in the Chicago headquarters of the agency, James McParlan. He had come from County Armagh only a few years before, but, as far as Pinkerton was concerned, he had already proved his mettle.

McParlan was a slim dark-haired man of medium height, but with massive shoulders. He had a fine Irish tenor, he could execute an expert Irish jig, he was adept with his fists, his blarney was elegant—he was, in fact, the kind of man every Irishman wanted to be. Before joining Pinkerton, he had been a teamster, deckhand, lumberman, bartender, cop, and proprietor of a liquor store. When he was handed the job of breaking up the Molly Maguires, he was just short of thirty years old.

And so it came to pass that McParlan, calling himself McKenna, arrived in Pottsville, Pennsylvania, in mid-1875. He hadn't been there long before learning that a man named Pat Dormer, the proprietor of a saloon, actually was the leader of a terrorist gang called The Sleepers. McParlan went straight to the saloon and flung open the swinging doors.

After a "shine" or so, as a straight drink was called, McParlan entertained the assembled guests with a few Irish airs, then danced a jig. His popularity was such that he was invited to sit at the table of the town bully, a huge Irishman named Frazier. McParlan, Frazier, and a character called Kelly the Bum engaged in a hand of cards, and it wasn't long before Frazier was accusing McParlan of cheating. McParlan called Frazier a string of names, and the assembled drinkers gathered round to see Frazier wipe up the floor with the cheeky young dancer.

Frazier had never been beaten in a fight, but he was beaten that day. His huge hamlike fists rammed empty air, as McParlan danced out of the way. McParlan, in turn, landed repeatedly, and in a few minutes Frazier was stretched full length on the floor. Dusting his hands McParlan said: "The drinks are on me, boys."

It wasn't long before the Pinkerton man was the hero of the coal fields. The scene at Pottsville was repeated elsewhere, as he toppled bullies, beat up company policemen and even disarmed a drunken knife-wielder. Finally, he got what he wanted —an invitation to join the Ancient Order of Hibernians.

Soon, he was in the thick of intrigue. As he met in secret council to plot murders and beatings, his reports went back to his boss, Allan Pinkerton, and then to the mine owners. As a result of these reports, a number of men accused of murders dating back ten years or more were rounded up. Trial of the cases, many of which went to the Supreme Court, continued for two years. During this period, McParlan spent much of his time in the witness chair. His testimony sent nineteen men to the gallows.

Many of the trials were conducted in such a high-handed manner that public sentiment, which had been running strongly against the Mollys, swung round. After the last man was hanged, it was generally conceded that the Molly Maguires were no more. There still were scattered murders, burnings, and beatings in the coal fields, but the public was satisfied that the Mollys were not behind them, that each was an individual case. Actually, of course, the Molly Maguires may never have existed in the first place.

After the downfall of the terrorists, the miners again turned to efforts at organizing a legitimate union. The United Mine Workers of America, organized in the late 1880s, finally succeeded where other unions had failed. In 1897, it called a strike of all soft or bituminous coal miners. The strike lasted three months, during which time the men and their families all but starved. In the end, they won a great victory—among other things, a 20 per cent rise in pay.

However, the growing young union soon ran into trouble. By this time the great tide of emigrants from Central and Southern Europe was in full flow. Management began quietly laying off the canny Irishmen and hiring the innocent newcomers— hoping to pit nationality against nationality and break the union. When Irishman John Mitchell became president of the United Mine Workers of America in 1898, he began a campaign to unite all ethnic groups. He discouraged the formation of nationality clubs, and made sure that all immigrant blocs were represented on committees and slates of candidates. Everywhere he went he preached the same message—the miners were no longer Irishmen or Poles or Italians, they were Americans.

Finally, with the union growing strong, Mitchell decided to hit the anthracite coal fields. He asked management for a conference to discuss wages, hours, and working conditions. Management refused. On May 15, 1902, he called his men out on strike. They obeyed without a word. For months, the strike dragged on. Hard coal disappeared from the market. Factories all over the country shut down. Still, management and Mitchell sat tight. Finally, with unemployment mounting, President Theodore Roosevelt decided to step into the picture. He invited Mitchell and the mine owners to a conference at the White House. Again, Mitchell offered to arbitrate. Again, the owners stood pat. The hot-headed Teddy Roosevelt quickly denounced management for its uncompromising attitude. He took strong issue with the owners' claim that the strike was the work of a gang of agitators.

The owners, stung by the rebuke, gave in. They agreed to the appointment of an impartial commission to look into the miners' grievances and make recommendations. Meanwhile, the men went back to work. In due time, the commission came up with its report, which the owners adopted. The fruits of victory were sweet: a 10 per cent wage increase, a promise from management that it would no longer discriminate between union and non-union employees and, sweetest of all, recognition of the United Mine Workers as the official bargaining agent for the anthracite miners. That victory, achieved when John L. Lewis was a lad of twelve, was the great breakthrough for American labor.

The first big attempt to organize an over-all national labor organization resulted in the Noble Order of the Knights of Labor, formed by a group of Philadelphia tailors in 1869. For many years, the organization was a secret one, which led to its condemnation by the Roman Catholic Church. James Cardinal Gibbons of Baltimore finally persuaded Pope Leo XIII and the Vatican hierarchy that it actually was not a secret organization in a canonical definition—that is, it had no pledge prejudicial to the confessional, and the ban was raised. In 1881, the Knights abandoned secrecy altogether.

The Knights reached their peak under Terence Vincent Powderly, the son of an Irish immigrant. While Powderly was Grand Master Workman, the Knights attained a membership of more than 700,000. They won two important strikes, on the Union Pacific in 1884 and the Wabash Railroad a year later. However, the union had several built-in weaknesses, one of which was its open-door policy. It admitted almost anyone to membership. The only groups excluded were bankers, lawyers, gamblers, and stockbrokers.

Under the slogan "An Injury to One Is the Concern of All," the Knights battled on a number of fronts—for an eight-hour day, for abolition of child labor, and equal pay for equal work. But the union was heavy on idealism, weak on finances. After several long-drawn-out strikes had drained its war chest, it began

Things grew so bad in Ireland that farmers could not feed their families.
Crop failures meant disaster. The poor were ragged and hungry. In 1848, a
newspaper pictured the alternatives: poverty in Ireland, or abundance
in America, and suggested that emigration was a remedy.

America offered new hope, but the immigrant learned quickly that the streets were not paved with gold and that the living conditions in the big city slums were as bad as those he had left behind. Tenements were filthy and overcrowded and the death rate was high.

OPPOSITE PAGE: The immigrant "runner" was always on hand to welcome the new arrivals and to offer help in finding rooms and jobs. But the "runner" often was an unscrupulous former immigrant, making his living by cheating his old countrymen.

Immigrant ships were crowded to capacity as they left
Liverpool and other ports. Bad food and water, unsanitary conditions, sickness
and death rode with the traveler to the shores of America. Hundreds
perished along the perilous route.

After weeks at sea, the long journey finally was over. This was the bay and harbor of New York in 1847. The round building at the left is Castle Garden, point of arrival for immigrants.

One of the immigrant's first aims was to find employment which would help him buy food and pay his rent. The Labor Exchange in front of Castle Garden, New York, was set up to aid the new arrival in his search for a job.

to wither away. By 1890, it was down to 100,000 members, and at the turn of the century it had virtually ceased to exist.

No sooner had it bowed out than the sturdy, successful American Federation of Labor rose to take its place. Samuel Gompers, who organized it in 1886, had as a lieutenant a young son of Cork immigrants, Peter McGuire. As founder of the Brotherhood of Carpenters and Joiners, he proposed, in an address before the annual A.F. of L. meeting, a yearly national holiday called "Labor Day." The union heartily endorsed the idea, and twelve years later Congress made it official.

Down through the years, the Irish have been leaders in the labor movement. Just as Irish immigrant worshipers wanted Irish priests, so Irish immigrant laborers wanted their unions run by Irishmen. And the Irishman, with a firsthand familiarity with the problems of labor and a natural bent for the give-and-take of politics, made an excellent organizer.

There have been many prominent Irish labor leaders down through the years—George Meany, president of the A.F. of L., for example, and that prototype of an Irishman, Michael J. Quill, president of the Transport Workers Union, whose carefully cultivated brogue has survived intact since he migrated in 1926. These—and others like them—are labor leaders for the Irish laboring man.

As time went on the Irish laborer, or his son—or his son's son—gradually worked his way up the economic ladder, but it was hard going. By 1880, some 29 per cent of Boston's Irish were still laborers, as contrasted to 48 per cent twenty years before.

There were three reasons why the Irishman found it hard to better his lot, the first of which was money. He had come here broke. It was all very well for priests, newspapers, and immigrant welfare organizations to tell him to leave the city—to go west where the opportunity was greater. He just didn't have the money. It took capital to get there and capital to get started. He didn't have it, and with his low wage, he couldn't save or borrow it.

The second reason was prejudice. Entrenched Americans had the Irish tagged as ignorant and lazy. "No Irish Need Apply" and similar phrases appeared in many an advertisement in newspapers of the early nineteenth century. For instance, the New York *Evening Post* of September 4, 1830: "Wanted—a cook or chambermaid. She must be American Scotch, Swiss or African—no Irish." It took time for the Irish to overcome the prejudice of fellow Americans, much of it inherited from their English ancestors. And it was time lost in getting ahead.

The third reason was education. The Irish, for the most part, believed the Church should provide education, and numbers of them refused to enroll their children in public schools. As parochial schools were inadequate or nonexistent, many of the children attended no school at all. In 1877, some 9000 of the 43,000 children in Boston between the ages of five and fifteen were not in school, and most of them were Irish. A first generation Irish son, deprived of his education by his parents' beliefs, often remained as ignorant as his immigrant father, who had been deprived of his education by the Irish Penal Laws.

An Irish-American did not necessarily need an education to become a successful businessman. Quite a few immigrants managed to build going enterprises, but many sank dismally back down into the laboring class when one of the periodic panics (as depressions were called in those days) whiplashed the country.

The first panic of the new machine age occurred in 1819. Another came ten years later. The most severe in the history of the United States up to that time began in 1837 and dragged on for five long years. A brief recovery turned out to be the prelude to a subsequent collapse in 1847. Ten years later, in 1857, still another severe depression settled over America. All of these happened during the time when the Irish were trying to gain an economic toehold in the New World. And, lacking capital, they suffered most.

In the old days, before the Industrial Revolution, things had been different. When times were hard a man could always scratch some sort of living from the earth. But you couldn't grow a life-saving potato in South Boston or the 6th Ward of New York. It was either a job or the almshouse.

And that's just where many Irish immigrants landed. The foreign population of the Boston almshouse jumped by 115 per cent from 1829 to 1834, while the native-born inmates declined 10 per cent. George Potter reports in his previously mentioned book *To the Golden Door* that of the 870 foreigners in the New York City almshouse in November 1834, some 305 were natives of Ireland. In that same year there were 1303 persons from Ireland among the 1895 foreign-born in the Philadelphia almshouse.

There was, of course, a great hue and cry—just as there is a hue and cry in New York City today over the proportion of Puerto Ricans on relief rolls. "This country," said the commissioners of the New York almshouse in 1835, "has become the great receptacle for the miserable outcasts from European society."

Little did they know, the editorial writers and speechmakers who complained about the high incidence of Irish poverty, how much the Irishman dreaded the almshouse. He associated it with the patronizing Protestantism of the old country—and his suspicions were fed by the fact that all of the poorhouses of America were operated by Protestants.

As time went on, of course, the Church, growing stronger, was better able to take care of its poor. And with the passing years the Irishman—saving his money, gaining in education and general acceptance—was able to push his way upward. Just as he had supplanted the old Yankee laborer—picked up the Yankee's shovel, as it were, while the Yankee became the straw boss—so a new army of immigrants—from Italy, Poland, Czechoslovakia, Greece, and the Balkans—was arriving to supplant him as a laborer. And the Irishman, who had been through it all, became, in turn, the straw boss.

Today, there no longer are any statistics on the ethnic division of the labor force—how many Irishmen are priests, publicans, or policemen. But one does not need statistics to realize that the Irish have left the labor gangs for every field of endeavor open to men. You will find Irish names lettered in gold on the outside of Wall Street offices and in the by-lines of your newspaper. A broad Irish face may smile out at you from under the brim of a policeman's cap. The Irish smile may belong to a soldier, sailor, or marine. An Irishman may fill your tooth, change your oil, set your broken arm, or hear your confession. His voice, still with the faint flutter of a brogue, tells you what his party will do when elected, and describes the glories of a new soap. With equal aplomb, he is in the drivers' seats of tractors, tanks, taxis, bulldozers, and jet planes.

In short, the Irishman does what other Americans do. But it would be wrong to imply that the Irish are equally spread through all professions, that they have not clustered in some and avoided others. Just as the Greeks seem to tend toward the restaurant business, the Italians toward barbering and masonry, the Chinese toward laundering, so the Irish have their chosen ways of earning a living.

What are the "Irish" occupations?

One, of course, is the priesthood, which we discuss in another chapter. Another is politics. All Irishmen are, of course, politicians, but some earn a living at it. That, too, we talk about in a separate chapter. Still another Irish occupation—and possibly the most important of all—is government service: the occupation embodied in the Irish cop.

Former Chicago Police Commissioner Timothy O'Connor once explained to me why so many Irish have joined the police force, down through the years. Lacking capital, often the victims of prejudice, they sought security. "In the old country," Commissioner O'Connor said, "they were denied the right of self-expression, so the one thing that every man that was a migrant craved was security. Security in his mind existed in two ways—the ownership of property or a Civil Service position. So they became either firemen, policemen, mailmen, or entered some other branch of government or municipal service."

There were other reasons, too. They had carried from Ireland a deep respect for the station of the policeman. He wore a uniform, he was part of the government—he had status. As the Irish became more and more prominent in politics, they were in a position to dispense the plums of patronage. And a job on the police force frequently was one such plum.

It worked the other way around, too. His excitable temperament often got the Irishman immigrant in trouble, and city fathers decided the best choice for keeping an Irishman out of trouble was another Irishman. The Irish made good cops for two reasons—they generally were strong and courageous.

By 1855, of New York City's more than 1000 policemen, 26 per cent were natives of Ireland. At about the same time 45 per cent of the Chicago force carried Irish names.

George Potter tells an amusing story about Boston's first Irish policeman. A group of prominent citizens urged Mayor Bigelow to appoint an Irishman to the force, and he chose one Barney McGinniskin, the driver of a hack in the Irish Ann Street section. There was a storm of protest over the appointment of an Irishman, and someone recalled that Barney had paid a ten-dollar fine for his part in an anti-Catholic riot. Someone else said Barney was a drunken bum, so the mayor asked Marshal Tukey to investigate. The marshal—who corresponded to the present-day police chief—did, and reported that Barney was a "temperate and quiet man." Barney got the job, but only two months had passed before he and the marshal fell out. Tukey said Barney regularly reported for duty as "Barney McGinniskin from the bogs of Ireland," which he said was designed to provoke trouble. He described Barney as "noisy, quarrelsome, and meddlesome." Barney sued for libel. When Bigelow stepped down as mayor, Marshal Tukey fired Barney, but the next mayor restored him. The marshal refused to recognize Barney as a member of the force. Barney refused to recognize the marshal. Finally, Barney was fired once and for all and went back to his cab.

As early as 1815, an Irishman, John McManus, headed New York City's police department. Most of the top brass since then have been Irish-Americans. A study of the New York department made before World War II revealed it to be 36 per cent Irish-American. It's doubtful if the proportions have changed much since then.

Newsman Frank Conniff, whose mother was in Connecticut politics and sponsored countless Irish cops, tells the story of the beet-faced immigrant who, upon stepping off the boat from Ireland, had his toe accidentally stepped on by someone on the pier.

"If that happened tomorrow I'd be able to pinch you," the newly arrived fumed indignantly.

The Irish, who loved excitement and uniforms in equal measure, also, down through the years, have constituted the bulk of our firemen. Of course, many undoubtedly enter the fire-fighting service for the same reason that has attracted the Irish to the police force—to obtain the protection of a job which, though not notoriously high in pay, nevertheless provides a maximum of security. Even if he makes captain, the cop or fireman can't afford Mediterranean cruises or minks for the wife. But if he keeps his nose clean, he's set for life. And to the Irish, who have known starvation in the old country and poverty in the new, this looks good—even today.

Fire-fighting was left to volunteers until after the Civil War. Each big city firehouse was staffed by an unpaid, but nevertheless gay company of firemen, and the Irish made up the bulk of these groups.

There was high rivalry among the various companies. Almost every alarm brought a mad race to see which could first reach the hydrant nearest the blaze. Many times the rivalry exploded in a fight which resulted in wounds and lacerations for both men and equipment. Guns and knives were sometimes brought into play. Quite often, the house burned down while the firemen fought to see which company would have the honor of fighting the fire.

When an alarm rang, a company usually sent its best fighters ahead to hold the hydrant while the rest of the group brought up the equipment. One vital piece of equipment was a barrel of whisky. A steward was on hand at all fires to ladle it out to the "fire laddies."

Another piece of equipment was the hand pump. There was bitter rivalry among the various companies to see which could throw the highest stream of water. The men pumped away with such a will that the hose often burst from the pressure—or was cut by members of a rival company.

The engines, or "machines," as they were called in the nineteenth century, were brightly painted, sometimes decorated with scenes, such as "The Battle of Bunker Hill," and almost always festooned with flowers and flags. Uniforms always were gay. In New York, the firemen wore red flannel shirts, dark pantaloons, boots, and helmets.

Fighting fires—and other firemen—was only a part of the volunteer's life. Parades and parties were equally important. Dances usually were held to raise money for the firemen's benefit fund. Sometimes they took place in the firehouse itself, sometimes at outside halls. Many of those in New York were staged in Niblo's Garden or at the Academy of Music on Fourteenth Street.

Some of the companies formed choruses, which entertained

the guests at their parties with such old standbys as "The Angel's Whisper" or "The Bells of Shannon." A favorite in New York, "The Clasped Hands of the Fire Brigade," told the volunteer's devotion to fire-fighting:

They came from the altar to face the flame,
From prayers to fight the fire;
And the flame which burns but never binds,
Was a bond to draw them nigher.

The volunteer companies took any opportunity for a parade. The Fourth of July brought them out in force, as did special occasions. In New York, for instance, they paraded in 1825 to mark the completion of the Erie Canal, and in 1858 to commemorate the laying of the first Atlantic cable. Most of the bigger companies had their own brass bands.

The firehouse also was a center for gambling and other strictly male pleasures. And, as such, it was a hangout for politicians. No man who aspired to climb the political ladder could afford to shun the volunteer fireman. New York's notorious Boss Tweed, for example, belonged to several companies.

Although the volunteer companies formed a gay, colorful aspect of nineteenth-century urban life they were not the answer in controlling the huge conflagrations that periodically razed great sections of our predominantly wooden cities. In 1853, Cincinnati created the first full-time professional fire department. St. Louis, Baltimore, Boston, New York, and Chicago soon followed suit.

The volunteers, of course, were outraged. Angry editorial writers in the Irish-American journals argued that it was great ingratitude to repay the companies for their heroism by abolishing them. However, professional methods and regulations soon ended the evils associated with the old volunteer companies. And the Fire Commissioners of New York, in their first report, were able to say: "Noise and confusion on our streets on the occasion of alarms of fire have ceased . . . raving and fighting between companies is unknown and the city police are relieved."

After their initial outrage had died down, many of the Irish volunteers became Irish professionals. As the years passed, more and more Irish, liking the combination of security and excitement the job provided, joined them. Today, you can read the roster of virtually any big city fire department in the nation and find it liberally decorated with Irish names.

The Irish have gone into every conceivable kind of work, from ditch-digging to finance. William R. Grace got his first job in America as a singing waiter, later became a longshoreman, finally launched the Grace Steamship Company, climaxing his career by twice being elected Mayor of New York City (1880 and 1884).

John Wolfe Ambrose dredged a deep-water channel into New York harbor, and the beacon that guides vessels into the anchorage, Ambrose Light, is named for him. John F. O'Rourke planned and built much of New York's subway system. Marcus Daly helped establish the Anaconda mining empire. John Mackay, Dublin-born, discovered the fabulous Comstock lode in Nevada in 1873 and later organized the Postal Telegraph Cable Company.

The Irish also have produced their giants in merchandising. Alexander Stewart, who landed in an immigrant ship in New York, remained to become proprietor of one of its most elegant department stores. James Butler founded the world's first big grocery chain.

They have clustered in jobs that require the Irishman's special characteristics: physical strength, courage, a love of excitement and an ability to get along with people. That's why more of them wield nightsticks than batons, why they prefer the law to medicine, politics to plowing.

When you consider the Irish in America—a busy, prosperous people, comfortable in their surroundings—it is hard to realize that less than a century and a half ago they were digging for shriveled potatoes in an ancient homeland no longer theirs. Less than one hundred years ago they were digging for shriveled paychecks in the canals and mines of a new homeland not yet theirs. Today, they dig no longer; others haul the water and hew the wood.

The Irishman hitched a ride with history. It was a long trip, and there were plenty of bumps. But today he has arrived.

7 POLITICKING IRISH:

From Ward to Presidency

At exactly 12:51 p.m. on January 20, 1961, America's Cath-
olic Irish reached the end of a long and difficult journey. When
John Fitzgerald Kennedy took the oath of office as the 35th
President of the United States, and delivered an address hailed
as an eloquent classic, they finally pulled abreast of the Protestant
English majority that had run the nation since its founding.

Over the previous half-century, Catholic Irishmen had won
prestige and prominence in every field of honorable endeavor.
But, despite their natural bent for politics, they had not been
able to elect one of their number President. That one final
achievement eluded them; the White House still was off-limits
to Catholics.

Kennedy changed all that—and he changed it despite a continuing though dwindling mass of anti-Catholic prejudice. With
his election, the Catholic Irish—despised, derided, denied even
the most menial jobs a century and a quarter before—at long
last reached the ultimate political and social pinnacle.

In the balloting of 1960, America did more than elect John

Fitzgerald Kennedy President; it also elected the Catholic Irish to full membership.

The Irish could have chosen no more fitting representative to try for the White House than John F. Kennedy. He was only three generations, or a little more than one hundred years, removed from the Irish ghettos of Boston.

President Kennedy's paternal great-grandfather, Patrick, landed in Boston in 1850, a penniless emigrant from the potato famine. Twelve years later, in 1862, his son Patrick was born. Pat, a saloonkeeper, also became a ward boss who rose to political power in Boston. Nothing was too good for his son Joseph, and he sent the boy to Boston Latin School and Harvard. When things were slow in Pat Kennedy's saloon, he usually could be found behind the bar, reading a book of American history.

Joseph P. Kennedy passed up saloonkeeping for finance. At twenty-six, two years out of Harvard, he became the nation's youngest bank president. By thirty-five, he had his first million. A few years ago, *Fortune* magazine estimated his total wealth at two hundred times that first million. He made it in motion pictures, whisky, real estate, and stocks.

Joe Kennedy waited until he had amassed his fortune before succumbing to the Irishman's traditional love of politics. In 1932, he became a supporter of Franklin D. Roosevelt and a heavy contributor to his campaign. F.D.R. made him first chairman of the Securities and Exchange Commission. Kennedy presided over the liquidation of market practices which had helped to make him rich. In 1938, Roosevelt—never one to honor old traditions or prejudices—named this grandson of a refugee from British misrule as Ambassador to the Court of St. James.

When World War II broke, Ambassador Kennedy expressed opinions that were regarded by some as on the side of appeasement, and he and Roosevelt parted. It has been said, but never confirmed, that Kennedy hoped to succeed Roosevelt, and when he saw that this was out of the question, decided to make his eldest son, Joe Jr., President. When that son was killed in World War II, the mantle fell on the next of the nine children—John Fitzgerald Kennedy.

Jack, separated by a year and a half from Joe, Jr., and by ten years (and four sisters) from his younger brother, Robert, accepted the challenge as a clear-cut duty. "If I had been killed," President Kennedy has said, "it would have been Bobby."

By this time, the elder Kennedy had set up million dollar trust funds for his children so any of them "financially speaking could look me in the eye and tell me to go to hell."

Despite their wealth, Kennedy demanded that his children give their best to everything they undertook. When Jack wrote home from prep school that he guessed his poor grades were a result of laziness, his father wrote back: "I would be lacking even as a friend if I did not urge you to take advantage of the qualities you have. It is very difficult to make up fundamentals that you have neglected when you are very young, and that is why I am always urging you to do the best you can. I am not expecting too much, and I will not be disappointed if you do not turn out to be a genius, but I think you can be a really worth-while citizen."

President Kennedy's middle name is derived from the other branch of the family tree. Maternal grandfather John F. Fitzgerald was born just a year after paternal grandfather Patrick Kennedy. "Honey Fitz," as he was called, became the first native American of Irish descent to be mayor of Boston. He sent daughter Rose to convent colleges in New York and Europe and saw her married in William Cardinal O'Connell's private chapel to Joseph Kennedy, son of Pat the saloonkeeper.

Two years later, in 1916, "Honey Fitz" was defeated for the United States Senate by a man whose names epitomized the narrow New England Puritanism many Boston Irish had grown to despise—Henry Cabot Lodge. But he lived to see Rose's shy, skinny son Jack defeat another Henry Cabot Lodge for the senate in a year the Eisenhower Republicans swept the nation.

As Ambassador to the Court of St. James', the elder Kennedy was determined that his children—notably the two eldest: his namesake and Jack—would then and there be given every chance to develop their minds and viewpoints. He sent them to the London School of Economics to study under the controversial Socialist Harold Laski ". . . to see what the other side has to offer." He dispatched them around Europe as it teetered into war, examining the impending conflict's causes, writing reports which he in turn passed along to the State Department. Out of those experiences, and his own keen eye as a reporter, John F. Kennedy wrote, at twenty-three, the masterly *Why England Slept*, an extraordinarily thoughtful and detailed expansion of his Harvard thesis on why Britain remained untroubled in the face of growing Nazi strength. The book sold 80,000 copies in the U.S. and abroad.

As the war engulfed America, the two elder Kennedy sons were commissioned in the Navy. Joe, Jr., was killed in a spectacular mishap. Though entitled to return home, having completed his required number of flying missions, he volunteered for one last crack at the enemy. He and an enlisted man were to fly a B-17 bomber—so loaded with TNT that it was, in effect, a flying bomb—to a point some miles from the intended target: impregnable U-boat pens in Belgium. There they were to parachute down in friendly territory, and the plane was to be guided by remote control to the target. It blew up with a hellish roar in mid-air before its little crew could abandon it.

Lieutenant John F. Kennedy's war on the other side of the world was all but equally vivid, except that he survived. The PT boat he commanded was slashed in two by the sharp prow of the Japanese destroyer, *Amagiri* one desperate night in 1943 in Blackett Strait, near New Georgia.

Two of the young skipper's crew of twelve were killed out-right. Kennedy was heavily thrown about and recalled later saying to himself, "This is how it feels to be killed."

But he was not killed. He kept his little band together for days and nights in an epochal feat of survival, aiding those who could not swim to reach land, moving from islet to islet in desperate search of food and water, avoiding capture or death at Japanese hands.

Back at his base on Rendova in the Solomon Islands, the Catholic chaplain said a Requiem Mass in his memory.

His rescue and that of his surviving crew was providential in character. Natives in longboats paddled the PT men past Japanese sentries unscathed: Kennedy and the others had been covered with palm fronds as they lay in the bottom of the boats.

He was awarded the Purple Heart and the Navy and Marine Corps Medal for his "courage, endurance and excellent leadership."

But having survived that, Kennedy nearly died of malaria. The impact of the ramming by the Japanese destroyer was also to cause him serious spinal trouble then and in later years.

Mustered out of service after long hospitalization in Boston, Kennedy picked up the threads of a career he hoped to follow—journalism. The Hearst newspapers assigned him to cover the formation of the United Nations in San Francisco in the spring of 1945. He was to present "The GI's Viewpoint." The viewpoint he took was dim: "The world organization that will come out of San Francisco will be the product of the same passions and selfishness that produced the Treaty of Versailles."

The death of Joe, Jr., who had been eager to enter politics after the war, and the repeated urgings of Joe, Sr., induced John Fitzgerald Kennedy to enter politics in 1946. He was thin as a pencil and still quaked from his malaria. No one gave him a chance when he set out to win a seat in the House of Representatives from the run-down Eleventh District of Massachusetts. But his opponents either did not know about or under-estimated the fierce clannishness of the Irish and particularly of an Irish-American family named Kennedy. The whole family pitched in with such fervor, drive, and irresistible charm, and Jack himself lined up such an effective organization beyond the family, that he swept to victory in the Democratic primary over nine opponents. That was tantamount to being handed his seat in the House, for Republicans were as scarce as Ku-Klux Klanners in the Eleventh—sprawled over Irish-dominated poor sections of Boston and Cambridge. In the November elections of 1946 he triumphed over his G.O.P. opponent by a 2-to-1 margin, and succeeded to the seat on Capitol Hill that had been warmed, uncomfortably, by one of the most colorful Irish-Americans ever to enter the unsteady realm of politics, James Michael Curley—who was to inspire the finest book ever written on the Irishman in politics, *The Last Hurrah.*

Representative Kennedy was unopposed in 1948, easily swamped four Italian-American opponents for the Democratic nomination in 1952, and, in the November contest against his Republican opponent, still another member of the burgeoning Italian-American political swell, he won by a 5-to-1 margin.

But six years in the House sufficed. He set his sights on bigger game—and in doing so settled an old score.

Nothing could have summed up the altered state of affairs in the "Athens of America" better than that 1952 election. On the one hand, the Protestant Republican candidate, whose two last names were redolent of Beacon Hill and "breeding." On the other, the Catholic Irish Democratic candidate, grandson of a saloonkeeper, whose illiterate ancestors were plowing potatoes in County Wexford when his opponents were founding colleges. Things have never been the same in that last remaining American citadel of aristocracy since a Kennedy defeated a Cabot Lodge for the United States Senate. He did it, of course, by a combination of know-how, gained in the House of Representatives, and hard work—for instance, he stumped every one of Massachusetts' 351 cities and towns.

Kennedy narrowly (and probably providentially) failed in his bid for the Democratic Vice-Presidential nomination in 1956. But that combination of know-how and hard work paid off four years later when he went for the big prize.

Robert S. McNamara, President Kennedy's Secretary of Defense, a Presbyterian, is part of the Irish-American success story. He has it made three ways—as a political and military leader, as a professor, and as a millionaire. After acquiring a Phi Beta Kappa key and diplomas from the University of California and Harvard School of Business, McNamara—an expert in statistics —joined the Harvard faculty. After the war, he shifted to the Ford Motor Company. There, he rose steadily, rank by rank, until, at forty-four, he reached the $400,000-a-year-presidency of Ford. A month later, President-elect Kennedy—after one talk with the dynamic, knowledgeable McNamara—chose him as the youngest man ever to hold the key job of Secretary of Defense. McNamara quickly accepted, though it cost him $3,000,000 in stock holdings.

Successful Irish-American politicians or appointees have included James F. Byrnes, head of the Office of War Mobilization under Roosevelt, Secretary of State and Supreme Court Justice under Truman; Admiral of the Fleet William D. Leahy, Roosevelt's personal chief-of-staff; Pat Brown, Governor of California; Major General Patrick J. Hurley, Secretary of War under Hoover, and Ambassador to China in the 1940s. And, of course, there's the epitome of the Irish politician, James Aloysius Farley, now a Coca-Cola executive.

James Aloysius was born in Grassy Point, New York, in 1888. Jim recalls that when he went to visit his father's people, in a town called Verplanck's Point, only a few miles away, he couldn't understand why all the Catholic Irish there were Republicans. He said:

"I couldn't understand how a Catholic could be a Republican because in the community where I was born and raised all the Catholics were Democrats. As a matter of fact, in Grassy Point we had difficulty finding enough Republicans to man the election boards."

Jim says he eventually learned that a Peekskill politician was helping the Catholic Irish get jobs in the local brickyard and enrolling them in the Republican party. As Jim says, the Irish largely voted as a bloc in the interests of self-protection, but they also sought the protective coloration of the dominant party. "In Boston," Jim says, "they became Democrats because there were Democrats in Boston. But in Philadelphia politics was dominated by the Republicans, and in a large measure they became Republicans."

Jim began his political career by getting himself elected district committeeman. He recalls that the other two members of the town committee were at odds. "They were not on speaking terms and they couldn't agree on who would be the chairman, secretary, or the treasurer of the town committee. Neither one of them would vote for the other, so they elected me to all three positions. So I started from there and I was elected town clerk and served eight years. Finally, supervisor. Went to the New York State Assembly one year, and now you know the rest of it."

"The rest of it" is one of America's great success stories: Farley became head of the New York State Democratic Committee in 1930 and two years later successfully pushed the presidential nomination of Franklin Delano Roosevelt. Becoming chairman of the National Committee, Farley managed F.D.R.'s presidential campaign with equal success and landed up in the cabinet as Postmaster General. He dropped out to mastermind Roosevelt's 1936 campaign after which he stepped back into his old cabinet job. By 1940, Jim had accumulated some presidential aspirations of his own, and when Roosevelt decided he wanted the job again, Jim dropped out of the cabinet and shed his party chairmanship.

It took twenty years for someone else to bring to reality the dream Jim had nurtured—to become the first Catholic Irish President. However, John Fitzgerald Kennedy was by no means the first man with Irish blood to take up residence in the White House. Andrew Jackson, James K. Polk, James Buchanan, Andrew Johnson, Chester A. Arthur, William McKinley, William Howard Taft, Woodrow Wilson, Grover Cleveland, Calvin Coolidge, and Harry Truman were mostly or partly of Irish descent.

The Catholic Irish loyalty to the Democratic party extends back to the beginnings of the republic and to the historic schism between Thomas Jefferson and Alexander Hamilton. Hamilton and his well-heeled friends favored the restriction of the franchise to the propertied classes. His sympathies lay with Great Britain, and he deplored the revolution which had toppled the throne of France. "Your people," he once said, "is a great beast."

Jefferson, on the other hand, leader of the Republican party (as the present Democratic party then was called) was an implacable foe of monarchy and the whole British social system. After the French Revolution ended in the Napoleonic dictatorship, his ardor for France cooled; but his dislike of English aristocracy never dimmed. The Irish, loving liberty and hating England, sided with Jefferson.

When George Washington refused to run for a third term, the Federalists turned to a man almost as conservative as Hamilton, John Adams. He defeated Jefferson by 71 to 68 electoral votes, but the margin was too close for comfort for the Federalists, and they made up their minds to stay in power by silencing the opposition. To that end, they rushed through Congress in 1798 several infamous laws.

The first, the Alien Act, gave the President the power for two years to expel from the country any alien he might deem dangerous to the "peace and safety" of the United States. Although Adams failed to deport a single person, passage of the law frightened the unnaturalized Irish and angered all Americans jealous of their liberties.

The second, the Sedition Act, placed heavy penalties on persons found guilty of trying to stir up "sedition" or who published anything "false, scandalous or malicious" against the President or Congress. Although the law clearly violated the first amendment of the Constitution forbidding any abridgment of free speech or press, the Federalists managed to imprison many critical Republican writers. First to run afoul of the law was an Irishman, Matthew Lyon of Vermont.

The Federalists then went one step further. They rammed through Congress a bill requiring all foreign-born residents to remain in the United States fourteen years before applying for citizenship, then wait another five years for naturalization. This clearly was a blow at the Irish, and those of them who had not yet joined the Republicans hastened to do so.

In time, the Republicans became Democrats, but whatever the party's name, the Irish gave it their loyalty. The Federalists became Whigs, then Republicans; but though the label changed, as far as most Irish were concerned, the product remained the same.

If the Irish had discovered a leader in Jefferson, they found in Andrew Jackson a great hero. Indeed, Jackson elicited from the Irish in America the same kind of veneration they reserved for such Nationalist leaders as Wolfe Tone and Daniel O'Connell. The reasons for this adulation are many.

Jackson was an Irishman, the son of penniless Presbyterian immigrants from Carrickfergus. His democracy was as pure as his blood. He believed, in the words of one of his followers, Orestes Brownson, a prominent clergyman and writer of the time, that "property should be held subordinate to man."

Jackson's hatred of England was deep. At the age of thirteen, he had joined the American Revolutionary Army and had been captured by the British. An English officer had ordered him to clean his boots, and when the boy refused, had slashed him on the arms with his saber. Jackson bore the scars, and his hatred of all things English, to his death.

Jackson was a military hero, and the Irish fancy bravery. In 1813, upon the outbreak of hostilities with the Creek Indians, he had raised a volunteer force of three thousand men and defeated them. Jackson's final victory in 1814 had broken the power of the Indians in North America. After appointment as a general in the United States Army, Jackson defended New Orleans against the British in 1815, a victory that earned him enduring popularity.

Jackson was described as "the most roaring, rollicking, game-cocking, horse-racing, card-playing, mischievous fellow in town." The historian Edward F. Roberts says "there is not in history a more conspicuous case of a man who embodied more completely the typical characteristics of the Celtic temperament, who had a greater share of Irish faults and Irish virtues."

But the Irish loved Andrew Jackson principally because he took the Constitution literally. As far as he was concerned, when it said equality, it *meant* equality. The founding fathers' theory about equality had remained just that—theory. The monied people still ran the country. All of that, Jackson and his followers set out to change. Said Orestes Brownson: "All classes, each in turn, have possessed the government, and the time has come for all predominance of class to end; for Man, the People, to rule." More than a century later, Franklin Roosevelt spoke of Jackson's success in attaining this goal. "It will never be possible for any length of time," he said in 1936, "for any group of the American people, either by reason of wealth or learning or inheritance or economic power, to retain any mandate, any permanent authority to arrogate to itself the political control of American life . . . This heritage . . . we owe to Jacksonian democracy."

Jackson's admirers swept him into office in 1828 and again in 1832. After his two terms, he passed the mantle to Martin Van Buren, who had started his career as a taproom boy in Kinderhook, New York. The Jacksonians, by now known officially as the Democratic party, carried every presidential election between 1828 and 1856, inclusive, except for the Whig victories of William Henry Harrison in 1840 and Zachary Taylor in 1848.

Quite obviously, the party would never have emerged as powerful as it is today had it not been for the political-minded Irish, who not only voted its ticket, but also rang doorbells, managed campaigns, and performed all the other chores necessary to get a candidate elected to office.

However, many of the big issues that deeply divided the parties through the years were of little or no interest to the Irish. The most bitterly fought question of the Jackson administration was the right of government to engage in banking. The Irish, with scant savings, couldn't care less who held the key to the vault. Nor was the tariff problem one that stirred their blood.

But on some issues they held strong and decisive opinions. One was the question of universal suffrage. Most of the founding fathers had believed in special privilege based on property qualifications. The Irish, behind Andrew Jackson, made universal suffrage the rule.

The Democrats, including the Irish, also believed in an "open door" immigration policy as opposed to the Whigs' "America for Americans." The Democratic platform of 1840 contained this plank, which was readopted in each succeeding campaign until the Civil War:

"Resolved, That the liberal principles embodied by Jefferson in the Declaration of Independence, and sanctioned in the Constitution, which make ours the land of liberty and the asylum of the oppressed of every nation, have ever been cardinal principles in the Democratic faith; and every attempt to abridge the present privilege of becoming citizens and the owners of soil

[128]

among us ought to be resisted with the same spirit which swept the Alien and Sedition laws from our statute books."

The Catholic Irish felt strongly on this issue because the so-called Know-Nothing party, dedicated to "checking the stride of the foreigner or alien, of thwarting the machinations and subverting the deadly plans of the Jesuit and the Papist," was becoming perilously powerful.

As a matter of fact, the Know-Nothings came very close to winning the Presidency. It happened this way: In 1852, the Democrats had won with Franklin Pierce. The Irish had worked hard for Pierce, and he rewarded them with the appointment of an Irishman, James Campbell, as Postmaster General. The Whigs, angry at the Irish, threw in their lot with the Know-Nothings. By 1855, some 75 congressmen had taken the Know-Nothing pledge, the party held sway in eight states and seemed a sure bet for the presidency.

The Know-Nothings picked as their candidate former President Millard Fillmore, who was abroad at the time. It is one of the ironies of history that the news of his selection reached Fillmore when he had just requested and been granted an invitation for an audience with Pope Pius IX. The Republicans chose John C. Frémont, and the Democrats pinned their hopes on the son of a Donegal farmer, James C. Buchanan, a Presbyterian. To make their position as clear as possible, they adopted the old "open door" plank of 1840 and added another:

"Resolved, That the foundation of this Union of States having been laid in, and its prosperity, expansion, and preeminent example of free government built upon, entire freedom in matters of religious concernment, and no respect of persons in regard to rank, or place of birth, or party can justly be deemed national, constitutional, or in accordance with American principles which bases its exclusive organization upon religious opinions and accidental birthplace. And hence a political crusade in the nineteenth century, and in the United States of America, against Catholics and foreign born, is neither justified by the past history or future prospects of the country, nor in unison with the spirit of toleration and enlightened freedom which peculiarly distinguishes the American system of popular government."

The Know-Nothing platform, on the other hand, said:

"Americans must rule America; and to this end native-born citizens should be selected for all state, federal and municipal offices of government employment, in preference to all others.

"A change in the laws of naturalization, making a continued residence of twenty-one years, of all not heretofore provided for, an indispensible requisite for citizenship hereafter, and excluding all paupers and persons convicted of crime from landing upon our shores."

There were celebrations in every *shabeen* and shanty when the results were in. The Know-Nothings had run a bad third. Buchanan won with a 1,927,995 popular vote against 1,391,555 for Frémont and 874,000 for Fillmore. The Know-Nothing party collapsed into insignificance after this defeat, and disappeared altogether before the outbreak of the Civil War.

This victory, resounding though it was, was the last for the Irish for many years. They opposed Abraham Lincoln—opposed the abolition of slavery, for the most part—but political differences were largely swallowed up in the Civil War. The years following Appomattox saw a decided change in the relative position of the Irish.

Because of the anti-Catholic and anti-Irish agitation in this country—and because economic conditions in Ireland had vastly improved—Irish immigration to the United States thinned to a trickle during and after the war. In 1850, the Irish had constituted 42.8 per cent of the foreign born in the United States. In 1890 the proportion was down to 20.2 per cent. And by the turn of the century, it was 15.6 per cent. The immigrants were still

coming, but after the Civil War the main stream was from Eastern and Southern Europe.

By this time, however, the Irish were running most of the
big city political machines. They knew well the inducements
that had persuaded them and their fathers into the Democratic
party in the early years of the century, so they were successful
in signing up most of the newcomers—except the Germans.
Because they were a cut above the other mid-European immigrants economically, the Germans preferred not to be identified
with them, and so voted Republican.

For many years after the Civil War, the Democratic party was
too weak to make itself felt nationally. But in time, with the
help of the Irish political machines—especially Tammany Hall
—it rose to power again.

The Irish took to big city machine politics like kids to candy.
As Edward F. Roberts in his *Ireland in America* says, "It is
probably true that the political machine was not invented by
the Irish or consciously by anyone, but it is certain that it was
developed to its greatest extent and has reached its highest degree of efficiency through the peculiar genius of the Irish for
political organization."

The strength of the Democratic party rested for many years
on twin pillars—the loyalty of the old Confederate states and the
big city machines. The patterns of political power have shifted
somewhat in recent years. The South is no longer solid; the
countryside and the cities are no longer monolithically Republican and Democratic respectively—in fact, the Irish themselves
moved into G.O.P. ranks in droves as their economic condition
bettered, especially during the Eisenhower years. Nevertheless,
the machines the Irish built and largely controlled for many
years still are powerful political instruments.

The once most notorious and still most powerful doubtlessly
is New York's Tammany Hall, currently run, significantly, by
an Italian-American, Carmine DeSapio. But it was the Irish

who dominated Tammany when it helped make Grover Cleveland the first Democratic president since the Civil War. Here is how it came about:

In 1884, when it began to look as if the Democrats might return to power, the alarmed Republicans sought a man with a large Irish following. They found him in James G. Blaine, who not only had a large number of Irish friends, but whose mother was Catholic Irish.

The Irish might well have changed sides—they weren't too happy with Cleveland's threats to replace Andrew Jackson's old spoils system with a civil service set-up based on merit—had it not been for an incident that occurred five days before election.

A New York Presbyterian minister named Samuel Dickinson Burchard told a Blaine rally: "We are Republicans and don't propose to leave our party and identify ourselves with the party whose antecedents are rum, Romanism and rebellion." The Democrats quickly seized on the phrase "rum, Romanism, and rebellion" and gave it wide publicity. The New York Irish, wavering up to then, massed solidly behind Cleveland. As a result, Blaine lost New York State by some one thousand votes. And New York's electoral votes lost him the election.

During Cleveland's term of office, the Irish came to regard him as an outright Anglophile. Surely they loathed his civil service reform. So they stayed away from the polls in sufficiently large numbers to insure his defeat by Benjamin Harrison four years later. However, Cleveland learned his lesson and came back in the succeeding election in 1892.

The Democrats, despite the Irish, lost the next four presidential elections—to William McKinley twice, Theodore Roosevelt, and William Howard Taft. And when they made their comeback in 1912 with Woodrow Wilson, the central question of relations with Germany overshadowed party differences.

After World War I, the Democrats saw more lean years. In fact, it wasn't until the advent of Alfred E. Smith in 1928 that they posed a serious threat. Four years before, the party had lost with John W. Davis, scion of an old American family, who had little appeal for the Democrats' northern big city vote but strong attraction for its southern rural branch. Davis lost so decisively to Calvin Coolidge that the Democrats decided next time to pick a favorite of the opposite, big-city wing of the party.

They could hardly have chosen a man better suited to represent the Catholic Irish voter. In his four terms as Governor of New York, Alfred E. Smith had demonstrated a progressivism, a regard for the common man, that harked back to the Irish immigrants' first American political hero, Andrew Jackson. Moreover, he was a Catholic, the faith of a vast majority of the big city immigrants. And, it should be noted, he deplored Prohibition.

Now, the country came face-to-face with the religious issue for the first time. In the White House, there had been nine Episcopalians, five Presbyterians, four Unitarians, four Methodists, two Reformed Dutch, and one each of the Disciples of Christ, Congregationalist and Baptist faiths, but no Catholic.

Actually, Smith wasn't the first Catholic candidate for the presidency. Charles O'Conor of New York, son of Irish immigrants, had headed an insurgent Democratic ticket in 1872. That was a politically complex year in which liberal Republicans bolted their party to endorse the regular Democratic ticket of Horace Greeley and B. Gratz Brown. O'Conor, a states' righter, was the candidate of the Straight-Out Democrats, a Southern-oriented group that couldn't take Greeley. Of course, the regular Republican candidates, Ulysses S. Grant and Henry Wilson, won handily.

But if the Irish in 1927 thought that the anti-Catholic feeling so bitterly epitomized by the Know-Nothings and the American Protective Association, had melted from the land, they had a sad awakening. This time it was the Ku-Klux Klan, an organization which had borrowed the name and rites of an anti-carpetbagger Southern guerrilla group active during the Reconstruction.

The Klan had grown so powerful politically that the Indiana Grand Dragon, D. C. Stevenson, was able to say without contradiction: "I am the law in Indiana." When Al Smith became the Democratic nominee, it trotted out all the old familiar pieces of anti-Catholic apparatus: whispering campaigns and leaflets imputing terrible immoralities inside convents, stories that the Knights of Columbus had a blood oath to kill all Protestants, tales that the Pope was preparing to take over America.

It should not be assumed that only the rabble in the Klan opposed Smith because of his faith. Many thoughtful Protestants sincerely were not prepared for a Catholic President. In the hope of quelling all doubt, Smith himself made his position clear in an article in the *Atlantic Monthly*:

"I believe in the worship of God according to the faith and practice of the Roman Catholic Church. I recognize no power in the institutions of my Church to interfere with the operations of the Constitution of the United States or the enforcement of the law of the land. I believe in absolute freedom of conscience for all men and in the equality of all churches, all sects and all beliefs before the law as a matter of right and not as a matter of favor. I believe in the absolute separation of Church and State and in the strict enforcement of the provisions of the Constitution that Congress shall make no law respecting an establishment or prohibiting the free exercise thereof . . . I believe in the common brotherhood of man under the common fatherhood of God."

The message did not get through in the electoral college. Smith lost, 444 to 87. But he polled seven million more popular votes than had Davis—the largest popular vote, in fact, of any Democratic candidate up to that time.

The central issue had *not* been religion, but Prohibition. The country may not yet have been ready to accept a Catholic President, but it was even less ready to accept the return of legal liquor. There were other determining factors: Smith was a big city product in a land still mainly small town in sentiment; his education had been limited, and his appearance and speech, many thought, would detract from the dignity of the Presidency. Herbert Hoover was everything that Smith was not: aloof of "politics as usual"; educated, polished; a great administrator, engineer and humanitarian, rather than a professional office seeker. The wonder is that Smith received as many votes as he did.

The campaign against Smith because of his religion reached its most ludicrous pitch with the widespread circulation in Southern rural areas of a picture showing him cutting the silk ribbon at the inauguration of service on New York City's Independent (or Eighth Avenue) subway. The caption that told of the occasion and Smith's participation in it had been removed and, in its stead, was one which stated flatly that the picture depicted Smith's opening a "secret underground tunnel to the Vatican."

The Democrats eventually did get back into power—and with a bang too. They elected Franklin Roosevelt to an unprecedented four terms. But before Roosevelt's death in 1945, the Irish had begun their second migration—this time out of the Democratic party. The causes were clear: the basic conservatism of the Catholic Irish rebelled at the experimentation of the New and Fair Deals, and their inherent piety recoiled at reports, not always confirmable, of the infiltration of government by godless communism. There was another reason too: the Republicans were the party of the Haves, as against the Democratic Have Nots, and many Irish were beginning to be Haves.

At any rate, many Irish-Americans cast their first Republican vote against Roosevelt, and later additional thousands followed the inclinations of their forebears during Andrew Jackson's day and voted for a military hero, General Dwight D. Eisenhower.

There are no unerring statistics to measure that sort of thing, but in the big-city generally Irish areas Kennedy brought many "errant" Irish back into the Democratic fold despite the more conservative platform of his opponent Richard Nixon. At any rate, the religious question again was a focal point of the election, but this time there were no such distracting issues as Prohibition to shift attention elsewhere.

Again in 1960, the question was placed squarely before the voters: could a Catholic be trusted to maintain religious equality in the full spirit of the Constitution? Senator Kennedy thought so. He said:

"I would think there is really only one issue involved in the whole question of a candidate's religion. That is, does a candidate believe in the Constitution, does he believe in the First Amendment, does he believe in the separation of Church and State? When the candidate gives his views on that question, and I think I have given my views fully, I think the subject is exhausted."

Dean John Bennett of the Union Theological Seminary of New York, agreed. He said: "The fear that Roman Catholics in American life may be agents of a centralized system is without foundation. It does not take into account the record of Catholics who do hold many of the highest offices; they do not conform to a single pattern, but are divided, as are other Americans, on most public issues." At the time Dean Bennett made the statement, there were twelve Catholic United States Senators, 90 Representatives, and ten Governors.

The National Council of Churches of Christ, the official association of the major Protestant denominations agreed with Bennett that there was no peril involved in the election of a Catholic President. But there was Protestant dissent, and plenty of it. The Reverend W. A. Criswell, pastor of the First Baptist Church of Dallas, the nation's largest all-white Baptist congregation, was one of the dissenters. Dr. Criswell whose 12,000 members include evangelist Billy Graham, said the election of a Catholic President would "spell the death of a free church in a free state and our hopes of continuance of full religious liberty in America."

There was also plenty of opposition on a less elevated level. Officials of the Department of Justice counted one hundred and forty-four producers of anti-Catholic literature during the Kennedy campaign. Estimates by the Fair Campaign Practices Committee placed the number of pieces in the tens of millions and the cost of distribution in the hundreds of thousands of dollars.

What kind of person produces this material? Well, there was Harvey Springer, "cowboy evangelist," the author of "Kennedy Cannot Win; The Roman Octopus." He wrote: "I ask: How many Catholics came over on the Mayflower? Not one. I maintain that the Constitution is a Protestant Constitution and let's keep it that way. I'm perfectly willing to admit I'm a bigot. But . . . the Catholics are just as bigoted against the Baptists."

Then there was a character named Rev. Harrison Parker. One of his productions states: "Civil War is possible in the U.S.A. because of the anti-American Catholic Party being formed with Joe Kennedy, the Roman Catholic millionaire whiskey merchant, as boss."

One perennial calumny cropped up in the campaign—the spurious and infamous "Knights of Columbus Oath." This purports to require Catholics among other duties, to wipe out Protestants, Masons, and "other heretics." The Knights have won criminal libel suits against distributors of this ancient hoax, but at least nine versions of it circulated during the Kennedy-Nixon campaign.

One of the most unusual pieces of literature was directed not against Kennedy but against Nixon. It claimed Nixon actually was a secret Catholic and, if elected, would turn the nation over to the Pope.

Many thoughtful Americans were of the opinion that this kind of opposition to Senator Kennedy did him more good than harm. The anti-Catholic bigots were going to vote against him anyway, and the literature was pitched too low to sway anyone sane. Besides, as they saw it, this type of campaign made it certain that angry Catholics, no matter what their past affiliation, would vote Democratic, even if it might be for one election only. And the country now was almost 25 per cent Catholic, as against 15 per cent when Smith was the nominee.

Interestingly enough, the Democrats chose Southern Protestants as running mates for both Smith and Kennedy—Senator Joseph T. Robinson of Arkansas in the case of Smith, Senator Lyndon B. Johnson of Texas in the case of Kennedy—perhaps to try to offset the inevitable opposition in the citadel of fundamental Protestantism south of the Mason-Dixon line. At any rate, the results speak for themselves.

As it turned out, the issue of religion cut both ways—perhaps helping Kennedy more than it hurt him. True, many Protestants voted against Kennedy's Catholicism. In fact his faith is believed to have been responsible for the loss of such states as Kentucky, Tennessee, and Oklahoma.

On the other hand, many a Catholic Republican crossed to the Democratic column. Fortunately for Kennedy, the Catholic Irish were strategically concentrated in the big Eastern States with their king-sized collection of electoral votes. Of the ten states with the greatest number of Catholics, Kennedy won seven, with a total of 103 electoral votes. Of the ten non-Southern states with the smallest number of Catholics, Nixon won eight, but with only 68 electoral votes.

What it adds up to is this: There probably were more Protestant votes against President Kennedy because he was a Catholic than Catholic votes for him for the same reason. But the Catholic votes packed more wallop. Not only were they massed in populous states with impressive totals of electoral votes, but also in those states' big cities, which any Democrat must win to offset the largely rural Protestant vote of "downstate" or "upstate" as the case may be.

Thus, Kennedy had a secret weapon: the Catholic Irish in the big industrial states of the North. In each of those key states, the Catholics—concentrated in the big cities—outvoted the rural Protestant Republicans to tip the balance of the state to Kennedy. And, collectively, those states, with their big electoral voltage, outvoted the rest of the fifty to tip the balance of the nation to Kennedy.

But this is not meant to suggest that the contest was one of Catholic versus Protestant. President Kennedy would never have won had he depended on the Catholic vote alone. His election signified his acceptance by all the people, Catholic, Protestant, and Jew. For example, the Boston *Pilot* said "the American people are more mature than their observers had imagined. . . . Plainly, the mass of American Protestants, with admirable and unpredicted maturity, placed the religious issue in a secondary or even lower place . . . Americans generally, and American Protestants specifically, demonstrated this week the truly democratic nature of our national elections. . . . The present social climate of America has, on a testing under pressure, shown itself to be far healthier than our commentators had assumed."

For the Irish, it was the end of a long road. The last "Man Wanted—No Irish Need Apply" sign had come down—the one that had hung on the White House.

8 WORSHIPING IRISH:

When All Else Failed,
There Was God

To the average Protestant or Jew, the members of that big family down the block—the one that goes to Mass and often Communion on Sundays or daily—are not simply Irish and Catholic; they are "Irishcatholic." It is as though the two words are eternally glued together.

The Germans, Italians, and French, although they may share the faith of the Irish, are, well, Germans, Italians, and Frenchmen. But as often as not, when we speak of the people whose culture forms one of the brightest strands in the fabric of American life, we mention not only the country of their ancestors but also their faith.

We certainly never describe the Irish-Catholic thus to distinguish them from the Protestant Irish, such as they are. If we did, we would use the same device for the Germans, who are more equally divided between the two great branches of Christianity. Without doubt we use the phrase simply because Irish and Catholic seem to go together like corned beef and cabbage, and "damn" and "Yankee."

There is no slide rule comprehensive enough to show what percentage of America's 40,871,302 (as of 1960) Roman Catholics trace their ancestry to the 26-thousand-square-mile Shamrock across the sea. One source suggests the Irish number about one-half the Roman Catholics in this country. But whatever their numerical strength, it is far outweighed by their influence in the Church.

The first Roman Catholic Cardinal in the United States, elevated by Pope Pius IX in 1875, was an Irish-American—John Cardinal McCloskey of New York, the son of a Brooklyn shipping clerk who had arrived in this country from County Derry early in the 1800s. From the installation of Cardinal McCloskey, for the next half a century every Cardinal in the United States was of Irish lineage. The great majority of today's 200 bishops and archbishops are of Irish background. One researcher has established that of 464 bishops appointed from 1789 to 1935, more than half had Irish names.

Irish influence extends into the Roman Catholic educational system. One historian has estimated that the Irish fill more than 90 per cent of the teaching posts in Catholic elementary schools. Read a roster of the Notre Dame or Fordham faculty and you might well be reading a page from the Dublin telephone book.

There are several reasons why the Father Murphys outnumber the Father Romanos. The Irish were the first over. Ireland gave America its huddled masses in the middle and late 1800s, Italy in the early and middle 1900s. By the time Tony got here, Pat was already running the Church. For a second reason, the Irish immigrant spoke English. True, it was an English thickened by brogue and laced with Gaelic idiom. But it gave him a leg-up over other newcomers in dealing with the older Americans.

Beyond that, there is a more basic reason for the Irish-

American's devotion to the church of Rome and his influence in it. Ireland, Catholicism's only English-speaking nation, may well be its most devout. The country is 94 per cent Catholic. It surely produces more priests and nuns per capita than any other country on earth.

For centuries, the Irish fought the Protestant ascendency, tooth, nail and shillelagh. The long battle not only sharpened their aggressiveness, it deepened their attachment to the Church. The Irishman who stepped ashore in America was a man looking for a break—not a faith. He had brought his faith with him. It had served him through persecution and starvation; it would see him past the pitfalls of a new land.

Watch a little girl, face aglow, every ribbon in place, trip off to her First Communion. Walk the hushed corridors of a great Catholic university. Look on while nursing sisters go silently about their tasks in the honeycomb of a big hospital. Step off Fifth Avenue's noisily crowded sidewalk in New York into the silent and breathtaking vastness of St. Patrick's Cathedral—far from a world ridden by rock-and-roll and Russia, divorce and delinquency—and let the peace of God magically infiltrate your soul. All this, St. Patrick started, and you can readily see how his name was chosen for the cathedral on Fifth Avenue. (The most famous of American Roman Catholic cathedrals, St. Patrick's cornerstone was laid in 1858 by Archbishop John J. Hughes. Construction work was temporarily halted during the Civil War, and it was not until May 25, 1879, that the cathedral was ready for dedication by John Cardinal McCloskey.)

St. Patrick possessed one tool essential to the successful missionary. He spoke the language of the country. Then as now, the Irish were enthusiasts. They embraced Patrick's new religion with ardor. Rude churches soon dotted the land. Before his death, the saint laid out a neat organization and pattern of parish, diocese, cathedral church, and bishop.

Actually, Catholicism took a turn in Ireland that, on first

glance, may seem strange. The penitent, the hermit, became the ideal. Monasticism flourished among a people known, then as now, for their love of social life. The abbot and his monastery became as important as the bishop and his cathedral.

But the early Irish ecclesiastics were more than men of reflection. They also were men of action. They didn't hesitate to take up arms in a cause they thought was just. For example more than 800 Irish monks died in a single internecine battle in 816.

Besides being celibates and soldiers, Irish priests and monks were statesmen and scholars. A millennium ago in Ireland, as today, the priest did not regard his responsibilities as ending at the church door. He was an often-consulted leader in civil affairs.

The monastery became the center of cultural life. It was school and library rolled into one—the repository of Ireland's culture as well as its religion. In the fifth and sixth centuries Ireland was the only country in Europe whose monks still knew Greek. Several of its monasteries became great universities. To them went earnest students from England and the Continent; from them, went missionaries to bring the light of Christianity to hoards of heathens. One of these, Columba, in 563 became the St. Patrick of Scotland, others Christianized the endless barbarians of Europe.

For four centuries, waves of barbarians had spilled across the Roman Empire. Except for isolated pockets here and there, Christian civilization had retreated to the edges and outposts of the Continent to, among a very few other places, Ireland. And it was from these outposts, that dedicated missionaries fought it back.

Alcuin, one of the most influential educators of the Dark Ages, for instance, came from England to the Irish monastery of Clonmaonoise for training, and went on to become tutor at the court of Charlemagne, the first Holy Roman Emperor. He presented to his royal pupil a sevenfold curriculum of studies (a trivium of grammar, dialectic, and rhetoric and a quadrivium of arithmetic, astronomy, geometry, and music) which became the basis of the Master of Arts degree all over Europe.

Alcuin was succeeded by a great Irish scholar, Johannes Scotus Erigena, who served the court of the Frankish King, Charles the Bald. His *De Divisione Natura* still is studied by philosophers and Medievalists. By now, Ireland was known all through Europe as the land of "saints and scholars."

The Norsemen came and, two centuries later, went. The Normans on the other hand came and stayed—to become, as has been said, "more Irish than the Irish." But through it all the Christian faith remained strong. Finally, in 1170, Henry II of England became ruler of Ireland, and the ancient faith of Christian Ireland began to undergo, at the hands of Christian England, its severest test.

At first the Church suffered but little. In fact, the English paid it virtually no attention at all until the fourteenth century when the notorious Statutes of Kilkenny forbade Irish clerics within the Pale from entering English Catholic churches. Then, a century and a half later, came the English Reformation.

Webster defines the Reformation as "the important religious movement in western Christendom beginning early in the sixteenth century which resulted in the formation of the various Protestant churches."

But, although they took place about the same time, there was a sharp difference between the Reformation on the Continent and in England. The Continental Reformation was doctrinal; the English, political.

In 1517 Martin Luther nailed to the door of the church at Wittenberg, Germany, the so-called 95 theses which attacked what he described as abuses in the administration of Papal indulgences. In time he denied Papal headship, and the necessity for the intervention of clergy between man and God for salvation. His movement began the trend toward religious sects which is continuing today. There now are 250 recognized religious denominations in the United States alone.

The writings of Luther and his followers, avidly read in English, in a sense provided the fertile soil for the later growth of the English version of the Reformation. The deeper cause was the power struggle among England, Spain, and France. But the immediate cause was more human than political or theoretical. For once history borrowed from fiction a plot worn threadbare by both low comedy and high tragedy—an old married man's lust for a servant girl. Henry VIII developed a passion for one of the queen's attendants, Anne Boleyn. He confidently applied for a divorce from Catherine of Aragon, whom he had never loved dearly anyway. But to his complete amazement, an ecclesiastical court shook its head and to the man Pope Leo X had designated "Defender of the Faith" for his treatise against Luther's defection, Henry was not one inclined automatically to take no for an answer. In high dudgeon, he abolished Papal control of the English church, and seized ecclesiastical, as well as temporal, power in his own hands.

After establishing the Church of England, Henry decided to tidy up Ireland. He dissolved the Irish monasteries, took over their lands for himself and his cronies, and declared himself head of the Anglican Church of Ireland as against "the usurped authority of the Bishop of Rome." England went along with Henry; Ireland balked. The seeds of the Reformation had fallen on a field fertile with discontent in England. Heresy had been growing for many years. In the reign of Henry VII, twenty-five heretics were condemned in London alone.

But conditions were different in Ireland. The pomp and grandeur of the medieval European Church were missing. As the people were poor, so was their Church. No rival sects had sprung up. Indeed, Bishop Tanner wrote in 1571 that "not a hundred Irishmen in all Ireland have been infested with heresy."

The English readily followed Henry into the Anglican church.

For one thing, England at the time was threatened by the Catholic powers of France and Spain. But just as it seemed the thing to do to become a Church of England man in Britain, so it was the essence of patriotism to remain a Catholic in Ireland. The old animosities between the people of the adjoining islands, became more than Englishman versus Irishman; it now was Protestant against Catholic.

Two wives later, when Henry VIII died of various excesses, he was succeeded for six years by his 10-year-old son Edward VI. Then his oldest daughter, Mary, who had despised her father, turned England Catholic again, but the switch meant more harm than good for Ireland. "Bloody Mary" burned so many Protestants at the stake—her executioners touched off perhaps three hundred human bonfires—that she engendered in the British people a terrible hatred for all things Catholic. The Irish were to feel the full extent of that hatred in the years to come. When her half-sister, Elizabeth (daughter of Henry and Anne Boleyn) succeeded her to the throne, England about-faced again and became militantly Protestant. Protestantism and patriotism became synonymous.

Under Elizabeth, events conspired to make England even more Protestant, Ireland (if this was possible) even more Catholic. Catholic Spain unsuccessfully sent an armada against England and Pope Pius V excommunicated Elizabeth, angering the British but having quite an opposite effect on the Gaels. "Irish history, till then fluid, ran into the mold where it hardened for three hundred years," says the British historian Trevelyan. "The native population conceived a novel enthusiasm for the Roman religion, which they identified with a passionate hatred of the English."

The Irish had high hopes of Elizabeth's successor, James I. He was believed to be secretly in sympathy with Catholicism. But he sorely let them down. He used the rebellion of a minor Irish chief as the excuse to seize most of Ulster—six counties embracing half a million acres. He split the province into estates of one to two thousand acres each and handed them to English and Scottish Protestants, deepening the bitterness of the Catholics.

The worst was yet to come. After James, came his son Charles I. Even the English found it hard to stomach him. However, his misrule had one beneficent effect. To get out, thousands of English fled or were sent to the new world—Puritans to Massachusetts, Catholics to Maryland, others to Virginia, and the West Indies.

Those that stayed behind in England split up—the Roundheads (Puritans, Presbyterians and the pro-parliament group) on one side; the Cavaliers (Royalists and Church of England supporters) stayed with Charles. While the Protestants were thus at one another's throats on their island, the Irish decided it was time to get rid of some Protestants on *their* island. The displaced Catholics fell on the new English and Scottish settlers in Ulster in what is described as "the great massacre." Estimates of the dead range from 10,000 to 100,000, depending on whose history book you read.

There was nothing, for the moment, that the English could do about the massacre. They were too busy slaughtering one another at home. As a matter of fact Charles decided to make friends of the Irish Catholics. He eased up on their restrictions and recruited a small Irish Catholic army.

But in the end Charles lost not only the civil war but also his head. A month after his execution—in February 1649—the Irish proclaimed as their king, Charles' exiled son, Charles II. The leader of the Parliament-Puritan-Presbyterian faction—an up-and-coming dictator (he called it "Lord Protector") named Oliver Cromwell—landed in Ireland and put down the rebellion with a viciousness that revealed the Puritan's deep-seated hatred of the Catholic. He stormed the center of the revolt and slaughtered everyone in the garrison, including women, children, and priests. When he conquered the land, he uprooted Catholics from the province of Ulster, Leinster, and Munster and planted them with Protestants. Rebels by the thousands were deprived of two-thirds of their land and given the remaining third in a different part of the country. For a while priests were hunted down like wolves, and deported to distant lands. Cromwell appropriated for his soldiers 11,000,000 of Ireland's 20,000,000 acres. Today, more than three hundred years later, the name Cromwell is a curse word in Ireland to an even greater extent than is Sherman in Georgia. In 1952 General Eisenhower, campaigning in New England, aimlessly called Oliver Cromwell a great hero—immediately losing a big Irish vote.

The Irish Catholics—by now experts at picking the wrong side in an English fight—almost immediately did it again. Just before the seventeenth century came to an end, they joined James II, England's last Catholic monarch, in his battle with William of Orange. This time they not only lost, but lost on their own soil, at the Battle of Boyne in 1690.

For a century and a half after that the Catholic Irish were not even second-class citizens in their own land. Catholics could belong to neither an Irish nor an English Parliament. They could neither hold office nor serve on a grand jury, and for a time they could not even vote. They were not allowed to operate public schools nor send their children to schools abroad. They could not bear arms, practice law or own a horse worth more than five pounds. If a Protestant woman married a Catholic man, she forfeited her land. Catholic bishops were, for a time, banished from the country, and a bounty of 50 pounds was placed on their heads. Anyone attending a Catholic pilgrimage was subject to a fine and a public whipping. And to add insult to injury, Catholics were taxed for the support of the Irish Protestant church, which represented only one-eighth of the population.

Thus the landless, impoverished peasant paid for the upkeep of a church attended only by his rich masters. In his fight to abolish the system, Daniel O'Connell told the House of Commons of eight parishes in which there was a total of 18,129 Catholics, and no Protestants, ten others in which there were 31,274 Catholics, and 70 Protestants. Not until 1838 was the crazy system abolished. Out of the persecution came a proverb: "For a man to be happy in this world and the next, he should live a Protestant and die a Catholic."

In time a Protestant in Ireland thought of himself as English, no matter if his blood was two-thirds Gaelic. Conversely, a Catholic regarded himself as an Irishman, even if his lineage was a mixture of Norse, Norman, and Scottish, with nary a drop of Irish blood. And, as O'Neill Daunt wrote, "Every Protestant cobbler and tinker conceived himself superior to the Catholic of ancient lineage and ample inheritance."

Through all the years of English rule the Irishman was sustained by his church. Beaumont, the traveling companion of De Tocqueville in the United States, wrote: "The Irish people exists in its church; there alone it is free; there alone it is sure of its rights; there it occupies the only ground that never has given way beneath its feet."

Temptation for the Catholic Irish was everywhere. Protestant landlords conceived it as their religious duty to entice the Catholic away from his faith with food and land. Many a man, watching the hunger of his children, found it hard to stand by the old faith. But just as Catholicism had stood by the Irish, so they overwhelmingly stood by it. Apostates were few and generally despised by other Catholics.

True, hunger drove a few Catholic Irish to Protestant ministers during the winter months. But almost invariably they returned to the chapel when the crops were safely in. On the estate of a few particularly zealous Protestants, some Catholics were "converted" four or five times a year to obtain allotments of food and clothes. Some of these "converts" solaced themselves

—and outraged the Protestant ministery—by saying the rosary during services.

During the famine period the Protestants set up soup kitchens with food going to the man who renounced his faith. The "converts" came to be known as "soupers." Hospitals, workhouses, orphanages, all run by Protestants, were busy hotbeds of proselytism. Orphans whose parents were unknown were automatically registered in foundling homes as Protestants.

Through all this the Church emerged triumphant. The Irish were Catholic to the bone. They had been Catholic for some fourteen centuries, and they would remain so through trials at home and tribulations abroad. When life became too much for him, the Catholic Irishman emigrated. He took along little else but his faith. But that was as much a part of him as his skin. Indeed, in many cases, the immigrant brought not only his faith, but its priests. Scores of clerics comforted the masses crouched in the reeking holds of emigrant ships as they rode out storms, sickness, and short rations. Once here, roaming Irish mission priests moved with gangs building canals and railroads to say Mass in the shanties of the laborers. As an example of their work, the sees of Albany, Buffalo, and Rochester have grown up around the great scar of the Erie Canal.

The Irish found America a land strange in many ways, none more than in its religion. Ironically they fled from persecution in a country predominantly Catholic to sanctuary in a country predominantly Protestant. At the end of the American Revolution there were 25,000 American Catholics. When the Vatican established the first see in the United States in Baltimore in 1789, embracing the entire nation and its territories, it contained no more than 40,000 communicants. Except for those few the population of the country, one hundred times as large, was solidly Protestant.

Then came the Irish. By 1840 the 40,000 Catholics had grown to 600,000, and by 1850 it was more than a million and a half with a million of them Irish. They took Communion from 2000 priests, supervised by 24 bishops and five archbishops. Another decade added another 600,000 Irish to the Church rolls.

The Irish coming ashore in America found themselves not only in a land with an alien faith, but also in a land where their own faith was, to some extent, alien. As America turned into the nineteenth century, the American Catholic Church, though small, numbered many wealthy planters and merchants. Its priests were preponderantly French—clerics driven from their native land by the French Revolution. Indeed, in 1817, all the bishops in the United States except one were French.

The "old Catholics"—rich, aristocratic, established—ran head-on into the new. Archbishop Ambrose Marechal spoke contemptuously of *"la canaille irlandaise"*—the Irish rabble— and protested because the Vatican sent him Irish priests and missionaries.

There were a number of reasons for the clash. The French had been Royalists; the Irish, with good reason, hated monarchy. The French came from a country of crown-supported religion, where church and state were one. The Irish, from the start, believed in the separation of Church and State. They recalled the words of Daniel O'Connell: "For my part, I would prefer death to consenting to the degradation of Catholicity, which a union of our Church with the State would necessarily produce." James Cardinal Gibbons was to say in 1916: "Sixteen millions of Catholics . . . accept the Constitution without any reserve with no desire as Catholics to see it changed in any feature. The separation of Church and State in this country seems to them the natural, the inevitable, and the best conceivable plan."

There was another point of difference between the old Catholics and the new. Some of the earliest American parishes had followed the lead of the Protestant denominations and vested control of church property in a board of trustees. This practice was directly contrary to that in Ireland and elsewhere in Europe, where such control rested with the bishop. The dispute over "trusteeism" shook the faith for years. A Buffalo church was placed under an interdict in 1851, and its trustees excommunicated three years later. St. Mary's Church in Philadelphia was riven for a decade (1820–30) by the dispute.

In the end the bishops—supported largely by the Irish immigrants, who, in most cases, did not know and, thus, mistrusted the well-heeled trustees—won. The Third Plenary Council in 1884 settled the matter once and for all. The Irish Catholics had won their first big battle in America.

They soon were to win an even more important one—Irish priests for Irish Catholics. Early in the nineteenth century, a large Irish Catholic community in western Pennsylvania petitioned Archbishop John Carroll for the replacement of its German priest by one from Ireland. The appeal read: "We would rather depend on Providence a little longer than get a German priest."

When the Reverend John Dubois, a French refugee, succeeded Archbishop John Connolly in the Diocese of New York in 1825, the Irish were up in arms. Father Dubois, founder and former president of Mount St. Mary's College in Emmitsburg, Maryland, was a famous churchman, but the Irish of New York had expected the Reverend John Power, vicar general of the diocese, to succeed as bishop; and when he didn't, they, almost literally, went on strike. Bishop Dubois couldn't garner a nickel for his pet projects. In fact, he went to Ireland to raise funds for an immigrant hospital—money his own parishioners in New York had refused to give him. In a pastoral, he asked why. He cited his record to show he'd actually favored the Irish in his appointments, and he continued: "Who are those who object to our foreign birth? Are they not in the same sense foreigners themselves? For the question was not why an American had not been appointed, but why it was not an Irishman." Father John J. Hughes of Philadelphia, a native of Ireland, finally was appointed coadjutor bishop of New York, and the opposition subsided.

In the end the Irish won their battle for Irish priests by sheer numbers. As they prospered their sons acquired the education necessary for priesthood. In time, more and more priests came out from Ireland. The hierarchy began to take on the Hibernian cast it has had ever since. Ironically, later immigrants—Italians, Germans, and Eastern Europeans—fought the same battle, this time, with the Irish as the "old Catholics." The parish-by-parish struggle often involved, not only the nationality of the priests, but also the language to be used, the saints days to be observed and the name of the church. The Irish liked such names as St. Patrick's; the Italians might prefer Our Lady of Carmel; the German's, St. Boniface's; the Croatians, St. Cyril's.

Many Protestants took advantage of the Catholic cleavage, and proselyting was rife. By 1918 there were some 25,000 converts to Protestantism among the Italians in New York City alone.

A German named Peter Paul Cahensly thought he saw a way out of it all: a church organization based on nationality rather than geography. Under his guidance, a Catholic meeting in Switzerland suggested to Pope Leo XIII in 1891 that the church in America be split up so that the Irishman, Italian, and German each would have his own hierarchy. This, he said, would cushion the shock of emigration and prevent Catholics from straying into Protestantism—prevent, for example, a German Catholic, dissatisfied on finding himself in a predominantly Irish church, from transferring his affiliation to the Lutheran church down the street where the service was conducted in German.

Cahenslyism was hotly discussed up and down the land for many months. In all such debates, the Irish were largely on the *con* side. For one thing they weren't the ones having trouble: they spoke English and found in almost any church a preponderance of their fellows. For another thing, as they saw it, a divided church would be a weakened church, and Catholicism would need all the strength it could muster in a predominantly Protestant land. In short, the Irish weren't about to let their Italian and German allies get away from them. Finally, the whole thing smacked of Protestantism; after all, the Catholic Church was supposed to be catholic. The Vatican, to whom this last reason was all-important, agreed, and denounced Cahensly-ism.

In the end, time solved this problem too. As the years passed, the immigrant groups which had tried to bring with them, as a comfort in an alien land, their own village church, with every local custom and seasonal celebration intact, grew more at home in America and no longer needed such solace. In time the Germans and Italians and Poles spoke German and Italian and Polish less and less, and spoke mainly English. Any priest who spoke English would do. In time the next generation came along, scorning the old ways and the old language, wanting a church that was homogenized American.

But the battles that Catholic fought against Catholic were as nothing to the ones Catholic fought against Protestant. America was, after all, a product of the Reformation. It had been settled, to a large extent, by dissenters. Before 1776, six colonies—Virginia, Maryland, the two Carolinas, Georgia, and New York—had the Church of England as the regulation religion. In three others—Massachusetts, Connecticut, and New Hampshire—the Congregationalists were correct; others were children of error. Massachusetts ruled that any priest crossing its border would be exiled and, on second offense, executed.

Maryland had been founded by Lord Baltimore for Catholics. But the Protestants, when they became a majority, banished his lordship, eliminated all Catholics from office and denied them protection under the law. Virginia quickly followed suit.

As time went on, things went from bad to worse. Catholic France and Spain and Protestant England all were fighting a colonial war in America. To the English colonist, as to the

Today, much of rural Ireland looks as it did in Cromwell's time. Today as then, the cottages are clean inside, neat outside, and their roofs are thatched.

One of the greatest champions of Irish freedom was American-born Eamon de Valera, who became free Ireland's first president. Moments after this picture was taken in 1923, De Valera, speaking in Ennis, County Clare, was arrested and put into jail.

Eire became a republic on April 17, 1949—the anniversary of the Rebellion of 1916. The General Post Office, on Dublin's O'Connell Street, was the focal point both of the uprising and of the independence celebration thirty-three years later. Here, the green, white, and orange flag was raised to the the singing of the Irish National Anthem.

It was a proud day for the Irish in America when they got their first red hat.
Here, a papal emissary announces to Brooklyn-born Archbishop
John McCloskey his elevation to the rank of Cardinal.

A century ago, as now, America's biggest city had its biggest St. Patrick's Day
parades. Here, in 1875, New York's Mayor William H. Wickham reviews
the marchers in front of City Hall.

69TH REG'T N. Y. S. M.

Col. MATHEW MURPHY.

THIS GALLANT CORPS WILL BE READY IN A FEW DAYS TO START FOR THE SEAT OF WAR!

200 PICKED, HEALTHY YOUNG MEN WANTED

To fill the Regiment to its maximum strength.

This Regiment is the **FIRST** of the **IRISH LEGION,** commanded by **GEN. MICHAEL CORCORAN.**

HEADQUARTERS,

Essex Market, cor. Grand & Essex Sts.

The Armed Forces actually didn't need posters like this one to attract Irishmen to the colors. With a fondness for fighting, they swarmed into such units as "The Fighting 69th" which distinguished itself in both the Civil War, under Colonel Mathew Murphy, and World War I, under Colonel William "Wild Bill" Donovan.

Elizabethan Englishman before him, Protestantism and patriotism became one and the same thing. New York made the Catholics disarm and post a bond for good behavior. Connecticut placed them outside the protection of its laws. New Hampshire required all inhabitants to swear an oath against Rome. Pennsylvania added a special tax against Catholics.

Then came the Revolution, and Catholics proved their loyalty by swarming to the colors. Not only that, Catholic France sided with the Revolutionists. As a result anti-Catholic feeling began to wane. The first state constitutions excluded the Catholic from the vote, but these provisions soon were eliminated. For a decade or so, anti-Catholic sentiment in the United States was at a low ebb. Early in the nineteenth century, the atmosphere changed.

In November 1829 the prospectus of a new Protestant journal thus outlined its aims: "To inculcate Gospel doctrines against Romish corruptions—to maintain the purity and sufficiency of the Holy Scriptures against Monkish traditions," etc., etc.

The reasons behind this new rise of anti-Catholic feeling were many. The Church seemed to have sprung up overnight in the United States—an alien shape in a landscape that had undergone only gradual change since the Revolution: between 1820 and 1865, some two million Irish flooded across this country, nearly all of them Catholic. The Catholic Irish concentrated in the big cities, where their numbers were plainly visible. But, most important of all, America had wrested its freedom from England without losing its English character. The Anglo-Saxon and the Gael—the Protestant Englishman and the Catholic Irishman—had been at odds for centuries. The two now faced each other in a single country, and the ancient animosities had not subsided.

The Protestant extremist used a special lexicon in discharging his anti-Catholic bile. The religion was called "Popery," the Catholic a "Papist." The Pope was "Antichrist," and the place of his residence was not Rome but Babylon. The worship itself was variously "idolatrous" and "pagan" and the rituals themselves "trumpery" or "mummery." Priests were accused of forbidding the reading of the Bible, and all Catholics were said to worship wooden idols.

Convents were "nunneries," and dark stories were told of what went on behind their walls. Indeed, there existed a literature of under-the-counter books, largely written by anonymous authors with pimply imaginations, whose smudged pages spun orgiastic tales of monastic wrongdoing. Three hundred thousand prurient Protestants bought copies of a book entitled, *Awful Disclosures of Maria Monk, as exhibited in a narrative of her sufferings during a residence of five years as a Black Nun in the Hotel Dieu Nunnery in Montreal,* published in New York in 1836. The book was a sordid tale of seduction and murder. As it turned out, Maria had been in a Montreal institution, all right, but it had been the Magdalen, a home for wayward women. Maria's mother disclosed the girl had suffered from mental lapses since the age of seven, and that she herself had refused £100 offered by the Reverend William Hoyt, Protestant author of the book, to swear Maria had been a nun. Two reputable Protestant clergymen, after a tour of the convent, reported the book a patent lie, and the editor of the New York *Courier and Enquirer* demolished the story in detail. Nonetheless, Maria has continued to sell right up to our own day. In 1928 it turned up in the campaign against Al Smith.

Samuel F. B. Morse, whose inventive capacities were not limited to matters telegraphic, was an anti-Catholic on another level. His objections to Catholicism were political, not moral. In *Foreign Conspiracy Against the Liberties of the United States,* he argued that Catholicism was at the root of a conspiracy among reactionary members of the Holy Alliance, headed by Austria. The object: to subvert the liberties of the United States. These governments, declared Morse, could never breathe easy so long as their dark despotism stood in sharp contrast to the shining example of the United States.

How was the combine to bring the United States to its knees? Easy, said Morse. Austria's St. Leopold Foundation, whose ostensible object was to raise money for the Church in the United States, actually was a creature of the Austrian government. Aided by funds from the Foundation, Jesuits came and went between the United States and Austria to carry out an evil design —subversion of the United States. This they hoped to accomplish by gaining control of education and by instructing the Catholic politically through the confessional. Strikes and disturbances were carried out by Irish Catholics, said Morse, to upset the harmony of the country. Morse concluded: "Our religion, the Protestant religion, and liberty are identical, and liberty keeps no terms with despotism."

The tide of opposition rolled on. The General Association of Congregational Churches of Massachusetts called on the people to save the United States from "Popery." Baptist groups distributed anti-Catholic literature among Irish settlers.

In the 1830s a number of anti-Catholic secret societies joined together to form "The Order of the Star-Spangled Banner." This name was revealed only to its members who, when asked about the organization, replied that they knew nothing; hence, the popular name the Know-Nothing party.

The war on Catholicism was fought not with words alone. Many a Protestant nose was bloodied and many a Catholic eye blackened before it was over. One of the ugliest incidents occurred on the night of August 11, 1834—the destruction of the Ursuline convent in Charlestown, Massachusetts.

The convent was a seminary, established in 1820, which attracted Protestant as well as Catholic girls. On the fateful day of its destruction the school had an enrollment of 46 girls, from six to eighteen years of age.

Charlestown's rabble regarded the convent with suspicion.

Why all the seclusion? Why the privacy? Surely it could be only because of dark deeds going on inside. Maybe these stories they had heard about "nunneries" were true. Maybe the black-robed sisters practiced medieval rites that would not stand the light of day. Maybe defenseless women were being held against their wills inside those thick, silent walls. Uninformed and diseased imaginations ran wild.

The *Boston Recorder* warned Protestants against enrolling their daughters in the institution. A snoopy neighbor called on the Mother Superior and swore that if any females were being kept inside against their wills, he'd see to it that they were freed.

On a night of shocking culmination, shouting rioters, fired with liquor, closed around the convent. The Mother Superior tried to talk them into going home, but to no avail. Seeing that the end was in sight, she herded the children to a summer house in the rear of the grounds. Finally the drunken mob broke into the building, stealing money, breaking furniture and religious objects, prancing about in the garments of the nuns. One man decked himself out in the bishop's robes, another burned his precious books one by one. Howling raiders ripped a rusty lock off a tomb and pushed their way in. They tore metal name plates off coffins, and ripped open one casket to expose the remains. The nuns had torn the mahogany tabernacle from the altar and hidden it in the shrubbery. But a group of pillagers found it, broke the ciborium, and scattered the sacred wafers in the field.

At half an hour after midnight the torches appeared. The marauders did a thorough job. They set fire to the main convent building, the chapel, the bishop's lodge, the farmhouse, the stables, and the barn. They shouted and pranced as the red firelight flickered over their sweating faces. Finally, at one-thirty in the morning, the roof of the convent collapsed with a hissing roar. The marauders stayed around until dawn, then stumbled home to fall into drunken sleep. Through the whole night of shame, not a hand—official or otherwise—had been raised against them.

Next day, reports spread through Boston that Irish laborers constructing three railroads radiating out from the city were organizing a revenge march on Charlestown. Hastily, Bishop Benedict J. Fenwick sent six priests out in different directions to turn back the angry Irishmen. That evening, in the Cathedral of the Holy Cross, he read from the fifth chapter of St. Matthew:

"You have heard that it hath been said, an eye for an eye, and a tooth for a tooth.

But I say to you not to resist evil: but if one strike thee on thy right cheek, turn to him also the other:

And if a man will contend with thee in judgment, and take away thy coat, let go thy cloak also unto him.

And whosoever will force thee one mile, go with him the other two . . .

You have heard it hath been said, Thou shalt love thy neighbour, and hate thy enemy.

But I say to you, Love your enemies: do good to them that hate you: and pray for them that persecute and calumniate you . . ."

In the months that followed pious Protestants formally announced that they deplored the whole thing. Both the city and the state launched investigations. But nothing came of them.

Bishop Fenwick asked the Massachusetts Legislature for indemnification. The lawmakers replied that no statute covered such a matter, and voted down the petition 412 to 67. All the Bishop got for his trouble was a bill for $79 covering taxes on the ruins. As the months and years went by other such petitions were presented to the state by both Catholics and Protestants. But to no avail. To this day, Massachusetts has not expunged the shame of that long-ago summer night.

In 1843 the state dedicated its Bunker Hill Memorial. At the ceremonies Daniel Webster spoke eloquently of the great liberties, including the freedom to worship as one pleased, the statue symbolized. The monument looked westward to the next hill which bore another monument that spoke of religious liberty —the ruins of the Ursuline convent.

But this was only one in a long chain of violent encounters that marked the rise of Irish Catholicism in America. It had been preceded, in 1831, by the burning of St. Mary's Church in New York. It was followed, in 1844, by three bloody days of rioting in Philadelphia over the issue of which Bible, Protestant or Catholic, should be read in the city's public schools. In that episode 40 persons were killed, more than 60 seriously injured, a Catholic seminary, two churches, and whole blocks of Irish Catholic homes went up in flames.

Ten persons died in anti-Catholic riots in St. Louis in 1854. A year later nearly 100 Catholics were killed in Louisville's "Bloody Monday." A church was blown up in Dorchester, Massachusetts, and another in Shelby County, Ohio. A mob broke up the cornerstone-laying ceremonies of a Catholic church in Bath, Maine, pulled down the cross, and hoisted an American flag in its place.

These battles continued right up until the Civil War, when disputants chose up sides again. This time, it was North versus South instead of Catholic versus Protestant. As had happened in the Revolution, Catholic willingness to fight lessened anti-Catholic feeling for a decade or so afterward. But, inevitably, it rose again.

The fraternal society of Catholic laymen, the Knights of Columbus, was founded by Father Michael J. McGivney and chartered by the General Assembly of Connecticut on March 29, 1882. To suspicious American nativists, this looked like an attempt to organize to take over the government. To meet this supposed threat an Iowan named Henry Bowers formed a secret society called the American Protective Association. Spreading through the West and Middle West, it published 70 anti-

Catholic journals and had 20 members in Congress. However, the A.P.A. never was an essentially political organization, as was the revived Ku-Klux Klan which rose during the 1920s.

Today, though many Americans oppose a Catholic as President of the United States, anti-Catholic feeling of the type that became virulent during the eighteenth, nineteenth, and early twentieth centuries is all but gone. President Kennedy has the awesome opportunity to exterminate the bias and allay honest doubt completely.

The antagonism between Catholics and Protestants probably was based more on economics and politics than on religion. It was a product of a twin fear—fear of Catholic numbers in the labor market and at the polling booth. A man who might be ashamed to denounce the Irish for lowering his wage or voting his candidate out of office did not hesitate to brand them the proponents of an un-American ideology—thus draping his argument with the sanctified mantles of patriotism and religious orthodoxy.

Irish Catholicism flourished in America despite this unpromising climate not only because of the unswerving allegiance of its followers but also because of the dedication of the cadre who led them. From Archbishop John Carroll to Francis Cardinal Spellman, the largely Irish leaders of the faith have been blessed with diplomacy, determination, and dedication. They have made it a point to get along with the Protestants who outnumbered them and, often, disliked them, but never at the expense of principle and the tenets of the faith.

Leader of this parade of illustrious clergymen, in point of time, was John Carroll, a prelate of towering proportions in church annals. As a first family of Maryland, the Carrolls were also a first family of Catholicism in America. Since secondary education was not allowed in Maryland when the Archbishop was a boy, he studied in France, where he became a Jesuit, and was ordained in 1769. When Pope Clement XIV suppressed the Jesuits, he returned to America and began touring the nation to minister to its scattered Catholics. At home, he maintained a private chapel, since Catholic churches were forbidden by law.

Archbishop John Carroll was an ardent supporter of the American Revolution, and accompanied Benjamin Franklin to Quebec in a fruitless attempt to persuade Canada to join up against the British. In 1784, Father Carroll was made superior of the missions in the United States, and in 1790 was consecrated Bishop of Baltimore. He founded Georgetown University in 1791, and in 1808 became archbishop, with suffragans at Boston, New York, Philadelphia, and Bardstown, Kentucky.

As Bishop of Baltimore he oversaw a diocese embracing the whole of the United States, where only one man in every one hundred was a Catholic. Understandably, he placed a heavy emphases during his administration on diplomacy—on explaining Catholicism to Protestant America.

Another of the great figures of the early church, Bishop John England of Charleston, South Carolina, also was dedicated to what, today, would be called good public relations. England began his ecclesiastical career in County Cork, where he ministered to several parishes. He was a vehement fighter for Catholic equality in Ireland, and his patriotic zeal spread his name throughout the island. Thus he was well-known before he was consecrated bishop of the new see of Charleston in 1820, embracing the two Carolinas and Georgia. Here, with the aid of two priests, he watched over a flock of 10,000, spread over an area the size of France, where Protestantism was diluted by only one Catholic in two hundred.

He was notable from the beginning for his interest in things American. Many of his writings and preachings touched the theme of the complete compatibility of Catholicism and Americanism. He was especially devoted to the needs of the Negroes and said a Mass for them each Sunday. Bishop England was, to some extent, the spokesman for the Catholic viewpoint that slavery was a natural disaster, like illness and war, but not a sin in itself. In 1841, a year before his death, he wrote that he was far from "friendly to the existence or continuation of slavery" but that he also saw "the impossibility of now abolishing it here."

Bishop England was a leader in the struggle to obtain Irish priests for Irish parishioners. "The Irish are largely amalgamated with the Americans," he said. "Their principles, their dispositions, their politics, their notions of government, their language and their appearance become American very easily, and they praise and prefer America to their oppressors at home. The French can never become American. Their language, manners, love of 'la belle France' their dress, air, carriage, notions, and mode of speaking of their religion, all, all are foreign. An American then says, 'It might be very good but 'tis foreign aristocracy.' Trivial as this might seem, it has impeded the progress of our religion here."

Notable biographies of Bishop England have been written by a contemporary, William George Read of Baltimore, Peter Guilday (1927), J. L. O'Brien (1934) and D. F. Grant (1949). A handsome red-brick Catholic high school in Charleston bears his name.

Two famous figures in the history of the early church in America share the same surname. The brothers Kenrick were born in Dublin, and the elder by ten years, Francis Patrick, came to America in 1821, following his education in Rome, to teach at the Catholic college in Bardstown, Kentucky. After eight years of it, he was handed what then was the toughest ecclesiastical job in the country—coadjutor bishop of Philadelphia. For ten years, since 1820, St. Mary's Church in the City of Brotherly Love had seen precious little of that commodity. It all began when the brand new bishop of Philadelphia, fresh out of Ireland, Henry Conwell, fired the Reverend William Hogan, the temporary pastor of St. Mary's, because of his false credentials as a priest. The trustees of the church defied the archbishop and supported Father Hogan, a fast-talking confidence man. The parish split down the middle—half for the bishop, half for Father Hogan. The brawl continued for a decade. At trustee elections, voting lists were padded, ballot boxes stuffed and fists used liberally. Before it was all over, the pro-Hogan side discovered their champion's true colors and dumped him, and Rome forceably retired the indecisive Bishop Conwell.

A year after Kenrick arrived, the St. Mary's trustees started causing trouble again. Kenrick, a very different man from Conwell, nipped it in the bud right away. He appeared before the congregation, made it clear that he, and he alone, was in command. Then he insisted that the trustees stay on to help him. There was no more trouble at St. Mary's.

Bishop Kenrick was to figure in another, more serious, episode some thirteen years later—the terrible Philadelphia riots. Throughout the bloodshed of 1844—when Catholic churches and homes were burned, and Catholics killed—he conducted himself with courage and dignity. In 1851, he was named archbishop of Baltimore. By this time his brother, Peter Richard Kenrick, whom he had brought over a dozen years after his arrival, was already an archbishop. Peter Kenrick was educated at Maynooth, and in 1833 his brother called him to become pastor of the Philadelphia cathedral. Archbishop Joseph Rosati of St. Louis asked for him in 1841, and he became his coadjutor. Two years later, he was made bishop, and four years after that, archbishop—four years before his older brother back East made the rank. He, too, had a mind of his own. At the Vatican council, he opposed the enunciation of Papal Infallibility as a dogma.

There isn't much doubt about the identity of the most colorful of the early clergymen. Hands down, the honors go to John J. Hughes, the famous fighting Irish bishop of New York, and its first archbishop. James Cardinal Gibbons called him "active, bold, vigorous, aggressive," and he certainly was all of that, although his enemies called him other names, including "Dagger John." Where Bishops Carroll and England had been conciliatory, Hughes was assertive.

Said one biographer: "He had the power of expressing scorn to a greater degree than any man I ever saw." He once told an opponent: "I will suffer no man in my diocese that I cannot control. I will either put him down, or he shall put me down." He was accused by some Catholics, as well as Protestants, of, among other things, nepotism, maladministration, arrogance, and meddling in matters that did not concern him. But no one ever accused him of weakness, of failing to fight for his faith. To a very great degree, he epitomized the Catholic Irishman.

John J. Hughes, of County Tyrone, joined his family in Pennsylvania in 1817. He got his first steady job in America as a gardener and laborer at Mount St. Mary's College, in Emmitsburg, Maryland. There, he was educated for the priesthood. After his ordination in 1826, he served for more than a decade in and around Philadelphia. It was here that he first attracted nationwide attention.

During this period, a journal titled *The Protestant* regularly published angry diatribes against the Catholic Church. Under the pseudonym Cranmer, Father Hughes finally began writing letters to *The Protestant*, furnishing it with alarming reports of the growth of Catholicism and exaggerated accounts of the Church's aims and rituals. *The Protestant* eagerly snatched up the letters, printing them word for word. "We hope," said the editor, "that our correspondent will furnish us with plenty of his Gospel ammunition." After four months as the poison pen pal to *The Protestant*, Father Hughes revealed his identity. The deception killed off *The Protestant*. But the disclosure also brought down lively criticism on the head of Father Hughes himself, much of it from Catholics, for resorting to dubious trickery to accomplish his purpose, worthy as that purpose might have been.

In 1838, Father Hughes was named coadjutor bishop of New York, where French-born Bishop John Dubois was running into strong opposition from his Irish parishioners. Father Hughes, who understood nothing if not the nature of the Irishman, quieted the contention and solved problems that the bumbling Bishop Dubois had found impossible to settle. Four years later, he succeeded the Frenchman as the Catholic spiritual leader of New York. Now he had power to match his drive.

New York, at the time, was a hotbed of anti-Catholicism. Charles G. Finney, an evangelist capable of whipping a crowd into wild-eyed excitement, thundered nightly against "the Beast" from the Broadway Tabernacle. Public debates between Catholic and Protestant clergymen became popular. Bishop Hughes enlisted his sharp wit and thunderous voice in the battle. Behind the scenes, he was forced to resort to these same tools to keep his hot-tempered parishioners from debating the issues with their fists. In 1835, a group of Irishmen had broken up a meeting in which Evangelist Finney was asking "Is Popery Compatible with Civil Liberty?"

But one of the bitterest battles Bishop Hughes fought was over the old problem of "trusteeism." A year after his consecration, the trustees of old St. Patrick's ordered the ouster of a Sunday school teacher appointed by the bishop. Hughes promptly called a meeting of all pew-holders for a Sunday afternoon. Summoning up his considerable powers as an orator, he spoke fondly of "poor Ireland, who upheld the freedom of her faith at the sacrifice of all that men hold dear beside." He contrasted that faith to the Church of England, "a gilded slave, chained to the crown." Did the parishioners want to adhere to the true religion of Ireland? Or did they prefer to sacrifice doctrine to their powers as a corporate body? Many an Irish cheek was dampened with tears that winter afternoon. And when Bishop

Hughes sat down, the battle over trusteeism was, to all intents and purposes, at an end.

Bishop Hughes, like virtually all the Catholic clergy, carried on perpetual war against secret societies that were the successors of the Ribbonman and Whiteboy organizations back in Ireland. Like many another Irish priest, he also was inclined to distrust Catholic clergymen who fraternized with non-Catholics. "Protestant priests," he called them. He remembered too well the bad days in Ireland when the Protestant proselytizer was likely to place as a price on the necessities of life, a shift in religious allegiance.

But by all odds the greatest battle Father Hughes fought was one that, to all intents and purposes, he lost. Nonetheless, it was a battle that placed his name on the lips of virtually every thoughtful man in America. That was the battle over public schools.

From the start, the immigrating Irishman had placed great emphasis on the education of his children. He remembered too well the old days in Ireland, when schooling was denied the Catholic. But even though the Catholic wanted his child to have an education, he wanted it to be a Catholic education—or at least, not a Protestant education.

Most Catholic Irish did not believe in secular schools in the first place. But even if they were forced to accept secular schools, they did not want them flavored with Protestantism. For, although American education was supposed to stand aloof from religion, it was in fact decidedly pro-Protestant. The King James version of the Bible, the Protestant form of the Lord's Prayer, Protestant hymns—all these were an almost daily part of school life.

The Catholic Irish responded in two ways—either by keeping his children out of classes altogether, or organizing Catholic parochial schools. One historian has estimated that in the mid-1800s one half the Catholic children in New York City went to no school at all. Many of the others attended crude classes maintained by individual parishes, usually in the church basement. Of the nine to twelve thousand Catholic school-age children in New York city in 1840, about five thousand attended such classes.

It was at this point that William Henry Seward stepped in. Seward, who two decades later was to become Abraham Lincoln's Secretary of State and later to negotiate the purchase of Alaska, in 1840 was beginning his second two-year term as Governor of New York. A likable, gregarious man with a number of intellectual interests, he was a sincere friend of the immigrant, especially the Irish. In his 1840 message to the state legislature, Seward suggested Irish Catholic schools for Irish Catholic children. Said he: "I desire to see the children of Catholics educated as well as those of Protestants; not because I want them Catholics, but because I want them to become good citizens."

In New York City at the time, a private organization supported by both public and private funds, the Public School Society, administered the schools. Taking their cue from Governor Seward, the trustees of seven parochial schools applied officially for a slice of the money going to the Society. The Common Council turned down the bid, saying public support of any organization where "religious tenets are taught to any extent" would do violence to the Constitution.

It was at this point that Bishop Hughes returned from a nine-month tour of Europe. Two days after stepping off the boat, he called to order a meeting in St. Patrick's schoolhouse to assume command of the fight. The upshot was that Bishop Hughes presented the Catholic case in person to the city fathers against a squadron of ministers and attorneys representing the Public School Society. Hughes said Catholics were willing to place parochial schools under the supervision of the Society, if they could share in school funds. By a vote of fifteen to one, the Board of Aldermen said no.

[168]

By this time the public was fully aroused. Press and pulpit accused Bishop Hughes of avarice for public money. Irish bully-boys broke up two meetings called to support the Public School Society. Finally, Bishop Hughes tried another tack. He petitioned the state to abolish the Public School Society and take over public education itself. The legislature asked the New York Secretary of State, John Spencer, to investigate the matter, and he came up with a new plan: Each ward in New York City would choose its own education commissioner, and thus would have the kind of education it wanted. Bishop Hughes liked the idea, but the legislature postponed acting until the elections were out of the way.

The two preponderant parties—Whigs and Democrats—came out for the Public School Society, and it looked as if the Catholic cause was doomed. But Bishop Hughes would not stop fighting. He called a meeting of Catholic voters four days before election and presented it with an independent ticket of candidates supporting the Spencer proposal for local option. A number of prominent Catholics accused him of playing politics and said they would stick to the regular Whig and Democratic organizations. As it turned out, only about one-third of the Catholics who normally would have voted Democratic, swung to the bishop's ticket—enough to throw the election to the bishop's worst enemies, the Whigs.

Not only Catholics but others sharply criticized Bishop Hughes for his political activity. The famous editor of the New York *Herald*, James Gordon Bennett, accused Bishop Hughes of trying to organize a Catholic party that he could swing to the Whigs or the Democrats "at the wave of his crosier." Even his friends conceded that the bishop had furnished what many New Yorkers considered proof positive that Samuel F. B. Morse was right about more things than the ability of an electric wire to carry a message.

In the end, Bishop Hughes won a kind of pyrrhic victory.

The state legislature passed a bill providing for control of public education in New York City by ward committeemen. But the bill's fine print said that no public funds could go to a school "in which any religious sectarian doctrine or tenet shall be taught." Bishop Hughes gave up the fight, and turned to the building of a better parochial school system.

Bishop Hughes belonged to what might be described as the conservative wing of the early Catholic clergy. Two others of that wing were Bernard John McQuaid, first Bishop of Rochester, and Michael Augustine Corrigan, Bishop of Newark and later Archbishop of New York. Both were second-generation Americans, McQuaid the son of a laborer killed in a fist fight with a fellow worker, Corrigan the son of a cabinetmaker.

The two most notable members of the opposite, and surely more worldly faction, were Bishop John Ireland of St. Paul and James Cardinal Gibbons of Baltimore, whom many regard as the most universally revered of all American Irish prelates.

Richard Ireland, a carpenter who immigrated to Chicago by way of Vermont, fell to talking with an old friend, John O'Gorman, on a Chicago street, and the two decided therewith to take their families West. They traveled by prairie schooner to Galena, Illinois, and thence by boat to St. Paul, then a frontier village, where they settled and prospered. Ireland's son John became St. Paul's first archbishop, and O'Gorman's son Thomas became the first Bishop of Sioux Falls.

After service as a Civil War chaplain, Father Ireland returned to St. Paul as Cathedral pastor. His fame spread as he thundered against liquor and denounced municipal vice and corruption. As time went on, he rose to coadjutor, bishop, then archbishop. He gained friends, as well as enemies, by his strong stands —for total abstinence, for the abolition of any foreign language in Catholic schools and churches, for the rights of organized labor. Archbishop Ireland was an ardent Republican and a close personal friend of Presidents William McKinley and Theodore Roosevelt.

Archbishop John Ireland and James Cardinal Gibbons bore many resemblances. Both spoke out often on national matters, both were friendly to the Knights of Labor. Both were close personal friends of a series of Presidents; in the case of Cardinal Gibbons, it was Grover Cleveland, Theodore Roosevelt, and William Howard Taft.

Thomas and Bridget Gibbons had come to Baltimore by way of Canada from County Mayo. Thomas died when his son was thirteen, and Bridget supported the boy during his studies for the priesthood. He was ordained in 1861 and seven years later became known as "the boy bishop of North Carolina." He rose step by step—secretary to the Archbishop of Baltimore, vicar apostolic of North Carolina, Bishop of Richmond, coadjutor to the Archbishop of Baltimore, archbishop, and, in 1886, was created a cardinal by Pope Leo XIII. In sharp contrast to Bishop Hughes, Cardinal Gibbons counted many friends among men of all levels of society and of all faiths. Invariably, he was on the side of conciliation and compromise, and in this sense he was something of a throwback to the earlier Bishops Carroll and England. He wrote a number of books, the most famous, *The Faith of Our Fathers*, a classic explanation of Catholicism for conservative Protestants. Cardinal Gibbons allayed the fears and suspicions of countless non-Catholics by speaking out with ringing clarity on separation of church and state and on patriotic issues.

This listing of famous early Irish-Catholic prelates is, of course, far from complete. A separate book could not do the subject justice. But such a scant sampling may be sufficient to show that one reason the Church became great in America was because it was blessed with great churchmen.

Today the American church, thanks in large part to the Irish, is the richest and perhaps most powerful of the numerous branches of world-wide Catholicism. In the decade ending in 1960 it increased by 47.2 per cent. Its parishes are scattered across our countryside. Its hospitals, homes, orphanages, schools, and colleges heal the sick, shield the helpless old and young, prepare youth for useful maturity and succor the poor.

The concerned or derisive Yankees, as they watched ragged mobs steaming from the sorry holds of immigrant ships, had no true way of knowing that nearly every member of this wretched parade was smuggling ashore a treasure. It was the treasure of faith, the same faith that had enabled them and their forebears to withstand war and starvation and death and all manner of tragedy.

Far more precious and negotiable than a full wallet, this treasure gave the Irish immigrant a start in America, gave him courage to make his way in a new land, to find his footing and walk a straight path. Just as his forebears had passed it on to him, so he handed it along to his sons and daughters. It has sustained them in ordeals private and public, from Bunker Hill to Korea's Porkchop Hill, through the wreckage of broken hopes and dissolving dreams. It will continue to light their path no matter what lies on the other side of tomorrow.

9 FIGHTING IRISH:

Fame in the Wars

Through the years, emigrating Irishmen have looked upon America as a suburb of heaven because it has given them the things they really need: a job, a chance to better themselves and an occasional rousing fight.

During the turbulent years of the mid-nineteenth century, a street-corner brawl was the immigrant Irishman's two-weeks-in-Miami. It benefited his body, nourished his nerves, and purged his psyche of frustrations and hidden angers. The Irishman found America a land filled, not only with opportunity but also with a Catholic-hating breed of Protestants. And if he was normally quick-tempered, he might reach advanced years before his knuckles had a chance properly to heal.

When they ran out of Protestants, the Irish battled one another. Preferably, Ulstermen fought men of the south, but when that was not feasible, men of one county fought men of another. Sometimes the Irish combined business with pleasure and did their fighting in the ring. But more often they restricted their roistering to the hours reserved for rest and relaxation.

[173]

America not only provided the Irishman with a plentiful supply of street-corner scuffles and barroom brawls, but every few years it threw in a real spectacular—such as the Civil War and World Wars I and II. These affairs provided the Irishman with an opportunity to purge, not alone the mere frustrations of the moment, but also the anger of a lifetime.

In the eighteenth century, the first wave was no sooner ashore than the startled immigrants were handed flintlocks and told to go fight the British. If they had not realized it before, they knew then that America was indeed another name for Paradise.

In the nineteenth century members of the second wave had a chance to take only a quick look around before they were issued rifles and told to go fight Southerners—or Northerners, depending on whether they had come ashore in New York or New Orleans. Since a North-South split was an old story to the Irish, they fell to with a will.

Later Irishmen, hearing rumors of high wages and intermittent bursts of gunfire from across the seas, flagged down the first boat to America, arriving in plenty of time for the twin World Wars.

When an Irishman gets in a fight it not only purges the anger of the Irishman, but also the anger *at* the Irishman. Anti-Catholic feeling ran high in colonial America, but the fingerling nation's 25,000 Catholics, Irish and otherwise, fought the British with such a will in the Revolution that the Constitution writers made religious tolerance not only popular but legal.

During the next century, America's Catholics increased 160-fold. And as Catholicism increased, so did anti-Catholicism. Then it was that "nativism" was born: the doctrine that Catholics, because they were obedient to the Pope, could never become fully loyal Americans.

Actually, except for the Revolution, in which they were fighting for their new home and against the British, the Catholic Irish have entered every American War with certain qualms.

They fought on the side of Protestant America against Catholic Mexico and Spain, although they themselves were Catholic. They fought on the side of the North in the Civil War though they feared freeing of the slaves, feeling that this would flood the market with cheaper labor. They fought on the side of the allies in World War I, though they were anti-British. They fought on the side of Russia in World War II, though they were anti-Communist. But the fact that they fought so long and so well despite these misgivings provided conclusive proof of their loyalty. It was not so much what they were fighting *with* or *against* as what they were fighting *for*, namely, America.

It is hard to imagine how colonial America could have shaken itself loose from Britain had it not been for the fighting Irish. It seems certain that at least half of Washington's armies were Irish. In 1779, a committee of the British House of Commons, investigating the causes of the Revolution, asked this question of Joseph Galloway, a delegate to the First Continental Congress who later joined the Loyalists: "What were the troops in the service of the Congress composed of? Were they natives of America or were the greatest part of them English, Scotch or Irish?"

Galloway replied: "I can answer that question with precision. They were scarcely one-fourth natives of America, about one-half Irish, the other fourth English or Scotch."

Testifying before the same committee, Major General Robertson said: "I remember Gen. Harry Lee telling me that half the rebel army were from Ireland."

In his *Personal Recollections*, George Washington Parke Custis has this to say about the composition of the Revolutionary army: "Up to the coming of the French, Ireland had furnished in the ratio of one hundred to one of every nation whatever."

Little wonder that when the surrender of Lord Cornwallis was announced to the British Parliament, Lord Mountjoy said: "England has lost America through the exertions of Irish immigrants."

Indeed, so solidly Hibernian was the most famous corps in the Revolutionary Army, "the Pennsylvania Line," that the doughty Light-Horse Harry Lee renamed it "the Line to Ireland." Lee said of the Irish: "Bold and daring they are impatient and refractory, and would always prefer an appeal to the bayonet to a toilsome march."

As so many fights, this one was started by the Irish. Major General John Sullivan opened the war by storming Fort William and Mary. There he captured the guns which armed the troops who fought at Bunker Hill.

Sullivan, one of Washington's most trusted officers, later commanded the American right wing at Trenton, Brandywine, and Germantown. After the war, he pursued a successful career as lawyer and judge in Durham, New Hampshire.

The Irish not only opened the war on land, but also at sea. In May 1775 the British sent the warship *Margaretta* along New England's coast. The purpose of the cruise seems to have been to impress the colonists with British might and thus keep them from joining the rebellion. In the course of its mission, the *Margaretta* entered Machias Bay, Maine, the home of Maurice O'Brien, late of Cork, and his five sons.

O'Brien and his boys gathered together a group of neighbors who, putting out into the bay in their fishing boats, boarded and captured the man-of-war. The angry British immediately sent two other vessels, the *Diligence* and the *Tapnaguish*, to recover the *Margaretta* and summerally punish the O'Briens and their neighbors. The result: the O'Briens captured these ships too. Maurice's oldest son, Jeremiah, sailed the three vessels to Waterville where the Maine provincial congress was in session. He was given a formal vote of thanks and his commission as a captain.

As such, he served under Irishman John Barry, who generally

is regarded as the father of the United States Navy. Barry was born in County Wexford in 1745 and emigrated to America when he was fifteen. He acquired wealth as the captain of a merchantman trading to Philadelphia.

When war broke out, Barry was appointed captain of the brig *Lexington* which, in April 1776, took the tender *Edward*, becoming the first United States vessel to capture an enemy ship. Barry's fame spread across the whole of the infant nation when he captured the armed schooner *Alert* in Delaware Bay with only a few men in rowboats.

Barry kept on fighting and kept on winning. In fact, he was victor in the last battle of the war, in 1782. Twelve years later, when Congress got around to providing for a Navy, he was chosen its first commander. He died in Philadelphia on September 13, 1803, at the age of fifty-eight, and his statue stands today in Independence Square.

The Irish provided leadership wherever the war was waged. One of the greatest of the Irish freedom fighters was Brigadier General Richard Montgomery, who gave his life for the freedom of his country.

There is a curious and tragic quirk in Montgomery's story. He began his career in the British Army in which he rose to the rank of colonel. As such, he took part under Major General James Wolfe in wresting Quebec from the French.

Virtually every schoolboy remembers the story of Wolfe and the Marquis de Montcalm, his French opponent. Though defeated in his first attempt to take Quebec, Wolfe scaled the cliffs with his army by night, and died in the moment of victory, while his brave antagonist Montcalm, dying too, said: "It is a great consolation to have been vanquished by so brave an enemy."

Montgomery, grieving at his general's death, could not know that a strangely parallel fate lay in his future. In 1772, Colonel Montgomery resigned his commission in the British Army to settle in America. When war broke out he threw in his lot with the Rebels, who were eager for the services of trained and experienced military leaders.

George Washington made Montgomery a general and handed him the assignment of invading Canada. Despite the small size of his force the Dublin-born soldier won victory after victory: Fort Chambly, Fort John, Montreal itself. Finally he turned on the citadel of Quebec. Rushing forward in advance of his men, he was killed by the first salvo fired by the British. His troops, seeing their leader fall, fled in all directions. But for the lucky shot that struck Montgomery down in 1775, Canada today might be a part of the United States.

Montgomery's body lay all night on the frozen Plains of Abraham where Wolfe and Montcalm had met their deaths. When the British recovered it the next day, it was frozen stiff. Montgomery's rigid right arm held a sword outstretched toward Quebec. He had died—as every Irish soldier would prefer to die—fighting in the van of battle.

Other Irishmen who served as generals under Washington were John Shee of County Meath, Richard Butler of Dublin, William Thompson of Londonderry, William Irvine of Fermanagh, and Andrew Lewis of Donegal. One historian has compiled from muster rolls of the Continental Army a list of 1500 officers whose names show them as unquestionably Irish. He also has found that 12,000 soldiers bore distinctly Irish names.

There is as little doubt about the quality of the Irish soldiers who fought in Washington's gallant army as there is about their quantity. The British historian and philosopher, William E. Lecky, says of those early Irish immigrants: "They supplied some of the best soldiers of Washington."

Washington himself recognized the worth of his Irish troops. In a graceful tribute to them, he made "St. Patrick" the watchword on the night of March 17, 1776, when British-held Boston,

1

2

3

4

5

6

7

8

9

10

11

12

1 F. Scott Fitzgerald
2 Colin P. Kelly, Jr.
3 George M. Cohan
4 Colonel William J. "Wild Bill" Donovan
5 Grace Kelly Grimaldi
6 President John F. Kennedy
7 Eugene O'Neill
8 John McCormack
9 Connie Mack
10 Supreme Court Justice Frank Murphy
11 Alfred E. Smith
12 John L. Sullivan

besieged by rebel forces for eight months, finally was occupied by the patriots. Later Washington was made a member of the New York chapter of the Friendly Sons of St. Patrick. In his letter of acceptance, he wrote:

"I accept with singular pleasure the Ensign of so worthy a fraternity as that of the Sons of St. Patrick in this city—a Society distinguished for the firm adherence of its members to the glorious cause in which we are embarked."

Washington knew that no colonists were more loyal to the fight for freedom than the Irish. Most Americans fail to realize how evenly balanced were the forces in America favoring independence of England and loyalty to it. Speaking of the work of the Continental Congress, John Adams observed: "Every important step was opposed and carried by bare majorities." But the English-hating Irish never swerved in their loyalty to the cause of independence. In 1780, when the colonies' fortunes and finances were at a low ebb—when Washington lacked money for supplies and desertions were at a peak—a group of Philadelphians pooled their resources and contributed the then huge sum of £300,000 to the rebel cause. One-third of that sum was raised by local members of the Friendly Sons of St. Patrick.

A generation after winning its independence by defeating England, the fledgling nation decided to take on its old foe again. The muddled little War of 1812 shed little glory on either England or the United States. But the war's one great victory was won by a son of Irish immigrants, Andrew Jackson. His second-in-command at New Orleans was another Irishman, General William Carroll, who twice served Tennessee as governor. In the ranks was an Irish soldier named Davy Crockett, later to gain glory at the Alamo. Though unable to read or write, Crockett won a seat in Congress because of his unparalleled ability as a storyteller, and later became an Alabama judge. One of his famous judicial findings was that correct spelling was "contrary to nature."

After two wars with a far-off foe, the young United States next tangled with a nearby neighbor, Mexico. The Irish distinguished themselves both as leaders and as rank-and-file fighting men during the Mexican War, which began in 1846 and lasted for two years. Approximately one-third of the men who fought under the American commander-in-chief, General Winfield Scott, and "Old Rough-and-Ready" Zachary Taylor were volunteers. And their ranks included a corps of two thousand native-born Irish. Writing about his Irish corps later Scott said: "Not one ever turned his back on the enemy or faltered in advancing to the charge."

George Potter in his *To the Golden Door* places the number of Irish-born enlisted men in the American forces at some 3500. And the *Freeman's Journal* said: "It must be a source of pride to Irish-Catholic citizens to know that General Taylor's army consists of more than one-half of their countrymen."

Irishmen enlisted not only by ones and twos, but also by companies. There were, for example, the Jasper Greens of Savannah, the Mobile Volunteers of Alabama, the Emmett Guards of Albany, the Montgomery Guards of Detroit and another company by the same name from Cincinnati. Three full companies of Irishmen enlisted in New Orleans and four in Philadelphia. The Boston Irish had a company, as did the Irish of St. Louis. The New York Volunteers, under the command of General James Shields, distinguished themselves in the storming of Chapultepec.

There had been much talk that Catholic Americans would not fight Catholic Mexicans. But the Albany *Evening Journal* pointed out: "If any thing was needed to wipe out this vile calumny, we have it in the long and fatal list of 'killed and wounded.' It is only necessary to read the names to see that two-thirds if not three-fourths of all who shed their blood in that gallant action were Irishmen."

The Irish produced, not only much of the American rank-

and-file during the war with Mexico, but also one of its great heroes. He was the aforementioned James Shields, born in County Tyrone in 1806. He was the second member of his family to go to war for America. As a boy in Ireland, he'd listened to the stories of an uncle who had returned from the United States after fighting in the Revolution and the War of 1812.

Shields' civilian life was distinguished by the fact that at various times he was elected to the United States Senate from three states—Illinois, Minnesota, and Missouri—and that he almost fought a duel with Abraham Lincoln. The near-duel came about when Shields was serving as auditor of Illinois. While he was trying to untangle the state's snarled finances, two anonymous articles in the *Sangamon Journal* sneered at his rustic manners and attacked him for the simple fact that he was an Irishman. The articles had been written by Lincoln's fiancée, Mary Todd, and her friend Julia Jayne.

When Shields asked the editor for the name of the author, he replied that Lincoln would assume responsibility for the articles. Shields immediately challenged Lincoln to a duel. Lincoln selected cavalry broadswords as the weapons, and a sand bar on the Missouri side of the Mississippi River as the site for the joust, to escape the Illinois law against such contests.

The two men met at the appointed time and place. And, while the seconds were conferring on procedure, they fell to talking. The result: they became fast friends and remained so through life. Lincoln later wrote an apology in the *Sangamon Journal* for the ungracious remarks of his future wife.

When war broke out, Shields was in Washington serving as Commissioner of the General Land Office. On the basis of his experience in the Florida war, he was made a general. Shields was wounded at Cerro Gordo, but he kept on fighting gamely and survived to distinguish himself in the storming of San Mateo on the outskirts of Mexico City in the most stubborn fighting of the war.

The war with Mexico produced other Irish heroes. One was Philip Kearny, whose last name fittingly is a corruption of the Celtic word for soldier. He began his fighting career by volunteering for France in her Algerian campaigns of 1839 and 1840. When the Mexican war broke out, he shuttled to the New World battlefield where he won a citation for gallant conduct and the rank of major. With Mexico defeated, Kearny returned to the French Army to take part in its war on Austria, and won honors on the field of Solferino. That war over, he made it back across the Atlantic in time for the Civil War in which he distinguished himself in the Peninsula Campaign and the Second Battle of Bull Run.

Kearny was a member of General George B. McClellan's staff when that overcautious Union general achieved one of his few victories over the Confederates, at Malvern Hill, on July 1, 1862. The triumph opened the way to Richmond, and there seems little doubt now but that, had McClellan pressed his advantage, he might have captured the rebel capital and shortened the war by years. But McClellan not only refused to advance, he actually ordered a retreat. Kearny was consumed by disgust. He told McClellan:

"I Philip Kearny, an old soldier of fortune, enter my solemn protest against this retreat. In full view of the responsibilities of such a declaration, I say to you that such an order can be prompted only by cowardice—or treason."

McClellan not only refused to take action against the Confederates, he also refused, despite the insult, to take action against his officer.

Another Kearny also distinguished himself in the Mexican War, by presenting New Mexico to the United States. He was General Stephen Watts Kearny, Philip's uncle. He was born in Newark, New Jersey, in 1794 and entered the army as a lieutenant at the age of eighteen. When the Mexican War broke out, he was commanding officer at Fort Leavenworth, Kansas. Hastily assembling a force of some 1700 men with the vaunted title of Army of the West, he marched on Mexico's province of New Mexico and seized it for the United States. Later he served as civil governor of California, which was ceded to the United States by Mexico as a result of the war.

Two Irish heroes cited for bravery during the Mexican War were as familiar with the pen as with the sword. They were Captain Mayne Reid and Major Theodore O'Hara. Reid, a hero at the storming of Chapultepec, became a writer of stirring adventure stories like *The Castaways* and *The Quadroon*. And O'Hara, a hero of Contreras and Churubusco, wrote the enduring poem "Bivouac of the Dead," a tribute to his fallen comrades:

> On Fame's eternal camping ground
> Their silent tents are spread,
> And glory guards with column round
> The bivouac of the dead.

Still another Irish hero of the Mexican War was Lieutenant John Paul O'Brien. At Buena Vista a section of artillery he commanded became isolated from the main part of the United States Army. But he refused to retreat and, although his guns were captured, he held off the Mexicans until American rein-forcements arrived. The guns, later recaptured, now stand at West Point.

If the Irish provided some of the war's great heroes, they also produced one of its blackest villains. He was Major John Riley, commander of Mexico's notorious San Patricio Battalion, a deserter and a traitor. Born in Ireland in 1817, he had served as a noncommissioned officer in England and, migrating to this country, joined the United States Army as a private. On Sunday April 12, 1846, before the war actually started, Riley was with General Taylor before Matamoros. That morning he asked his captain for permission to attend Catholic religious services. And when it was granted, he disappeared.

Later at his trial Riley said he'd been captured by the Mexicans and given the choice of execution or accepting a commission. At any rate he turned up as a major and the second-in-command under a Florida-born Mexican colonel of a group that called itself The Legion of Strangers or the San Patricio Battalion. This Mexican Foreign Legion consisted of two hundred Americans who, for various reasons, had deserted to the enemy. Some had gotten drunk and wandered into Mexican lines. Others had lingered too long with native girls. Still others had gone over the hill to escape punishment or a cruel officer.

The Legion of Strangers fought long and hard until its remnants, including Major Riley, were captured at Churubusco by another Catholic Irishman, General Shields. Of the seventy-two men that survived, twenty-seven were natives of Ireland, fifteen of the United States, six of Germany, three of Scotland, and two each of Canada, England, and France.

No sooner had the men been captured, than two military courts were set up to try them on the spot. Hour after hour, they came up with the same verdict, "guilty of desertion to the enemy." In forty-nine cases the sentence was: "to be hanged by the neck until dead." Of those hanged, seventeen were natives of Ireland.

Ironically, the life of the most hated of them all, Riley himself, was spared because of the technicality that he had deserted before the war had actually started. Nonetheless, the court gave him the stiffest sentence within its power: "fifty lashes with a rawhide whip well laid on the back," and the letter "D" for deserter branded on his cheek. After he was drummed out of service Riley returned to the Mexican Army as a colonel.

Even while the war with Mexico was going on the nation was moving inexorably toward a war with itself. America was alive with controversy over slavery, and it was becoming clearer by the day that only a resort to arms would decide the issue.

It is, on the surface at least, one of the anomalies of history that the propertyless Irish, huddled in the slums of America's Northern cities, should have sided in the debate over slavery with the landed, aristocratic Southern planters. But such was the case. The Irish, who ironically had fled from tyranny in their own land, wanted the black man to remain a chattel.

Slavery had been outlawed in Ireland since the twelfth century. No slave ship had ever sailed from an Irish port. When the question of emancipating the West Indian Negroes came up in the House of Commons, every Irish member voted "aye." Daniel O'Connell, the heroic leader of Ireland's fight for freedom from England, was bitter in his denunciation of the pro-slavery American Irish. "It was not in Ireland that you learned this cruelty," he told them. "How can you have become so depraved?" Yet despite all this, the American Irish favored slavery.

There were several reasons for this attitude. First, there was the matter of economics. The vast majority of Irish Americans were laborers. They were afraid that a great hoard of freed slaves would become the new labor force of America. After all, a man accustomed to working for nothing would be happy enough to work for next to nothing. Second, the Irish automatically took the opposite side of the Abolitionists. The Abolitionist movement was a product of the Protestant evangelical churches. Its leaders were largely members of the Protestant clergy, many of whom denounced slavery and "Popery" with equal fervor. Abolitionist societies, said the *Boston Pilot*, are "thronged with bigoted and persecuting religionists, with men, who, in their private capacity, desire the extermination of Catholics by fire and sword."

The third reason for the Irish position was political The Democratic party had been good to the Irish immigrant; he rewarded it with his loyalty and his votes. And the Democratic party was the party of slavery. Besides, the opposing party, whether Whig or Republican, had never hesitated to welcome to its bosom such anti-Irish factions as the Know-Nothings. In short, if the Democratic party wanted a continuation of slavery, the Irish wanted it too.

The fourth reason for the Irish attitude was religious. Officially, the Catholic Church neither condemned nor condoned slavery. In May 1858 the pastoral letter of the Ninth Provincial Council of Baltimore summed up the Church's position: "Our clergy have wisely abstained from all interference with the judgment of the faithful which should be free on all questions of polity and social order, within the limits of the doctrine and law of the church."

Perhaps the Irish attitude on slavery was basically a product of the Irish character. Very aptly, author Potter puts it this way: "The Irishman, by nature as well as by the teachings of his church, opposed innovations, had little patience with reform and reformers and put small faith in the use of the law to change or perfect human beings."

Whatever the Irishman's attitude had been in the years of debate before the war, when the bell rang to start the fight he was in there punching. Arguing the slavery issue was one thing, fighting for one's country was quite another. President Lincoln, in his first call for volunteers, wisely said nothing about slavery, but emphasized only that troops were needed to "save the Union." That was enough for the Irishman. As the war wore on, and England began to lean toward the Confederacy, the Irishman knew that his instinct had been correct.

In the South, of course, other Irishmen found other reasons for their loyalties. Wasn't the Confederacy being kept within the United States against its will, just as Ireland was imprisoned within the United Kingdom?

There is little doubt of the part the Irish played on both sides of the Civil War. Cogently, they had not migrated in large numbers to the South because the available unskilled laboring jobs were held by slaves, so their Civil War contribution was largest on the side of the North.

There are no hard-and-fast statistics to show how many Irishmen fought on the side of the North in the Civil War, but the available facts seem to indicate there were about 300,000. Records of the Army Medical Department show that of the 501,537 men whose place of birth was recorded when they were examined during the war, 50,537 were natives of Ireland. If that ratio held true for total Union enlistments of 2,778,304, the Irish-born men in blue would number just short of 300,000.

Fox, in his *History of Regimental Loss*, supports this estimate. He says 150,000 men of Irish birth are numbered among those who fell and an equal number were returned to civilian life.

As in all wars, the Irish also provided abundant leadership. The Union generals of Irish blood included Philip H. Sheridan, who won the Shenandoah Valley for the North and whose parents were from County Cavan; George G. Meade, the victor of Gettysburg, whose Irish-born grandfather fought in the Revolution; Thomas Francis Meagher, the exiled Irish patriot and the leader of the famous Irish Brigade recruited in New York City; Philip Kearny, Michael Corcoran, C. C. Sullivan, George Croghan, John Logan, and Robert Patterson.

The most famous Gaelic unit in the United States Army during the Civil War was the Irish Brigade. It consisted of the 23rd, 29th and 88th New York Regiments, the 116th Pennsylvania, and the 28th Massachusetts—solidly Irish, every one of them. The brigade formed part of General Israel Richardson's division.

Then there was the 69th New York Regiment, commanded by General Corcoran, which became the core of the later Corcoran Brigade and also fought as part of the Irish Brigade. Colonel Timothy O'Meara led the 19th Illinois, which called it-

self the "Irish Legion." The 9th Massachusetts was labeled
"The Irish 9th." Other all-Irish or nearly all-Irish units included
the 15th Maine; the 9th, 37th and 63rd New York; the 2nd and
69th Pennsylvania; the 9th Connecticut; the 10th Ohio; the
11th and 17th Wisconsin; the 35th and 61st Indiana; the 7th
Missouri; the 23rd Illinois; the 5th Minnesota; and the 1st
Rhode Island.

Like the Union Army, the Confederates kept no records to
show the number of Irish-born troops in their ranks. However,
the Irish patriot John Mitchell, who after his exile took up
residence in Richmond, says 40,000 Irishmen fought in Confederate ranks. Mitchell himself lost two sons on the Confederate
side in the war. General Patrick Finnegan, the defender of
Florida, and General Patrick Cleburne, who died in action at
Franklin, Tennessee, were both born in Ireland. The Postmaster
General of the Confederacy, John Reagan, was of Irish blood
although born in Tennessee.

The story is told of General Cleburne that at Franklin he saw
a young soldier struggling across the battlefield in bare and
bloody feet. The general leaped from his horse, removed his
boots and gave them to the private. "Here," he said, "you need
them more than I do." And he rode off to his death.

Among the Irish units in the Confederate Army were the
Emerald Light Infantry of South Carolina, the Emerald Guards
of Alabama, the Emmett Guards and the Montgomery Guards
of Virginia.

However, of all the Irish units on both sides, the Union
Army's Irish Brigade was by far the largest and best known.
Leonard Wibberley in his Coming of the Green tells an amusing
story of the brigade's introduction to General Richardson, their
new non-Irish divisional commander. Captain Jack Gosson of
Dublin, concerned lest the men snub a commanding officer who
had the effrontery to be born outside the mother isle, called
the men together and said:

"Sure, he's a wonderful old feller with an Irish heart and never mind his name. Hasn't he sent up three barrels of whisky for the brigade and paid for them out of his own pocket? Now what would you say to a man like that?"

When the general finally arrived, the Irish gave him a noisy welcome. It was many weeks later before they realized that those three barrels of whisky had never materialized. Richardson himself was killed in the bloody fighting at Antietam —the battle in which the great Irish Brigade became immortal.

The time was September 17, 1862. The place: the small Antietam Creek, which flows into the Potomac near Sharpsburg, Maryland. On one side the Confederates under Robert E. Lee. On the other, the Federals, under McClellan.

The Irish Brigade occupied a position in, roughly, the center of the line. Opposite them, under General James Longstreet, the Confederates were strongly entrenched along a sunken road, behind a breastwork of fence rails. Unit after unit had attacked that position—the 132nd Pennsylvania, the 118th Pennsylvania, the 8th Ohio, for instance—and had been forced back by a withering Confederate fire.

By this time, Bloody Lane, as the Confederate position was called, had become the focal point of the battle. Either the position would be taken, or the Federals would lose the whole battle, with only a lengthy casualty list to show for their efforts.

Finally, the Irish Brigade was ordered to attack. With green banners flying in the crisp fall air, the Irish marched across the crest of a hill and down the far side, toward Bloody Lane. In a few minutes, the battle was joined.

The long, low line of Confederate breastwork soon disappeared in a thick cloud of smoke, shot through with stabbing streaks of fire. The roar of the guns shook the hill, but above the din the Federal reserves watching the grim battle could hear the agonized screams of the wounded and dying.

Finally, General Richardson sent another brigade forward to

pull his troops back over the hill, accept his losses, and chalk up the Irish Brigade's first defeat, or he could charge. For if the Irishmen remained where they were, they would surely be wiped out.

Above the thunder of battle came Meagher's bullhorn voice. "Follow me, boys, follow me." Into the cloud of smoke the Irish Brigade plunged. Half of a New York regiment was wiped out in the first volley. Within a few hundred yards of Bloody Lane General Meagher's horse was shot out from under him. The dead were piling up, forming a breastwork of their own.

Finally, General Richardson sent another brigade forward to hold the grimly won position while the Irish fell back to replenish their ammunition. Only a remnant of the men who had marched so proudly down the hill managed to stagger back to the rear. When they had rested, they went back for the final charge that swept the Confederates out of the Bloody Lane. The brigade lost one-fourth of its officers and one-third of its men that day.

Years later General McClellan wrote in his memoirs: "On the left of the center we were also hotly engaged in front of Roulette's house and continued to advance under heavy fire nearly to the crest of the hill overlooking Piper's house, the enemy being posted in a continuation of the sunken road and the cornfield. Here the brave Irish Brigade opened upon the enemy a terrific musketry fire and sustained its well-earned reputation. After suffering terribly in officers and men, and strewing the ground with their enemies as they drove them back, their ammunition nearly expended and their commander, General Meagher, disabled by the fall of his horse shot under him, this brigade was ordered to the rear."

Author Wibberley quotes a soldier of the 118th Pennsylvania Volunteers, to whose rescue the Irish Brigade had come, as writing: "The gallant Irishmen moved into battle array with the precision of parade. Prominent in its place beside the national

standard, the green harp of Erin was distinctly observed. As the
scathing fire cut out its fearful gaps, the line halted with deliberation to adjust itself. The dead and wounded strewed the
ground, thickening as the distance from the enemy lessened.
Twice and again the green standard fell, but only to be promptly
seized again. A vast curtain of smoke concealed the enemy, rising at intervals, disclosing him holding firmly to his post. The
deadly moment of impact came, the line impinged and the
enemy, in irreparable confusion, broke for the friendly cover of
the timber. The Irishmen, still maintaining their organization
with commendable exactitude, pressed them in their helpless
flight until finally, with shout and cheer, friend and foe were
lost to view in the woods."

The Federals lost 12,000 men on the shores of tiny Antietam
Creek, the Confederates 11,000. Historians say the battle was
badly generaled on both sides, but they award the biggest
booby prize to McClellan for failing, once Bloody Lane was
breached, to turn a standoff into a brilliant victory by pouring
in his reserves. Whatever the final judgment of the battle, no
one has ever questioned the courage of the noble Irish Brigade,
many of whose members, far from the bogs of their birth, laid
down their lives for a land they had known only a few brief
years.

The two thousand members of the Irish Brigade who survived
Antietam went on to win more fame at Fredericksburg. President Lincoln had sent McClellan to the showers and called in
General Ambrose Burnside to take command of the Army of
the Potomac. If McClellan had bungled Antietam, Burnside
made a shambles of Fredericksburg.

The quiet little Virginia town lies on the banks of the Rappa-
hannock River. To the south stretched a plain, cross-hatched by
fences. Behind the plain stood a hill, Marye's Heights. Across
the face of the hill stretched a road, and in front of it, a stone
fence.

Burnside advanced on Fredericksburg. The Confederates fell back out of the town, across the plain, and behind the stone fence, halfway up Marye's Heights. From there, they commanded the town and the plain below. They knew the position could never be taken by frontal assault. Burnside's advisers knew it too and suggested a flanking maneuver. But the general said no, they'd take it by storm.

The Federals were all but defeated before the battle actually began. Assembling on the plain before the hill, they were hammered by Rebel artillery fire from the Heights. As they battered down the crisscrossed fences, round shot, then canister, tore gaping holes in their ranks.

Yet on they came.

When the Federals were within a few hundred yards of the stone fence, the 2500 Rebel infantrymen crouched behind it, on a signal, opened fire. The Federal line completely disappeared, as though swallowed up in the smoke that billowed out over the scene. Scattered in a line along the hillside lay the blue-clad dead and wounded, "like the debris left by the highest wave of the tide."

Despite the defeat, Burnside stuck to his plan. Marye's Heights must fall by assault. And, as at Antietam, it was the Irish Brigade that drew the honor of saving the day. Their ranks were bolstered by a largely Irish Zouave regiment consisting of New York firemen.

Before they went into battle, General Meagher called his men together in the streets of Fredericksburg and said:

"Fellow exiles of Erin, the flags of our native land have been shot to pieces; the green color is all gone from them, but there is plenty of boxwood in the streets of Fredericksburg. Pluck it, place it in your hats and you will still fight for your adopted land beneath the immortal banner of green."

Thus adorned, they moved over the frozen plain toward the stone wall stretching like a thin scar across the face of the hill.

The Rebels opened fire. Here, there, yonder, gaps appeared in the slow-advancing blue line. Still it came slowly on—across the line of dead from the earlier charge, straight toward the stone wall itself. Twenty-five paces from the wall, the Irishmen could go no farther. Two-thirds of their number lay dead or dying. Slowly, suffering more casualties all the time, they fell back.

Five more times that cold December day the Irish, and other troops, tried to take Marye's Heights. Five more times they failed. None got closer than twenty-five yards from the wall, the high-water mark set by the Irish Brigade and their Zouave brothers. At the end of the day, the brigade added up its casualties and found that its five regiments had been melted down to some two hundred men. But if they had done nothing else, they had convinced Burnside that the position could not be taken by assault.

The correspondent of the *Times* of London was moved by the bravery of the Irish to write: "Never at Fontenoy, Albuera, or at Waterloo was more undaunted courage displayed by the sons of Erin than in those six frantic dashes which they delivered against the almost impregnable position of their foe . . . The bodies which lie in dense masses . . . are the best evidence of what manner of men they were who pressed on to death with the dauntlessness of a race which has gained glory on a thousand battlefields and never more richly deserved it than at the foot of Marye's Heights on the 13th day of December, 1862."

Antietam and Fredericksburg were only two of the Irish Brigade's finest hours. Before them had been both Bull Runs, Yorktown, Fair Oaks, and Seven Days. After them was bloody Chancellorsville.

Chancellorsville! Three days of hell in the bright spring of 1863. The historians who keep score on Civil War battles chalk it up as a victory for the Confederates, who fought under two of the most brilliant generals modern warfare has produced—Robert E. Lee and Stonewall Jackson. But was it a victory? Both sides lost heavily. And numbered among the Confederate dead was Jackson himself.

The Irish Brigade had been handed the task of defending a battery threatened by the enemy. They did it, right enough, but at a terrible cost. So depleted were their ranks after Chancellorsville that Meagher asked permission to go North to recruit more Irishmen. At the time, he suspected that the brass was about to do what the enemy had failed to accomplish—wipe out the Irish Brigade. A rumor circulated that its few remaining troops would be spread out among other units. When the higher-ups turned down Meagher's request, he resigned his commission.

As it turned out, the brigade was not broken up. Its thin ranks were in the thick of it at Gettysburg. And eventually recruits from the New York and Boston Irish brought the organization back up to its full strength.

The great fighting team stayed in the battle, not only until the end of the war, but after it. Its last action was a little skirmish at Skinner's Farm two weeks after Lee's surrender.

One story best illustrates how their comrades looked on the fighting members of the Irish Brigade. After Marye's Heights a chaplain told a survivor: "It must have been a great consolation to you in your hour of danger to have known that you were supported by Divine Providence." Said the survivor: "We were supported by the Irish Brigade and that was consolation enough."

Quite often, Irish troops faced one another on the battlefield. A number of Irish companies were among the Confederates who turned back the Irish Brigade before Marye's Heights. Later, at Petersburg, author Wibberley relates, Irish soldiers on both sides called an unofficial truce.

Someone asked if there were any Limerick men present.

"Enough to take care of the whole of County Cork," came the reply.

"Ah, the divil with war. We're short of tobacco. Have ye a pipe to spare?"

Soon the men met between the lines to trade tobacco and newspapers. Someone opened up with "Colleen Bawn" and men from the North and South of Ireland—and the North and South of the United States—joined in. There were more songs and a jig or two. And finally, at dusk, the men returned to their lines to resume the war.

Indeed, the Irish gained the reputation of being the war's best soldiers on the battlefield, and its worst off. Back in camp, they resisted discipline, were often drunk, and passed the time between formal battles with private battles of their own. But once the advance had started, they were the fightingest fighting men a general could want. Theirs was a gay, offhand courage that bespoke their real joy in battle. This, they seemed to be saying, was the proper life for an Irishman—a life that required courage and strength, a life of risk and danger; in short, a man's life.

Not that it wasn't a woman's life too. Sister Anthony of Limerick became the Florence Nightingale of the Civil War. She led a group of nursing nuns into the battlefield hospitals which, in those pre-penicillin days, when anesthetics were in their infancy and modern medicine had not yet caught up with modern warfare, were as close an approximation of Hell as man had been afforded up to that time.

The nuns weren't the only Irishwomen on the battlefield. Many a wife followed her man to war. Colonel W. W. H. Davis of the 104th Pennsylvania Volunteers, tells of one.

"An Irish camp woman, belonging to a New York regiment, made herself quite conspicuous during the action. She remained close to the side of her husband and refused to retire to a place of security. Occasionally, she would notice some fellow sneaking to the rear, when she would run after him, seize him by the nape of his neck, and place him in the ranks again, calling him a 'dirty, cowardly spalpeen' and other choice epithets. The flying shells had no terrors for her. During the hottest of the cannonade this courageous woman walked fearlessly about among the troops, encouraging them to stand up to their work. Her only weapon, offensive or defensive, was a large umbrella she carried under her arm."

And, he might have added, her sharp Irish tongue.

The Irishman fought so well during the Civil War because he was better armed than other troops. In addition to the conventional weapons, he also bore into battle his great Irish sense of humor. Stories by and about the Irish, many of them no doubt apocryphal, circulated by the hundreds during the Civil War.

For instance, there was the story of the Irish soldier who asked his commanding officer for a furlough. He explained that his wife was sick and there was no one to look out for the children.

"Pat," said the officer, "that's very strange, for the chaplain has a letter from your wife asking us not to send you home. She says every time you go home on leave you get drunk and frighten the children."

"Faith," said Pat, "there's two of the most splendid liars in the army in this room. I was never married in me life."

Likewise the story of the Irishman carrying a comrade suffering with a leg wound to a first-aid station. Unknown to him, a cannon ball took the man's head off while he was carrying him. When the Irishman reached the station and dumped the corpse down on a cot someone pointed out to him that it lacked a head.

"Why, the deceivin' creature," he said. "He told me it was his leg that was botherin' him."

And so, armed with his courage and his unshakable sense of the comedy of life, the Irishman saw America through the Civil War. The United States was officially at peace for half a century after it ended, but not the Irishman. If the United States would not provide him with a war, he would cook up his own. After all, he had a clear-cut cause: the freedom of Ireland.

Soldiers of all wars have found it difficult to settle back into peacetime civilian ways after the fighting is over. Many, missing the excitement that sustained them during the conflict, have fretted at the placid ways of the civilian, hedged in as they are by restraints. Some have stayed on in the peacetime army. Some have sought out other wars in other lands. Others have found their kicks in a life of crime. Most, after a difficult period of readjustment, have decided that occasional boredom is not too high a price to pay for the comforts of security.

The Irish too had their troubles settling down after the Civil War. Since the United States seemed determined to stay at peace for a while, the Irish dreamed up a war of their own. They invaded Canada.

During the Civil War, a new revolutionary movement called the Irish Republican Brotherhood had appeared in Ireland. After the war, the movement spread to the United States. On this side of the Atlantic, its members were called Fenians, a word derived from Fiann, the name of the legendary group that fought for the Irish hero Finn.

The Fenians decided that the best way to free Ireland was to wage war on England. This, of course, was illegal. Congress insists that it alone has the right to declare war on another country. But no one bothered to explain this to the Fenians—not that they would have listened had anyone taken the trouble. So they discussed in open and widely publicized meetings their strategy for defeating their old foe.

If the Fenians thought about it at all, they probably figured the United States would be only too happy to see them slap down England. After all, the British had sympathized with the Confederacy during the Civil War. Not only that, the two nations had been squabbling over certain fishing rights and over the northwest boundary between the United States and Canada ("Fifty-four forty or fight," cried an American faction that wanted the boundary set at 54 degrees, 40 minutes).

The Fenians, led by William O'Mahoney, an exiled revolutionary, decided to raise money, set up an Irish government-in-exile, establish an army, and invade England. As simple as that. First came the money. This the Fenians raised by issuing bonds promising six per cent interest, redeemable six months after Irish independence, and by other devices, such as promoting picnics.

Money, contributed by the largely poor Irish, flooded in, and in October 1865, a Fenian convention, attended by representatives of thousands of clubs from coast to coast, was held in Philadelphia. The delegates drew up a constitution, modeled on that of the United States, and picked O'Mahoney as President. And old Indian fighter named Tom Sweeney, who had lost an arm in the Mexican War but fought heroically in the Civil War nonetheless, was chosen Secretary of War.

O'Mahoney rented a mansion in New York as headquarters until such time as England could be defeated and the seat of government established in Dublin. The Fenian flag, together with the Stars and Stripes, fluttered above the headquarters in Union Square.

Next, with money in the bank and a going "government" behind them, the Fenians had to decide on a strategy for defeating England. O'Mahoney, a direct man who favored direct methods, proposed an invasion of England mounted from Boston and New York. But William Roberts, a New York dry-goods merchant, had another idea. Why not capture Canada and swap it to England for Ireland? Roberts' idea was enthusiastically adopted.

The Fenians, making no secret of their plans, set the date for the invasion as the first week in June and announced that it would be mounted from Buffalo, New York, and St. Albans, Vermont. Fighting-age Fenians from all quarters of the United States were asked to report to those two cities. General Sweeney was to head up the invasion from St. Albans and General John O'Neill, who had commanded a Negro regiment in the Union

Army, was placed in charge of the Buffalo force, which was conceived as a diversion for the main invasion from Vermont.

Largely because they were a trump to play against England,
President Andrew Johnson had kept his hands off the Fenians,
but now things were getting out of control. Fund-raising picnics
and thunderous speeches denouncing England were one thing,
an invasion of Canada was quite another. So he sent General
George G. Meade, the hero of Gettysburg, to St. Albans to disarm the Fenians. Ironically, General Meade rode to St. Albans
on the same train as General Sweeney.

Meade disarmed most of the Fenians, but a few managed to
retain their weapons. Under Sweeney, they slipped across the
border into Canada and took up positions on a hill. However,
when the Canadians sent a militia force against them, they retired back into the United States, where they were arrested.

In Buffalo, General O'Neill, who knew nothing of the fate of
the St. Albans group, assembled his eight hundred men and prepared to cross into Canada. But the night before D day, two
hundred of them celebrated too enthusiastically and missed the
invasion barges. Nevertheless the remaining six hundred crossed
into Canada, occupied abandoned Fort Erie and advanced four
miles inland.

By this time, two thousand Canadian troops were marching
on the Fenians in two groups. O'Neill decided to place his little
army between the twin Canadian forces to keep them from linking up. At the town of Ridgeway, the Irishmen retired behind
a breastworks of fence rails and waited for the first of the Canadian units, consisting of eight hundred and fifty men, to come
up.

When the Canadians arrived, the Irishmen, battle-hardened by
the Civil War, quickly put them to rout. However, O'Neill was
without reinforcements and was running short on supplies, so
he decided to fall back to Fort Erie. When the Fenians returned,

they found a group of Canadians had retaken the fort, but they quickly evicted them.

However, after settling down in the fort, O'Neill learned the dismal news that O'Mahoney had been defeated and he would get no reinforcements. So he freed his prisoners and recrossed the Niagara to the United States. There his whole army was promptly arrested by the crew of the gunboat *Michigan*.

The invasion set off howls of protest in England—and among the Fenians, who accused President Johnson of being a tool of the British. Since a national election was coming up, the United States dropped charges against the invaders. In fact, the government even hired lawyers to defend the thirty-three luckless Fenians captured by the Canadians. Twenty-six were acquitted and seven sentenced to death, but their punishment was commuted to twenty-years' imprisonment.

The invasion had been an abject failure, but the fact did not dampen General O'Neill's enthusiasm for the plan. Twice more he tried to invade Canada, in 1870 and again the following year, but both attempts fizzled. After that, the Fenian organization in the United States dwindled to nothing.

One odd result of the movement was the development of the modern submarine. John Philip Holland, a Limerick schoolteacher who had emigrated to the United States in 1873, obtained money from the Fenians to build an underwater fighting ship capable of sinking the British Navy. After much work, he succeeded, but by this time the Fenian movement was dead.

After the American Celts had closed out their own comic opera war, America sighed and settled down to a long period of peace. It was broken only by the quickie Spanish-American conflict of 1898—"That splendid little war," Theodore Roosevelt called it—and some trouble on the Mexican border. Finally, in the early years of the twentieth century, the world exploded into its greatest holocaust up to that time, World War I. The Irish, rested by the long peace, were ready.

Leaf through the fading records of that war and you'll find Gaelic names in the records of every combat unit. But the fighting men who drew the most attention were members of a great team—"The Irish 69th."

The New York National Guard regiment had distinguished itself in the Civil War. So heavy had been its casualties that it had been necessary to bring it up to war strength nine times. At Bloody Lane and Marye's Heights, at Gettysburg and Chancellorsville, the 69th Regiment had displayed its valor.

The 69th next saw duty in the Spanish-American War and again in the Mexican border campaign, but its time of greatest glory was World War I. The 69th had only been back from the Mexican border six months when it was drafted into the Regular Army. Right away, the 69th began a recruiting campaign to boost its strength from fewer than a thousand to 3500 men.

Poet Joyce Kilmer, who was a sergeant in the 69th and whose history of its deeds was interrupted by his death, said: "It was desired to enlist strong, intelligent, decent-living men, men whose sturdy Americanism was strengthened and vivified by their Celtic blood, men who would be worthy successors of those forgotten patriots who at Bloody Lane and on Marye's Heights earned the title of 'The Fighting Irish.'"

The regiment's machine gun trucks toured Irish sections of New York displaying a placard reading: DON'T JOIN THE 69TH UNLESS YOU WANT TO BE AMONG THE FIRST TO GO TO FRANCE. The Catholic clergy was asked to send in good men from the parish athletic clubs.

Father Francis Patrick Duffy, the beloved and heroic chaplain of the 69th—whose statue commands Duffy Square, just north of Times Square in New York—recalled later: "An Irish regiment has its troubles in time of peace. But when the call to arms was sounding we knew that if they would let us we could easily offer them an Irish Brigade for the service."

A number of Frenchmen, Italians, and Poles joined the regiment because of its Catholic character. "The 69th never attempted to set up any religious test," Father Duffy said. "It was an institution offered to the nation by a people grateful for liberty, and it always welcomed and made part of it any American citizen who desired to serve in it. But, naturally, men of Irish birth or blood were attracted to the traditions of the 69th, and many Catholics wanted to be with a regiment where they could be sure of being able to attend to their religious duties." As it turned out, he said, only about five per cent of the regiment was "Irish neither by race or racial creed."

The 69th was indeed among the very first fighting units sent overseas in World War I. After training at Camp Mills on Long Island, the regiment was shipped to France in two boatloads. All told, it was in direct contact with the enemy an unprecedented one hundred and eighty days. The records show that it changed its headquarters eighty-three times and gained in battle a total of fifty-five kilometers. It went overseas with some 3500 men, and it suffered exactly 3501 casualties—644 killed, 2857 wounded.

The regiment was gassed at Luneville only a short time after reaching France. But it went on to distinguish itself in the Aisne-Marne push, the St. Mihiel offensive and the crucial Argonne-Meuse drive. The heroic deeds of its brave soldiers are too many to list. But many of them are recorded with loving care in a diary Father Duffy published shortly after the war.

None in that courageous regiment distinguished himself more than the man who rose to become its leader, Colonel (later General) William J. "Wild Bill" Donovan. The Buffalo lawyer, who gained his nickname as a college football star, went on to win more glory as chief of the Office of Strategic Services during World War II. In his diary, Father Duffy says: "The richest gain that I have gotten out of the war is the friendship of William J. Donovan."

Donovan, as a boy, reveled in stories of the great deeds of

General Meagher's Irish Brigade in the Civil War, and he dreamed that someday he too might command an Irish Brigade in the service of his country. As it turned out, his dream more than came true, for the 69th in World War I was larger than the Irish Brigade ever was. But, as Father Duffy pointed out after the war, it wasn't mere dreaming or Irish luck that brought Donovan to the top. "He is always physically fit," the priest wrote in his diary, "always alert, ready to do without food, sleep, rest, in the most matter of fact way, thinking of nothing but the work at hand. He has mind and manners and varied experience of life and resoluteness of purpose. He has kept himself clean and sane and whole for whatever adventure life might bring him." As it turned out, his adventures brought him fame in the two greatest wars in history.

The second of those wars also brought fame to other Irishmen. However, in World War II, the Irish were fairly well dispersed through all the fighting forces. There was no Irish Brigade in this greatest of wars, but there were individual Irish heroes beyond count.

Colin P. Kelly, a 26-year-old West Pointer, was the war's first hero. Early on the morning of December 10, 1941, when the war was three days old, Captain Kelly took his Flying Fortress aloft from Clark Field in the Philippines. So hasty was the take-off—the Japs were overhead at the time—that the crew only managed to load three bombs. The mission, Kelly explained to his men as they roared aloft, was to look for a Japanese aircraft carrier reported operating north of Luzon. The Fortress was supposed to be joined by the remainder of the squadron, but when it failed to show up Kelly headed north alone.

Suddenly, through the haze, they spotted two small Jap transports, then three more transports, then three destroyers, finally an enemy battleship! Only three bombs, but Captain Kelly determined to make them count. They were at 20,000 feet. Corporal Meyer Levin, the bombardier, placed one bomb to the starboard of the giant battleship, the 29,000-ton *Haruna*. Then he laid the second bomb squarely on the deck and the third slightly to port.

As the great fighting ship headed for the bottom, Kelly's Flying Fortress headed for Clark Field and home. But at 10,000 feet it ran into trouble. Two Japanese Zeros emerged from behind a bank of haze and bore in on the big Fortress from the rear. Shells and tracer bullets spattered through the ship, shattering the radio equipment, knocking out the oxygen supply, setting the left wing afire.

With the Fortress blazing fiercely, Captain Kelly dove for the shelter of a mountain range of clouds. Seeing he couldn't make it, he ordered his crew to bail out. They did, but before Captain Kelly could get away the plane exploded. Thus died America's first hero of World War II. General Douglas MacArthur posthumously awarded Kelly the Distinguished Service Cross.

There were so many, many others. John W. Finn, a well-named aviation ordnance man at Pearl Harbor. When the alert sounded, he seized a machine gun used for instruction and mounted it on a parking ramp. Then, as bombs fell around him, he organized a supply chain for ammunition, and hour on hour poured a deadly fire at the enemy. In the words of his citation, he collected "many wounds," and once was blown off his feet by a bomb. But he kept at it. Finally a medical officer ordered him to sick bay. His wounds patched, he returned to supervise the rearming of American planes as they flew in from battle. Finn —a fitting scion of the Irish legandary hero of the same name— won the nation's highest award, the Congressional Medal of Honor.

Then there was Lieutenant John D. Bulkeley, commanding a squadron of PT boats in the Philippines, and his sidekicks, Lieutenant Robert B. Kelly and Ensign George Cox. The squadron was given a vague order: find and attack hostile shipping. The results were anything but vague. The record: one cruiser damaged and beached, two cruisers damaged by torpedo hits, two 5000-ton ships sunk, an oil tanker set afire, two barges loaded with enemy troops sunk, three dive-bombers and one seaplane destroyed by machine-gun fire. It was Lieutenant Bulkeley's group that slipped General MacArthur off Corregidor to carry on the war from Australia.

We could go on for another book relating the heroism of individual Americans of Irish blood during the Great War. It is sufficient to say that the Irish were provided an enormous opportunity to indulge their inherited love of combat, and they took advantage of it; and that America was provided with more heroic fighting men than any nation has a reasonable right to expect. General James M. Gavin, later U. S. Ambassador to France, was the intrepid leader of the great development of the war in Europe—Paratroops. General Anthony McAuliffe uttered the single most significant word of the conflict—his reply of "Nuts!" to German surrender demands at beleaguered Bastogne.

The same blood and spirit laced U.S. forces in Korea, and will wherever Americans are forced to fight.

If the Cold war can be said to have opened in Berlin in the days that followed World War II then the image of America's posture in that ideological conflict was best exemplified by the U.S. commandant of the Berlin Allied Kommandatura, Brigadier General Frank L. Howley, soldier's-soldier, author, and now vice-president of New York University. Howley was one of the first spokesmen of the West to recognize and condemn Soviet meddling and intransigence.

Father Duffy, in his diary, speaks of the curious blend of piety and pugnacity that goes into the makeup of the fighting Irishman. "The religion of the Irish has characterstics of its own," he says. "They make the Sign of the Cross with the right hand, while holding the left hand ready to give a jab to anybody who needs it for his own or the general good. I cannot say that it is an ideal type of Christianity; but considering the sort of world we have to live in yet, it is as near as we can come at present to perfection for the generality of men. It was into the mouth of an Irish soldier that Kipling put the motto, 'Help a woman, and hit a man; and you won't go far wrong either way.'"

10 "IRISH" IRISH:
The Irish Character

What is an Irishman?

Noah Webster says simply that he is "a man born in Ireland or of the Irish race." Which is like defining Brigitte Bardot as a form of animal life. True but hardly adequate.

What are the Irish *really* like? Or, to put the question another way, Do the real-life Irish bear any resemblance to the stereotype Irish of song, story, and barroom joke?

George Bernard Shaw thought not. "Of all the tricks," he said, "which the Irish nation has played on the slow-witted Saxon, the most outrageous is the palming off on him of the imaginary Irishman of romance."

Yet Shaw shared some of the traits of that Irish stereotype— wit and willingness to exaggerate for the sake of a good argument. Consequently, anything he might say on the matter is subject to suspicion.

I once asked Dr. David Greene, a man who had pondered the question for many years, whether he thought the stock Irishman and the real-life Irishman shared any common traits.

He answered that he thought the stereotypes of the American Irishman "whether he comes from a Pat and Mike story or whether he comes from the novels of a James T. Farrell" are basically true, though exaggerated.

"After all," he added, "what is wrong with being a man who falls in love easily, and who has emotions and emotional depths?"

He believed that the Irish should be very happy that such a stereotype exists—that they've been the subject of so many stories. "This alone indicates that they've got something to be proud of," he said. "At least they've been worth writing about."

But that still doesn't answer our question: What are the Irish *really* like? I think the answer I like best comes from the eminent historian, Carl Wittke. Here is how he describes the Irish temperament in his *The Irish in America*:

"The so-called Irish temperament is a mixture of flaming ego, hot temper, stubbornness, great personal charm and warmth, and a wit that shines through adversity. An irrepressible buoyancy, a vivacious spirit, a kindliness and tolerance for the common frailties of man, and a feeling that 'it is time enough to bid the devil good morning when you meet him' are character traits which Americans have associated with their Irish neighbors for more than a century."

One will get contrary opinions. Just as the Irish never do anything by half-measures, so opinion of them is often all to the good or all to the bad. Jonathan Swift, who wrote *Gulliver's Travels* and was Episcopal dean of St. Patrick's in Dublin sang of the Irish:

A servile race in folly nursed,
Who truckle most when treated worst.

Samuel Johnson sneered "The Irish are a fair people; they never speak well of one another." Heywood Broun called them "the cry-babies of the Western World." In 1868, the *Chicago Post* said: "An Irishman is a born savage, a brutal ruffian. He never knew an hour in civilized society. Scratch a convict or a pauper, and the chances are that you scratch the skin of an Irishman."

A description current in the early nineteenth century in America said:

"The children of bigoted Catholic Ireland, like the frogs which were sent out as a plague against Pharaoh, have come into our homes, bed-chambers, and ovens and kneading-troughs. Unlike the Swedes, the Germans, the Scots, and the English, the Irish when they arrive among us, too idle and vicious to clear and cultivate the land, and earn a comfortable home, dump themselves down in our large villages and towns, crowding the meaner of tenements and filling them with wretchedness and disease. In a political point of view, what are they but marketable cattle?"

One thing must be remembered about such comments as the one above. They were uttered by Americans, largely of English descent, who had not lost their Elizabethan prejudice against Catholicism. The shortcomings of Protestant Irish immigrants were regarded with more tolerance.

These same nineteenth-century Americans, as a matter of fact, liked to poke fun at all foreigners—at the stolid Germans, the perfumed Frenchmen, and the dense Englishmen. One method of baiting the Irishman was called "Paddy making." An effigy dressed in rags, with a whisky bottle in one pocket and a potato in another, was set up in a public place, usually the night before St. Patrick's Day. "Paddy making" led to a riot in Utica, New York, in which several persons were killed and many injured. It was outlawed in New York State in 1812.

No doubt of it, when you think of the Irish, certain adjectives pop up to qualify the word. "The Fighting Irish," for example. An old song goes:

"Wherever there's Kellys there's trouble," said Burke.
"Wherever fighting's the game,
Or a spice of danger in grown men's work,"
Said Kelly: "You'll find my name."

Kipling wrote:

For where there are Irish there's loving and fighting,
And when we stop either, it's Ireland no more.

In the mid-1800s, the New York *Journal of Commerce*, commenting on crime among the Irish, put it neatly:

"You will scarcely ever find an Irishman dabbling in counterfeit money, or breaking into houses, or swindling; but if there is any fighting to be done, he is very apt to have a hand in it."

This joy in combat was summed up by Gilbert K. Chesterton in "The Ballad of the White Horse":

For the great Gaels of Ireland
Are the men that God made mad,
For all their wars are merry,
And all their songs are sad.

For all their love of fighting, the Irish were—and are—far from truculent. In fact, sociability is perhaps their chief characteristic. It is this central trait that kept them from heeding the advice of their leaders to leave their warrens in the cities for farms. It was this trait—practiced on Sunday—that so outraged their Sabbitarian neighbors, particularly in Puritan New England.

Sunday was a big day among the immigrant Irish. When Mass was over, relatives and guests sat down to huge spreads. After the dinner dishes were cleared, the menfolk gathered at a shabeen for a friendly drink or game of cards. The women gossiped, the children played. To the more rigid Protestants, to whom Sunday was an occasion for solemnity, this seemed a desecration of the Lord's Day.

The Irish, who had led rural lives in the old country, took to city living like birds to air. They loved the close neighbors, the constant gossip, the politics, the close-by church, the crowds, noise, and excitement. When they left Ireland, they were determined to abandon not only their homeland, but also its rural way of life. That's why the Irish clotted together in the big cities—why the Irish Broad Street section of Boston was described, before the turn of the century, as the most thickly populated place in the world, with the exception of an area in Liverpool.

Being gregarious, the Irish were—and are—great "joiners." Almost to a man, they are members of the neighborhood Catholic church, and to one or more of its societies. Tens of thousands of them, over the years, have belonged to the Ancient Order of Hibernians, founded in 1836. The Hibernians have plumped for Irish freedom, support of the Church, charity, and a stirring show of hands on St. Patrick's Day. Originally, the organization was open only to natives of Ireland, but since just before the turn of the century, all Roman Catholics of Irish lineage have been eligible. It numbers more than 150,000 members.

Many Catholic Irish also have been active in the Knights of Columbus, the Catholic Knights of America, the Catholic Mutual Benefit Association, and other such groups. The World Almanac lists sixteen large national associations and societies whose names begin with the word "Catholic," and the Irish make up a sizable proportion of the membership of each. Through the years, the number of Irish "total abstinence" and "temperance" clubs also have been legion—which brings up another facet of the Irish character.

Mark Twain said: "Give an Irishman lager for a month and he's a dead man. An Irishman is lined with copper, and the beer corrodes it. But whiskey polishes the copper and is the saving of him."

On the other hand, John Maguire, the Irish journalist who visited the United States after the Civil War, wrote: "Were I asked to say what I believed to be the most serious obstacle to the advancement of the Irish in America, I would unhesitatingly answer—drink!"

No one knows who invented whisky, or when, but the Irish gave it a name (from the Celtic *uisgebeatha* meaning "water of life") and have been putting it to use ever since. There seems to be solid support for the belief that, of all our ethnic groups, the Irish are fondest of the cup that cheers. In his *Commonsense Book of Drinking*, Leon Adams says flatly: "The lowest incidence of addictive drinking found in any group in the United States is among people of the Jewish faith. The highest rate is among Americans of Irish origin."

His findings coincide with those of a study made in New York some years ago. It showed that of various foreign-born nations represented among first admissions to New York State hospitals for alcoholic psychosis, the Jews, with .5 per cent per 100,000, were at the bottom of the list, and the Irish, with 25.6 per cent, were at the top.

Why is this so? Why did the Penal Laws Irishman, in the midst of his squalor, resort to poteen (from the Irish word for pot)? Some say the Irish turned to drink because, over the years, they had such a hard time of it. Because they lost the land of their forefathers and were ill-received wherever they went; because they endured poverty, privation, and persecution.

Some say the nineteenth-century Irish resorted to poteen to blot out the sight of their mean life. But actually, as Author Potter points out, "the hardest drinkers in Catholic Ireland were the small farmers possessed of money on market and fair days; the so-called tradesmen or skilled workers, such as stonemasons, carpenters, tailors and the like, with money wages; the colliery workers, with a steady wage; and the fishermen with shillings in their pockets. The peasant was not rated a hard or consistent drinker simply because he could not afford it."

Similarly, it was not poverty in America that turned the Irish to drink. In Ireland, a quart of whisky had cost six times an average day's wage. In America it cost about one-fourth, or a little more than twenty-five cents. Thus, it was relative prosperity, not poverty, that induced the Irishman to drink. Quite simply, he drank whenever he could afford it.

One fact should be made transparently clear. It was the Irish*man* who was the drinker, not his colleen. The 1836 Poor Inquiry Commission, discussing drunkenness in Ireland, said: "Females are generally exemplary in their abstinence from stimulating whiskey." And it's been that way through the years.

So the emotional, imaginative immigrant Irishman drank. When he landed in America, his higher wage gave him more means to buy whisky, his harder work more need to drink it. Whisky, completely untaxed, has never since been so cheap. Labor contractors primed their men with it to get every ounce of work out of them. On the canal and rail gangs, the first drink went down the hatch at sunrise, when work started. It was chased by another at mid-morning, a third at noon, a fourth in mid-afternoon, a fifth before supper—all on the house. As often as not, the Irish workman had a supplementary supply in his shanty for evenings and Sundays.

The Irish not only drank whisky, they sold it. In 1852, Michael Tukey of the Boston police reported that nearly two-thirds of the grog shops were owned by Irish. Walk Third Avenue, New York's prime saloon street, today and you'll notice that the majority of names over the doors are Irish.

In the nineteenth-century American whisky and politics went hand in hand. The whisky dispenser was, perforce, a politician. In New York, for instance, Tammany decided whether or not his license was renewed. Hence he gladly chipped in a barrel at election time so doubtful voters might be refreshed into casting the right ballot.

The Irish have a saying that drink is a good man's weakness. The terrible tragedy that the racial curse has brought into the lives of so many good men is summed up in the epitaph of a glassworker accidentally killed while drunk, which Potter quotes in his *To the Golden Door*. "*If we except one thing*," the obituary said, "he was a valuable man, ingenious, industrious, and always ready and willing to do his part in any difficult work." How many Irish lives that "one thing" has blighted!

When they first landed, the Irish thought it strange that native Americans attached a moral stigma to the selling, and even consumption, of whisky. The drinker or dispenser bore no such onus in Ireland, except, of course, among advocates of abstinence.

As time went on those advocates grew more numerous. The Roman Catholic clergy always had been engaged in a bitter struggle with Demon Rum. Gradually, other Irish leaders entered the fray.

As early as 1817, the Shamrock Society of New York warned Irish immigrants against the "pernicious habit" of drink. Three years later a mission priest among the Erie Canal work gangs formed a temperance society in Troy, New York. Within a few years, others were flourishing in Utica, Albany, Rochester, and Boston.

But the man who gave the temperance movement its greatest boost was a gentle Capuchin friar, Father Theobald Mathew, who was known as the "Apostle of Temperance." In 1839, he began a teetotal movement in Ireland that snowballed into enormous proportions. Within two years, he claimed to have administered the pledge to half of the country.

Finally, in 1849, he came to America. Everywhere Father Mathew went, his reception was tumultuous. He was greeted by mayors and governors; and in Washington, the House of Representatives voted him a seat on the floor—General Lafayette had been the only foreigner so honored up to that time. In the two years and four months Father Mathew spent in America, he administered the pledge to an estimated half a million persons. In the wake of his visit, scores of Hibernian temperance societies sprang up. They opened libraries, game rooms, bowling alleys, and gymnasiums in an effort to supplant the tavern as the "poor man's club."

The Catholic Total Abstinence Union of America published its own newspapers, songbooks and pamphlets during the period just before the turn of the century. However, many of its members—and many of the Irish generally—believed in temperance rather than total abstinence, and regarded Prohibition as a form of fanaticism. Archbishop John Ireland of St. Paul certainly was not one of them. For him, one drink was too many. He called for the exclusion of liquor dealers from Catholic societies and said a "tidal wave of abstinence" was essential "for the future of Irishmen in America."

In *John Bull's Other Island*, Bernard Shaw once had something to say about drinking and the Irish temperament:

"Oh, the dreaming! the dreaming! the torturing, heart-scalding, never-satisfying dreaming, dreaming, dreaming, dreaming. No debauchery that ever coarsened and brutalized an Englishman can take the worth and usefulness out of him like that dreaming. An Irishman's imagination never lets him alone, never convinces him, never satisfies him; but it makes him that he can't face reality, nor deal with it, nor handle it, nor conquer it: he can only sneer at them that do, and be 'agreeable to strangers' like a good-for-nothing woman on the streets. It's all dreaming, all imagination. He can't be religious. The inspired churchman that teaches him the sanctity of life and the importance of conduct is sent away empty, while the poor village priest that gives him a miracle or a sentimental story of a saint has cathedrals built for him out of the pennies of the poor. He can't be intelligently political: he dreams of what the Shan Van Vocht said in '98. If you want to interest him in Ireland you've got to call the unfortunate island Kathleen ni Hoolihan and pretend she's a little old woman. It saves thinking. It saves working. It saves everything except imagination, imagination, imagination; and imagination's such a torture that you can't bear it without whiskey."

In or out of his cups, the Irishman was—and is—a great talker. He admires oratory, and virtually every eighteenth-century son of old Erin was at least an amateur in the art of forensics. The novelist George Moore said: "My one claim to originality among Irishmen is that I have never made a speech."

Of course, the subject that most quickly stirred the Irish American to high flights of oratory was Ireland. Potter quotes two excellent examples of this oratory. At an Irish freedom rally in Washington attended by Abraham Lincoln, Senator Edward A. Hannegan of Indiana spoke thus of Ireland:

"I trust in God that before the sun shall again have reached this point in his yearly revolution, he will, as he brightens with his radiance the bright verdure of her soil, look down upon a still more glorious spectacle—her own green flag floating free on every hill and rampart."

And a young boy orator, speaking on St. Patrick's Day in Worcester, Massachusetts:

"Though I never breathed the invigorating air of the land of happiness, or witnessed the recreation which so many experience in the land of virtue, yet, sir, from my infancy my father has instilled in my mind and impressed it so deep on my heart, that for his sake and in detestation of the wrongs inflicted by the hand of tyranny, it shall never be erased from my memory."

No Irishman, no matter if he is three generations removed from the land of his forefathers, and has approached no closer to it than Coney Island, ever seems to lose this feeling of reverence, which is so well expressed in John Locke's "The Exile's Return":

> O Ireland, isn't it grand you look—
> Like a bride in her rich adornin'?
> With all the pent-up love in my heart
> I bid you top 'o the mornin'!

Of course, there are dissenting opinions. Bernard Shaw, an Irishman who lived in England, said:

> At last I went to Ireland,
> 'Twas raining cats and dogs:
> I found no music in the glens,
> Nor purple in the bogs.
> And as for angels' laughter in
> The smelly Liffey's tide—
> Well, my Irish daddy said it,
> But the dear old humbug lied.

The enormously gifted son of that dear old humbug was fond of shocking people, particularly his own fellow Irishmen. He had, like so many Irishmen, the gift of blarney.

Webster's Dictionary defines blarney as "smooth, wheedling talk; cajoling flattery." I like much better Monsignor Fulton J. Sheen's definition. He once said, "Baloney is flattery so thick it cannot be true, and blarney is flattery so thin we like it."

At any rate, the word derives from fifteenth-century Blarney Castle, near Cork. The old legend says that he who kisses the Blarney stone, placed in an almost inaccessible position near the top of the thick stone wall, will gain marvelous powers of persuasion. An anonymous poem, quoted in John Gibson Lockhart's *Life of Sir Walter Scott*, pledges:

The stone this is,
Whoever kisses,
He never misses
To grow eloquent.
'Tis he may clamber
To my lady's chamber.
Or be a member
Of Parliament.

One somewhat paradoxical Irish-American trait that is far less noticeable today than it was in the eighteenth century goes under the five-dollar label of xenophobia. It means, simply, a fear of strangers.

Oddly enough, the early Irish did not think of themselves as foreigners because, like the people born here, they spoke English. In Irish eyes, the Germans were the foreigners, as were the Swedes, Danes, French, and Italians.

In practice it worked out that way, too. The Irish blended easily into the American background. A week after they'd been off the boat, you couldn't have distinguished many of them from second-generation Americans. Not so the Germans and others who spoke no English. Their difficulties with the language sometimes carried over into the second and third generations.

The Germans and Irish sometimes got along fairly well. They both loved the bottle, and in 1855, staged a joint riot in Davenport, Iowa, to grab several barrels of beer confiscated by the local authorities. Twelve years later, they teamed up to vote down a law in New York City that would close down saloons on Sunday.

But often, too, they were at loggerheads. Shrewd entrepreneurs played off one group against the other to keep wages down. Sometimes gangs of Germans were used to break an Irish strike, or vice versa. The Germans generally regarded the Irish as barbarians, the Irish looked on the Germans as dangerous radicals.

But the Irish reserved their heartiest dislike for the Italians. When they started coming over, around the turn of the century, jobs were scarce. The Irish looked on aghast as Romans and Florentines who knew no word of English took over their jobs at lower wages.

The Irish adopted the attitude so aptly expressed by Mr. Dooley: "As a pilgrim father that missed the first boats, I must raise me claryon voice again' th' arnychists iv effete Europe. Ye bet I must—because I'm here first."

The Irish—oddly teamed up with their old enemies, the nativists—campaigned for legislation to close America's golden door, or at least leave only a small crack. One gimmick designed to do this was a literacy test. The Irish themselves were safe. Between 1900 and 1910, only two and one-half per cent of the Irish immigrants were illiterate, while the Italians knew little English.

A bill to establish such a test was successively vetoed by Presidents Grover Cleveland, William Howard Taft, and Woodrow Wilson, but the latter's veto was finally overridden by Congress in 1917.

After the Armistice a succession of quota systems limited immigration to a certain percentage of each nationality in the United States in a given year. However, by now, most of the Irish who wanted over had come. By this time, too, the Irish had moved up out of the lowest laboring class, and no longer competed for jobs with illiterates just off the boat.

The most obvious explanation for the early Irish-American's attitude toward other alien peoples is an economic one. The meanest tasks in the land, aside from those assigned the slave, went to newly arrived immigrants. The Irishman was at a disadvantage as far as the German was concerned because the German was generally better educated. Later, he was at disadvantage vis-a-vis the Italian, because the Italian—and the Chinese —were willing to work for less money. So he feared the other immigrant because he might take his job. And like most of us, he had a tendency to mask his fear of a person or a situation by pretended contempt.

Much, if not all, of this early xenophobia (if you'll pardon that word again) has disappeared among the Irish, perhaps because they no longer feel that "galling sense of inferiority." Today's Irish-American is as free of unreasoning race prejudice as Americans of other stock—which is to say some of them are and some of them aren't. Perhaps better than most, the Irish-man is able to sympathize with other minority groups. For one thing, he knows what it's like to be the object of prejudice. For another—because of his imagination—he is able to "feel" for the other fellow.

This one trait—imagination—runs all through the Irish character. Because of this imagination the Irish have profoundly affected American life. They have provided their adopted homeland with songs and singers, writers and actors, wits and curbstone comedians.

For centuries, this imagination peopled Gaelic Ireland with a race of wee folk existing nowhere else. The grass was filled with fairies, all fond of dancing and singing, prone to pranks, mischievous and wily. Fairy paths were known to all the residents of the countryside, and roadbuilders were careful to avoid them —even at the expense of constructing a longer, more circuitous highway.

At milking time, a bit of milk was usually spilled for "the good people." Part of the first run of the poteen still was splashed on the ground for them. Whenever someone sneezed, whoever was handling food at the time dropped a morsel for the wee folk. It did not lead to sanitation during hard winters or blustery springs.

The supreme creation of the Irish imagination was the shoemaker of the fairy world. He was called the cluricaune in County Cork, the luridadawne in Tipperary, the luricaune in Kerry, the logheryman in Ulster—and everywhere, the leprechaun. He was a merry, singing, whistling fellow, much given to drink, the uneasy custodian of the fairy world's crocks of gold. Certain leprechauns attached themselves to families, remaining with them generation after generation, familiar to the household down through the centuries.

Another all-too-familiar-figure of the invisible world of Ireland was the banshee (from the Gaelic for fairy woman). When death approached some member of a household, the family banshee began her long, lamentable wail—a beautiful yet fearful sound.

After death had come, the banshee's cry ceased—but there was another—the "keen" (from the Irish *caoine*, a wail for the dead). At some time during the wake, interrupting its subdued gaiety, a professional keener, or perhaps the wife or mother of the deceased, began a chanting, shrieking wail. Swaying to and fro, she improvised a cadenced recitative of his good qualities in a high wailing voice. The Arabs, the Jews, the Southern Negroes all mourn the passing of loved ones in a similar way—the disparity of races and origins making it clear that the practice, instead of having a common origin, was rather a natural one to primitive peoples.

As she rocked to and fro, the keener might "sing" in her mournful shriek:

"He was a good man. A good man. Now cold and silent is he. My life now is as cold as his body. No more will the sun shine for me, no more the moon pour his loveliness over me. For he is gone and will never return. And my life is as dead as his body. He was good, he was kind, he was generous. Now he is no more. No more."

And so on and on. The keen occupied but a small part of the

usual two-day wake. The rest was given up to sociability. There was good food, mellow tobacco, strong whisky, and plenteous talk. By sheer sociability, the grieving family's friends and neighbors tried to lessen the terrible impact of its loss.

Then came the funeral. As with primitive peoples everywhere, funerals among the pre-famine Irish were big affairs. Everyone who knew the deceased attended his funeral, and the procession might stretch a mile down the dusty road.

Lengthy funeral processions also became a mark of the early Irish in America. It was the collision of just such a procession and a volunteer fire department that caused the terrible Broad Street riot in Boston in 1837.

The Irish seem to take a paradoxical pleasure in sadness. Their folk songs are prone to sentimental sorrow. However, it is a beautiful melancholy, usually celebrating the singer's lost love—or the lost love of all overseas Irishmen, Ireland itself. For example, Dion Boucicault's "The Wearin' o' the Green":

> Then take the shamrock from your hat and cast it on the
> sod,
> It will take root and flourish still, though underfoot it's trod.

And, of course, every American is familiar with "the little bit of Heaven that fell from out the sky one day," sung, as often as not, in a high wavering tenor.

Many of the Irishman's songs spoke, not only of the old country, but of the new. For instance, a song called "Pat Malloy," popular before the turn of the century:

> From Ireland to America
> Across the seas I roam,
> And every shilling that I got,
> Ah, sure, I sent it home.

My mother couldn't write, but, Ah,
There came from Father Boyce:
"Oh, heaven bless you, Pat!" says she—
I hear my mother's voice.

Even the sheerest tragedy was an occasion for song. Witness this Irish famine song of 1846, whose author is unknown:

Oh, the praties they are small—
Over here, over here.
Oh, the praties they are small
When we dig 'em in the fall,
And we eat 'em, coats and all,
Full of fear, full of fear.

Through the centuries, the Irish have refused to truckle to the inevitable tragedy of life. They've turned it into a song—or a joke.

The Irishman's love of humor is, of course, famous. The Irish brought to America a capacity to laugh, not only at the foibles of others, but also at themselves. As many stories starting "Once there were two Irishmen, Pat and Mike" were told by Irishmen as by others.

There were certain stock jokes told over and over among immigrant Irish. Pat liked to say his house was so small "you can put your hand down the chimney and open the door from the inside." Or to tell of the two Irishmen, traveling on foot, who learned they still had ten miles to go. "Take heart," said one. "'Tis only five miles apiece."

Most frequently told, perhaps, was the story of the Irish immigrant girl who lost a certificate of character on the ship to the United States. When she arrived, a friend offered to provide her with another. He wrote: "She had a good character before she left the old country, but lost it on shipboard coming over."

The significant part about this joke is that it was just that—a joke. For the womenfolk which Ireland contributed to America were almost universally virtuous. You found numerous immigrant names in the rosters of the red-light houses of America's pre-Civil War cities, but seldom Irish names. The Irish servant girl—Irish immigrant women were "girls" even in their sixties—may have been unlettered and unfamiliar with nineteenth-century amenities, but she could be trusted, and she was virtuous. As one contemporary said, she might be bold in answering her mistress back, but she was safe when men were about. And the pillow cases wouldn't disappear.

Not only the women, but the men as well were straitlaced in matters of morality. At any rate, the Irish, given to grog and song, seldom got into trouble over women. This virtue served them well during the immigration years. The Catholic Irish developed a successful system for the care of unescorted single women in the crowded quarters of the immigrant ships. Before an unmarried girl left home, her parents entrusted her to the care of a male friend of the family in whom they had complete trust. He saw to it that she was not molested. In fact, they might share a berth at night for the sake of economy as well as her safety. There is no record that the system gave rise to any impropriety.

What *is* an Irishman? As ever, it is hazardous to generalize. But how many red-haired American Indians does one see through a lifetime? It is surely safe to say that Indians are given to black hair? And if we can say that, can't we also say that the Irish are given to certain traits: conviviality, sentiment, wit, sociability, to name a few?

Of course there are exceptions. Look hard enough, and you may find a taciturn Irishman, stolid, devoid of emotion, dull of wit, empty of sentiment. Look hard enough and you may find such an Irishman. Chances are he pals around with that red-haired Indian.

[224]

11 TALENTED IRISH:
A Gift for Many Things

America has given the immigrant Irishman a great deal: a chance to make a new life for himself, an opportunity to provide his children with a better break than he himself received. But what has the immigrant Irishman, in turn, given America?

The answer, in a word, is much. He has deepened America's faith, quickened its humor, hardened its muscle, and broadened its culture. He has leavened the largely stolid English character of American life with color and gaiety. The nineteenth-century English historian Goldwin Smith put it this way:

"The endowments of the Celt supplement those of the Saxon. What the Saxon lacks in liveliness, grace and warmth, the Celt can supply. What the Celt lacks in firmness, judgment, perseverance and the more solid elements of character, the Saxon can afford. The two races blended together may well be expected to produce a great and gifted nation."

The Dictionary of American Biography lists nearly five hundred well-known Americans who were born in Ireland, and literally thousands of others who are of Irish descent. For the truth of the matter is, you cannot pick a field of honorable human endeavor in which Irish-Americans have not been outstanding.

Medicine? Well, there was Dr. William J. MacNeven, a nineteenth-century Irish exile who became a professor at the College of Physicians and Surgeons. Also, Dr. Ephraim McDowell who in 1809 performed the first operation in ovarian surgery in the United States, and Dr. John B. Murphy who first removed an appendix.

Few, if any, American doctors had more impact on the mind and heart of men than Tom Dooley, who died of cancer early in 1961 at the age of thirty-four. In an extraordinary short period of time, Dooley created an indelible image at home and around the world. Virtually unknown in 1954, after premedical training at Notre Dame and graduation from St. Louis University's School of Medicine, Dooley became just another young doctor in the Navy. Once his military service was attended to, he planned to establish himself in St. Louis, where his good looks, bubbling personality, and skill would certainly have won him a wide and rewarding practice.

Fate ruled otherwise. His ship was assigned to participate in the evacuation of scores of thousands of Vietnamese fleeing southward in the wake of a Communist takeover of the northern portion of that land. Dooley was the only doctor on his particular ship, and now he found himself engulfed in utter human misery. Among his patients were children whose eardrums had been punctured by chopsticks driven into them for the "crime" of listening to the Lord's Prayer being recited.

In time, young Dooley commanded a handful of Navy corpsmen in a camp that processed 600,000 refugees. He drove himself recklessly to the edge of skin and bones but found his burdens enchanting, inspiring. The Navy gave him its Legion of Merit, making him the youngest medico ever to receive the award.

Mustered out of service, Dooley returned to the U.S. to begin his private career but he had left too much of himself in Southeast Asia. He wrote the first of his three best-selling books and used the $30,000 he made to launch a return to the other side of the world. By dint of sheer personality he rounded up his old staff of Navy corpsmen, secured mountains of contributed medical supplies, and set sail for Laos. In that primitive and Red-imperiled land he set up a hospital and won the respect and love of the people.

But he knew it was a drop in the bucket. He returned to the U.S., wrote another book, lectured, appeared on television and, with Dr. Robert Commanduras, created the organization known as MEDICO. He never spared himself, even after learning that a cancer of the chest had developed after a fall he took from a bicycle while peddling along a jungle road on an errand of mercy. His fund-raising campaign made possible the establishment of 18 hospitals and clinics in 12 countries. He worked feverishly, for his days were now numbered. The operation he had undergone for cancer did not succeed in eradicating the malignant growth.

Francis Cardinal Spellman was one of the last to call on Dr. Dooley, and said of him, the day he died that Tom Dooley crowded into his few years more goodness and love of his fellow man than most men exert through long lifetimes.

Law? Famous Irish-American attorneys—from the controversial criminal lawyer, William J. Fallon, at one end of the scale, to Supreme Court Justices Pierce Butler, William J. Brennan, Jr., and Frank Murphy, at the other—have been far too numerous to mention. As we said before, the law comes naturally to the Irish.

The Irishman's love of action, which made him a proficient policeman and soldier, also brought him into another field. The early Irish discovered, to their joy, that they could get paid for fighting, and so turned a pleasure into a business. They had

[227]

always been prone to settle arguments with fists. Coming over on the immigrant ships, they'd fought for the best bunk. Once here, they'd battled to see which volunteer fire department put out the fire. Now the Fighting Irish could fight for the living.

And fight they did. Bare knuckle bouts in the mid-nineteenth century, under London Prize Ring rules, continued until one man no longer could answer the bell, and some of them ran as many as 150 rounds. Fights often ended when one contestant killed another, or when one of them died of exhaustion.

The first Irish-American heavyweight champion was "Yankee" Sullivan who took over when native-born Tom Hyer retired from the ring. Sullivan won the title in a bout in which his opponent died of fatigue. He, in turn, was beaten in 1853 by another Irishman, John Morrissey, who was succeeded, five years later, by still a third, John Heenan.

After the Civil War, boxing adopted more respectable ways with the advent of the great John L. Sullivan. In 1882, he defeated Paddy Ryan to win the bare knuckle title. He then abandoned bare knuckle fighting and toured the country taking on all comers under the Marquis of Queensberry rules. Sullivan repeatedly returned to bare knuckle fighting to defend his title, but after 1889 there were no contenders for the London Prize Ring crown.

Three years later, Sullivan met James J. Corbett, another Irishman, for the Queensberry title. Sullivan, characteristically, had trained for the fight in saloons and at parties, and when Corbett knocked him out after 21 rounds, it was generally agreed that John Barleycorn, not Gentleman Jim, was the real winner.

Coming to after the count, "the Boston Strong Boy" waved his hand for silence, and told his audience through puffed lips:

"Gentlemen, I got one thing to say. I came into the ring once too often. But if I had to get licked, I'm glad it was by an

American. I remain your warm and personal friend, John L. Sullivan."

Sullivan had earned a half-million dollars in a dozen years, and spent every cent. But, as he said, "I was a lucky man to have it to spend in the first place."

There have been other great Irish-American fighters galore: Jake Kilrain, Mike McTigue, Terry McGovern, Tom Sharkey, Packy McFarland, Tommy Gibbons, Mike Gibbons, Mike McDowd, Billy Conn, Jack Dempsey, (who is also part English, Indian and Jewish) Gene Tunney, Tommy Burns, Jack Sharkey, Jim Braddock.

Gene Tunney told me his story of why the Irish once dominated professional boxing, as the Negro does today. It was economics by and large, he said, and boxing offered quick money. An Irishman is more or less a rarity in boxing today, Gene continued, because the Irish have more opportunity for an education. "Where they show any skills whatever in athletics," he said, "they can always get some kind of an offer from a college."

Incidentally, when Gene was born, on May 25, 1897, his father went to the corner saloon, bought a drink for all hands, and said: "This afternoon a future heavyweight champion of the world was born."

The Irish went in for college football with enormous zest as their educational levels rose after the turn of the century. Notre Dame, Fordham, St. Mary's of California, Georgetown, Holy Cross, Villanova etc. became gridiron giants but priestly educators in recent years have done much to de-emphasize participation.

The sports-loving Irish also have gone in numbers into professional baseball. John J. McGraw became manager of the New York Giants in 1902 at the age of twenty-seven, and won ten National League pennants. Cornelius McGillicuddy, better known as Connie Mack, managed the Philadelphia Athletics to 8 flags and had a hand in baseball until his death in 1956 at the age of ninety-three. Other big league managers included Joe McCarthy, Hugh Jennings, Pat Moran, Joe Cronin, Steve O'Neill. McCarthy won seven World Series.

One of the game's early greats was Michael J. "King" Kelly, who inspired the popular song "Slide, Kelly, Slide." He led his league in batting in 1886, but his greatest claim to fame was as a base runner.

Then, too, the legendary Delahanty brothers of Cleveland. Five of them played in the major leagues. A sixth was so seriously injured by a pitched ball just as he was about to step up into the big time that he was forced to drop out of baseball altogether. The eldest, Big Ed, once hit four home runs in one game, and was the only player to win the batting championship of both leagues.

The list of great Irish ball players knows no end. There was Iron Man Joseph McGinnity, the pitcher, outfielder Jim O'Rourke, catcher Roger Bresnahan, and many more.

Another of the all-time greats was Charles A. Comiskey. "The Old Roman" was the son of an Irish immigrant of 1848. The boy was apprenticed to a plumber, but at seventeen he began to play third base for Milwaukee. After a long career as a player, he helped organize the American League and was the president of the Chicago White Sox from its organization in 1900 until his death in 1931.

Plaques in Baseball's Hall of Fame, in Cooperstown, New York, betoken the fame of Bresnahan, the "Duke of Tralee," battery mate of Christy Mathewson and later a manager; Mickey Cochrane, another of the game's great catchers; Ed Delahanty; Hugh Duffy, who batted .438 in 1894; Kelly; McGinnity; Connie Mack, who was a great catcher before he became a great manager; and O'Rourke, who played until he was past fifty. Even baseball's mythical heroes are Irish—witness Ernest L. Thayer's "Casey at the Bat."

No list of professional Irish athletes is complete without the redoubtable name of William Muldoon, whose career was about as varied as a bowl of Irish stew. He worked as a bouncer in New York dance halls, as a laborer, longshoreman, and cab driver before becoming, in 1876, a policeman. He was an organizer of the famous Police Athletic League and, as a sideline, became a wrestler. Once he wrestled an opponent eight hours without a decision.

After retiring from the force in 1900, he opened the saloon and became a trainer of wrestlers and boxers. But he really reached the pinnacle of his fame when he established a health center on a Westchester estate for tired businessmen. Here, he invented the medicine ball, which became a standard part of the equipment of gyms everywhere.

Augustus Saint-Gaudens, the sculptor, was born in Dublin of an Irish mother and a French father. Then, there's Georgia O'Keeffe, the painter, and Louis Sullivan, the architect of skyscrapers.

One of the greatest contributions the Irish have made to life in America is in the field of education. Few realize how pervasive this influence has been and how far back it extends.

One obvious way in which the Irish have contributed to education in America is through their great seats of learning, such as Georgetown, Catholic University, Notre Dame, and Holy Cross, and through their elementary and secondary parochial schools. And lest we forget, the Irish schoolmasters formed an important part of life in colonial America.

The story begins with the Penal Laws. As we have said, England—in order to make sure of Ireland's subservience— virtually denied all educational facilities to the Catholic Irish. This was a hard blow for a land whose people, for more than a thousand years, had looked upon learning as one of the highest pursuits of life; a land where great universities had flourished before the poor people of England could count their fingers.

So, as best they could, the Irish educated their children anyway. So-called "hedge schools"—conducted in wooded glens—sprang up. But the English were stern. When a schoolmaster was caught, he was banished to the colonies—usually to the wilderness of America. Many of them, discouraged by the opposition in their native land, came to America voluntarily.

They were welcome. There was no school system, as such, in the colonies, and few parents could afford to send their children back to Europe for an education. A Pennsylvania scholar of the eighteenth century wrote:

"Forty years ago our people scarcely knew what a school was, but in later times there have come over young men from Ireland, some Presbyterians and some Roman Catholics, who commenced with school teaching, but as they saw better openings they gave that up."

Undeniably, these intinerant Catholic scholars taught, along with Latin and math, a hatred of England that contributed to the colonies' final resolution to break away from the mother country. Certainly, they supplied at least one signer of the Declaration of Independence, George Taylor.

Taylor's is one of America's first great rags-to-riches success stories. The twenty-year-old Irishman, of good family and impeccable education, came to America about 1736 as an indentured laborer. Fortunately, he found an employer who recognized the worth of his learning, canceled his indentures, and provided him with the financial backing to open a school.

Taylor married his benefactor's widow and eventually left the schoolroom for more lucrative pursuits. In the end, he became one of the wealthiest men in the colonies as an ironmonger in Bucks County, Pennsylvania. Unlike so many of the new nation's new rich, however, he sided with the rebels—against the established order.

One of the most famous signatures on the Declaration of Independence—that of John Hancock—owed its calligraphic character to an Irish schoolmaster, Peter MacLouth, a graduate of Maynooth College.

Other famous Americans also received their introduction to learning from Irish schoolmasters. Abraham Lincoln's first schoolmaster was an Irishman named Riney. U. S. Supeme Court Chief Justice 1836–64, Roger Brooke Taney, has recorded that his early education came from "an Irishman, a ripe scholar and an amiable and accomplished man."

The pioneer educator of Illinois was an Irish schoolmaster with the picturesque name of Thomas Halfpenny. After fighting in Washington's army, he traveled west as an itinerant teacher, finally settling in Illinois. Governor John Reynolds, in a history of Illinois, says: "Thomas Halfpenny was the Schoolmaster General of Illinois. This perceptor taught almost all the American children in Illinois in his day that received any education at all." Through the past 60 years teeming thousands of American boys have been schooled by Irish Christian Brothers, a teaching Order founded in Waterford in the early 1800s by a well-to-do widower, Edmund Ignatius Rice.

The Irish also have contributed to the establishment and well-being of many non-Catholic colleges. William Barton Rogers, the son of an Irish exile, founded the Massachusetts Institute of Technology. New York's Hunter College was named for Thomas Hunter, born in Ireland. Episcopal Bishop George Berkeley, whose diocese was Cloyne, County Cork, spent three years in America in the early eighteenth century, and contributed much, financially and otherwise, to Harvard, Yale, and Columbia (then King's College).

Another field in which the richly imaginative Irish have been most prominent is the theater. Irish plays began appearing on the New York stage as early as the 1820s. *Brian Boroihme, or the Maid of Erin*, by the Irish playwright James Sheridan Knowles, appeared in 1827. In the next few years, New York audiences also saw such works as *Kathleen O'Neill, or a Picture of Feudal Times in Ireland* and *The Red Branch Knight, or Ireland Triumphant.*

By 1849, a New York newspaper was able to report that "the largest number of Irish actors ever assembled" is "amongst us." Among the Celtic stars who thrilled nineteenth-century American audiences was Tyrone Power—William Grattan Tyrone Power, to be exact. He visited the United States repeatedly, starting in 1833. After appearances in New York, he usually toured the country starring in such plays as *The Irish Ambassador, Teddy the Tiler, The Irish Lion, How to Pay the Rent,* and *Rory O'More.* Power specialized in portraying the stage Irishman—smoking his clay pipe, swigging from his bottle, cracking his jokes in thick brogue, perhaps even leading a pig by a string.

Power died in 1841, but his grandson, Frederick Tyrone Power, became an even more distinguished actor. He was leading man for Mrs. Fiske, Mrs. Leslie Carter, and Julia Marlowe. *His* son, Tyrone Edmond Power, born in 1914, became a celebrated star of the American stage and screen. He died of a heart attack in 1959 while making *Solomon and Sheba* in Spain.

One of the most famous of the early Irish performers was John Brougham, whose field was parody. Among other things, he played *Hamlet* with a heavy brogue. Then there was Barney Williams, a native of Cork, who rose from the circus and Negro minstrels to serious roles in the legitimate theater. Also William Jermyn Florence, born Bernard Conlin, who was considered one of the top dramatic actors of the mid-nineteenth century. With his wife, he starred in *The Irish Boy and the Yankee Girl.*

Dublin-born Dion Boucicault combined writing (*The Wearin' o' the Green*) with acting. At nineteen, he had a success with his play *London Assurance* at Covent Garden. In 1853 he came to the United States, where he wrote or adapted more than three hundred farces, comedies and melodramas, in many of which he acted himself. The most notable of these was *The Colleen*

Bawn, which enjoyed a half-century of popularity. His 1859 melodrama *The Octoroon* was successfully revived in New York in 1961.

When Boucicault died in 1890, George M. Cohan had just received his first starring role—at the age of twelve. Born in Providence, Rhode Island, on the 3rd of July, 1878, he first appeared on the stage at the age of nine. He achieved considerable success two years later when he toured in the title role in *Peck's Bad Boy*.

Later, as one of "The Four Cohans," he became popular in vaudeville. Beginning at the turn of the century and continuing right up to World War I, Cohan wrote, produced, and starred in a long series of hits. Among them were: *The Wise Guy, The Governor's Son, Little Johnny Jones, Forty-five Minutes from Broadway, The Yankee Prince, Get-Rich-Quick Wallingford, Broadway Jones, Seven Keys to Baldpate, The Miracle Man,* and *Gambling.* Cohan, a jack-of-all-theatrical-trades, also wrote a long list of song hits, including "Over There," which propelled tens of thousands of Irish- and other Americans into World War I.

Probably the greatest of all Irish-American composers was the inimitable Victor Herbert. The immortal tunesmith was born in Dublin in 1859. When he was a young man he did what all would-be musicians did in those days—he went to Germany to study. He learned his craft well and stayed on there as principal violin-cello player in the court orchestra at Stuttgart. In 1886, the Metropolitan Opera Company in New York, hearing of his fame, decided to hire, not one Herbert, but two. It engaged Victor as a cellist and Mrs. Herbert as a singer.

Victor prospered in music-hungry America. He was connected with a number of American orchestras, either as soloist or conductor, including the Pittsburgh Symphony, which he founded and led for five years, However, he quit in 1904 and devoted himself almost exclusively to the work that was to make him famous—the composition of light operas. As the new century gathered momentum, people all over the land began whistling tunes from such hits as *The Fortune Teller, Babes in Toyland, Mlle. Modiste, The Red Mill, Naughty Marietta,* and *Sweethearts.* They still move the people.

Today, the movie, theater, and television pages of your daily paper are filled with Irish names—Bill Gargan, Peter Lind Hayes and Mary Healy, Morton Downey, Phil Regan, Jim Barton, Jackie Gleason, Frank Fay, Ed Sullivan, Arthur Godfrey, Horace MacMahon, Anthony Quinn, Pat O'Brien, the Pat Harringtons, Peggy Cass, Barbara Stanwyck (born Ruby Stevens), and Helen Hayes, the First Lady of the American theater. And, of course, there was the late Fred Allen.

Peggy Cass, who appeared on Broadway in *Auntie Mame* and *A Thurber Carnival,* grew up in an Irish neighborhood in Cambridge, Massachusetts.

"My mother," she once told me, "came from an even more tightly knit community, which was South Boston, which was where the people would get off the boat with an address in their hand and say, 'Your cousin Mary said you would put me up for a few days,' and then, you know, they'd stay put and never never move outside South Boston. They never even went across the bridge into Boston. The children did. That's when my mother met my father, when she crossed that bridge."

Peggy's mother militantly kept her brogue come thick or thin as the Cass's grew. She grew up in this country. "When I was about seventeen I started to go out with boys. One of them called me up one day and said, 'Oh Peggy, it was just awful. You know, I called you up, I wanted to take you out, but I couldn't understand a word the maid said. When did she get off the boat?' I said, 'We don't have any maid.' And then—oh, my mother! It was my mother's voice."

Another successful Irish stage and screen star who looks back with fondness on a happy childhood is James Cagney. "It was not an Irish neighborhood as such," Jimmy told me not long ago. "For example, from 72nd Street on up to, let's say, 88th Street in New York City there were Irish, Germans, Jews, Italians, Hungarians, name 'em, you had 'em. There was every kind of nationality represented. I'd say it was a great advantage to have been raised there because all the various dialects that I learned at an early age have certainly stood me in good stead since then, and no dialect is unfamiliar to me."

Jimmy not only learned dialects—he learned to speak undiluted Yiddish. "I went to school, Stuyvesant High School in New York City, and most of the students there were from the East Side, and I would say ninety per cent were Jewish. I studied German there under Professor Mankiewicz—the father of the motion picture Mankiewicz—and as I learned the German, I learned the Yiddish equivalents. And as Yiddish was a whole lot more fun, I became more familiar with the Yiddish than I did with the German."

Barbara Stanwyck was another product of the spreading "mixed" neighborhood. "As a youngster in Brooklyn," she recalls, "there were minority groups—Irish and Jewish—and at school, we were called 'shanties' and the Jews were called by various and other nasty names. And as a result we kind of stuck together. I think the Irish and the Jewish people get along very very well, always have and I think they always will. Maybe that's because of the background of used-to-be persecution, I don't know. I think the Irish and the Jewish people are deeply, deeply religious, and very very sincere about their religion; and I think this is another factor that binds them together."

Barbara thinks her Irish blood stood her in good stead in her rise to the top. "The Irish," she says, "are a fighting race, fighting for survival. I am one of them; I wanted something out of life, and I worked very hard for it, and fought for it."

Then there was Philadelphia's John B. Kelly, father of Her Serene Highness Princess Grace of Monaco.

Some years ago, I had the pleasure of interviewing the late Mr. Kelly on NBC's "Image-minorities." He told me something of his family history.

"My grandfather," he said, "was in the Civil War, but before that I had two great-uncles who came over and fought in Washington's army. Those two were willing to fight England at any time, so they just came over here to join the American army, and then went back home again when they helped finish the job."

He was proud of Grandfather Kelly, politically, too: "He told me when he came over he lived in Vermont. Of course, there were no Democrats in Vermont, but he registered Democrat, and he was the only one. Unluckily, on Election Day, they found two Democratic votes in the box, so they arrested him for repeating."

I asked him how he felt about his daughter's wedding. He said: "I think that my daughter marrying a Prince over there was sort of universally accepted. There were just as many Protestants as Catholics who were happy over it, and we got, I would say, a hundred to one letters in praise and happiness rather than criticism."

Before Kelly died of cancer on June 20, 1960 he composed a will that smacked of his buoyant spirit; and, in a sense, Ireland's.

In leaving $1000 to Godfrey Ford, his chauffeur for years, he stipulated that Ford was to be kept in employment by his heirs "so long as he behaves himself well, making due allowances for minor errors of the flesh." He made it plain, too, that none of his fortune was intended for the husbands of his three daughters —including the husband of the daughter he playfully called "Her Serene Highness, Princess Grace."

He anticipated trouble over the informal phrasing of his will. But he met the expected trouble head on:

"For years I have been reading last wills and testaments and

[238]

I have never been able to clearly understand any of them at one reading. Therefore, I will attempt to write my own will with the hope that it will be understandable and legal.

"Kids will be called 'kids' and not 'issue,' and it will not be cluttered up with 'parties of the first part,' 'per stirpes,' 'perpetuities,' 'quasijudicial,' 'to wit' and a lot of other terms that I am sure are only used to confuse those for those benefit it was written.

"Some lawyers will question this when they read my will; however, I have my opinion of some of them, so that makes it even . . . I hope I am making myself clear. I don't want anyone to twist what I am trying to say.

". . . I don't want to give the impression that I am against sons-in-law. If they are the right type, they will provide for themselves and their families and what I am able to give my daughters will help pay the dress shop bills which, if they continue as they have started out, under the able tutelage of their mother, will be quite considerable.

". . . I can think of nothing more ghastly than the heirs sitting around, listening to some representative reading a will. They always remind me of buzzards and vultures awaiting the last breath of the stricken. Therefore, I will try to spare you that ordeal and let you read the will before I go to my reward."

To his son, like the father a champion oarsman and, further like him, interested in flat and harness racing (Kelly, Sr., was president of the Atlantic City, New Jersey, Race Course) Kelly observed:

"I want to say that if there is anything to this Mendelian theory, you will probably like to bet on a horse or indulge in other forms of gambling—so, if you do, never bet what you cannot afford to lose, and if you are a loser don't plunge to try to recoup. That is wherein the danger lies.

"As for me, just shed a respectful tear if you think I merit it, but I am sure that you are all intelligent enough not to weep all over the place. I have watched a few emotional acts at graves, such as trying to jump into same, fainting, etc., but the thoroughbred grieves in the heart.

"Not that my passing should occasion any 'scenes,' for the simple reason that life owes me nothing. I have ranged far and wide, have really run the gamut of life. I have known great sorrow and great joy. I had more than my share of success.

". . . I worked hard in my early life, but I was well paid for that effort. [He was proprietor of the nation's largest bricklaying concern, this man who had once wielded a trowel himself and been barred from rowing at Henley, in England, because he was "in trade."]

"In this document I can only give you things, but if I had the choice to give you worldly goods or characters, I would give you character. The reason I say that is, with character, you will get wordly goods, because character is loyalty, honesty, ability, sportsmanship and, I hope, a sense of humor.

"If I don't stop soon this will be as long as 'Gone with the Wind.' So just remember, when I shove off for greener pastures or whatever it is on the other side of the curtain, that I do it unafraid, and, if you must know, a little curious."

He signed his name in green ink.

The Irish often have combined their talent for music with their talent for the theater. The contribution of the Irish to America's music has largely been in popular rather than classical forms and on the side of performance rather than composition. But there have been noteworthy exceptions.

One of the Celtic singers who gave American audiences the most enjoyment was that archetype of the Irish tenor, John Mc-Cormack. Born in Athlone, he studied in Milan and made his operatic debut in London in *Cavalleria Rusticana* in 1907 at the age of twenty-three. Two years later, impresario Oscar Hammerstein brought him to the United States, where he became a towering success.

After appearances with New York, Boston, and Chicago opera companies, he turned in 1914, to concert work, for which his voice was best suited. McCormack's popularity coincided with the first surge of interest in the phonograph, and his recordings of "Mother Machree" "Somewhere a Voice Is Calling," "Galway Bay," "When You and I Were Young, Maggie," and "A Little Bit of Heaven" were universal favorites on hand-cranked Victrolas.

McCormack became an American citizen in 1919 and a Papal count nine years later. With his voice showing the effects of age, he retired at fifty-four and died in 1945 at the age of sixty-one.

There is no telling to what heights of popularity John McCormack might have risen had he been born into the Age of Television instead of the Age of the Phonograph. Still, he remains the *ne plus ultra*.

One Irish singer whose popularity never seems to wane has made it big not only with recordings and on the radio but also on television and in movies, golf, business and big and active family life.

He is, needless to say, the ever-young Harry Lillis Crosby. Born in Tacoma, Washington, in 1904, Bing put in five years singing with dance bands before hitting the big time in radio and movies in 1931. He has been a major personality in American entertainment ever since, and as this book is being written shows not the slightest sign of fading. His *Going My Way* with the late great Barry Fitzgerald and Ingrid Bergman, produced by Leo McCarey, remains the Church's *Gone with the Wind*.

However, the Irish have not confined themselves to popular music, as the career of Edward MacDowell amply shows. Born in the early days of the Civil War to Scottish and Irish parents in New York, he began to take music lessons when he was eight.

He had such a tendency to decorate the margins of his music pages with pictures that there was some question whether his career would be art or music.

By the time he was fifteen he had settled on music, and his mother took him abroad to study. At the Paris Conservatory he was a fellow pupil of the French composer Claude Debussy. He next studied in Germany and at twenty became an instructor at the Conservatory at Darmstadt. There he married one of his pupils, an American girl named Marian Nevins.

After a dozen years in Europe, during which time he won fame as a pianist and composer, he returned to America. In 1896, he became a professor of music at Columbia University, remaining until 1904, when ill health forced him to resign. He died four years later.

During the last years of his life, he acquired a tract of woodland in Peterborough, N.H., finding release from the strain of city life. There he worked. Mrs. MacDowell carried out a wish of his last illness. She converted the estate into the MacDowell Colony. Here, composers, writers, painters, and sculptors may spend summers in creative work.

Among MacDowell's best-known works are "Woodland Sketches," "Indian Suite," "Sea Pieces," "Sonata Eroica," "Norse Sonata," and "Keltic (or Celtic) Sonata."

The Irish imagination, which peopled the old country with a gay race of invisible mischief-makers, has done much for writing as well as for music. Just as the Irish gave Jonathan Swift, Oscar Wilde, and George Bernard Shaw to English literature, so they have given James T. Farrell, F. Scott Fitzgerald, and John O'Hara to American literature. And not them alone. There also have been Betty Smith (A Tree Grows in Brooklyn), Jim Tully (Shanty Irish), Edwin O'Connor, and many more.

The Irish have perhaps been more prominent in journalism than in literature, as such. Back in the nineteenth century, the Irish-American journalist was a man of considerable importance, because the Catholic Irish newspaper ranked next to the Church as a cultural influence.

Peter Fenelon Collier founded a magazine which bore his name for more than half a century, (and Michael Cuhahy a meat-packing empire, John Robert Gregg a shorthand system, and Humphrey O'Sullivan a rubber heel).

The newspaper was the immigrant Irishman's school, library and friend. It counseled him in politics and furnished him with endless subjects for discussion at the corner saloon. Mr. Dooley's discourses on topics of the day were in the form of a conversation with his friend, Mr. Hennessy. Almost all of them started with a mention of something they had read in the newspapers:

" 'Well, I see Congress has got to wurruk again,' said Mr. Dooley."

" 'The Lord save us from harm,' said Mr. Hennessy."

The pre-Civil War Irish-American newspapers had many sepa-rate faults but several common virtues. Every one of them cau-tioned the Irishman about his thirst; every one of them crusaded to get the Irish out of the city tenements into the country—even though the success of the crusade would have meant a severe loss of subscribers; every one of them plugged for naturali-zation, for loyalty to America despite attachments to the old country.

The most important of these newspapers was the Boston *Pilot*, still very much alive and kicking a century and a quarter after its founding. It now is the official organ of the Archdiocese of Boston, though in its early days it was a newspaper of general interest to Catholic Irishmen all over the country. A decade after its founding, it could truthfully boast that it circulated "in every town in the United States, Canada, British Provinces, Mexico &c., where there is an Irishman."

The paper's stated purpose was "the elevation of the Irish character in this country, the Independence of Ireland, and the overthrow of sectarian prejudice." In 1841 it said: "We wish it to be distinctly understood that our paper is emphatically an Irish and Catholic journal."

Generally, the *Pilot* furnished Irish-Americans with a varied menu of news from Ireland; stories about the Irish in America; Church information, such as the transfer of priests and the appointment of bishops; and forthright editorials on the issues of the day, particularly those affecting the Catholic Irishman. Its long parade of editors included such distinguished journalists as James Jeffrey Roche and John Boyle O'Reilly.

Inevitably, one of the leading Irish newspapers was named *The Shamrock*. It was established in New York in 1810. The paper's masthead displayed an eagle and a harp with the words, "Fostered under thy wing, we die in thy defense." Generally, the paper was far more staid than its Boston contemporary. Perhaps that's why it survived only a few years.

That New York clarion, *Freeman's Journal*, was started in 1840 and passed six years later under the control of Bishop John J. Hughes. As might be expected, it placed a heavy emphasis on ecclesiastical matters. The *Journal* survived sturdily for 68 years, became a casualty of World War I.

More than any other ethnic group, the Irish have been prominent in American journalism. It is a profession that offers many features attractive to the Irish temperament—status, excitement, a chance to participate actively in the give-and-take of political life, and an opportunity to meet and know all kinds of people.

It is difficult to begin or complete any list of U.S. newsmen and news hens, as *Time* calls them, who point (or pointed) with pride and affection to an Irish ancestor.

There was Frank Ward O'Malley, who might be called the father of today's newspaper feature story. And Bill McGeehan, who gave the art of sportswriting tremendous punch, wit and erudition. And Boston's testy and tremendously talented Dave Egan, Harvard-bred but the epitome of hammer and tongs sports columning. And gentle Bill Slocum, the master baseball writer whose son and namesake is the newest and wittiest of the Hearst columnists.

The immortal Damon Runyon used to boast of Irish forebears, as did Heywood Broun, who was converted to Catholicism shortly before his death by Bishop Fulton J. Sheen. Anne O'Hare McCormick of the *New York Times* was America's greatest woman political writer and foreign correspondent for years. Margaret Mitchell, writing features for Atlanta newspapers, worked for years on an off-hours writing project which became so voluminous in manuscript form that friends who dropped in for a drink would sometimes use a bale of it as a seat or hassock. It became *Gone with the Wind*.

William Randolph Hearst, Sr., who pioneered in revolutionizing and vitalizing U.S. journalism, had Irish blood in him, which his Pulitzer Prize-winning son and namesake carries on. One of Hearst's top bygone editors and officials in features and news was Joseph V. Connolly. At the top of the colossal Hearst empire today stand two executives of Irish background, Richard E. Berlin and Harold Kern. The editor of their 11,000,000 circulation *American Weekly* in John O'Connell. The national editor of the Hearst papers is Frank Conniff, famed war correspondent and Pulitzer Prize winner.

Three of the most gifted and surely most vigorous writers in present-day journalism—Westbrook Pegler, Dan Parker, and Jimmy Cannon—are part of the Hearst chain, which has, since its inception with the San Francisco *Examiner* in the 1890s, specialized in the flair of Irish-scented prose. The tart tracts of Davis J. Walsh must be read by any youth who contemplates a career in sportswriting. The enormous writing range of Curley Grieve, sports editor of the San Francisco *Examiner*, and the hard-hitting Prescott Sullivan of the same paper, help to preserve the eminence of the founding paper. In Los Angeles, Vincent Xavier Flaherty of the L.A. *Examiner*, overcoming all manner of opposition at home and abroad, all but singlehandedly forced organized baseball to forget its traditional insularity and send major league teams to California. He could be called the father of big league baseball of today. His perseverance made the National Pastime national.

American journalism is richer today because of Notre Dame's Red Smith and Fordham's Arthur Daley, a rarity in his field for he is a sports columnist (*New York Times*) with a Pulitzer Prize. Ed Lahey of the Knight papers and Ed Folliard of the *Washington Post and Times Herald* (again a Pulitzer Prize winner) are enormously respected newsmen, as are colleagues in the Washington press corps as Marguerite Higgins, Mary McGrory, Robert Donovan, Michael O'Neill, John O'Brien, and Jerry Greene.

There has been an outstanding Sullivan in U.S. newspaper work since the rise of the late great Mark Sullivan, one of the most astute political observers in the annals of the craft. Frank Sullivan continues to bring wit and whimsy to his public, through *The New Yorker* magazine. Ed Sullivan combines his Broadway column with his now solidly entrenched career as the outstanding variety show master of ceremonies on television. Walter Sullivan is the *New York Times* science and research reporter. Still another Ed Sullivan is one of the top motion picture publicists and, since 1961, a Knight of Malta.

Jimmy Powers is sports editor of the nation's largest newspaper, the New York *Daily News*. Jim Roach is sports editor of the *Times*, whose sports column was once superbly manned by that repository of colossal scholarship, John Kieran. The Scripps newspapers similarly abound in Irish stars: Inez Robb, Andrew Tully, Joe Williams, Charles Lucey, and Willard Mullin, as well as having produced an imposing list of creative writers—Quentin Reynolds, Tom Meany, Tom O'Reilly, Joe Mitchell, etc.

The list drifts toward endlessness. The First Lady of Hollywood journalism, Louella Parsons, is perpetually proud of her Irish blood. So, of course, are the famed Kilgallens, Jim and daughter Dorothy. Kathleen McLaughlin of the *New York Times* is one of America's most honored reporters. The two brightest and sharpest stars to emerge from a new department in today's newspapers, television criticism, are John Crosby of the New York *Herald Tribune* and Jack O'Brian of the New York *Journal-American*. The world's largest news service, the Associated Press, has for its featured columnist Pulitzer Prize winner Hal Boyle. Tom Deegan, who once wrote sports for the *Times*, is chairman of the board of New York's billion dollar World's Fair of 1964.

And as for the funny section of the newspaper—probably the most popular comic strip in the history of American journalism has been "Bringing up Father," created by George McManus. For nearly half a century the more-than-Irish characters, Jiggs, and Maggie, have been household names.

And on and on and on . . .

Perhaps one factor that has enabled the Irish to excel in journalism is their flair for words—not only for using them, but also for coining them. For instance, they have given us such words as *speakeasy* and *smithereens*, as well, naturally, as *shillelagh*. The late H. L. Mencken also thought the Irish may have passed *lallapalooza* on to us. As he traced the history of the word, it comes from a County Mayo expression *allay-foozee*, meaning a stout fellow. *Allay-foozee*, in turn, probably came from the French *allez-fusil* meaning "forward the muskets." This, he insisted had been picked up from the French after they landed at Killala in 1798.

In his monumental *The American Language*, Mencken, who tended toward agnosticism but considered Cardinal Gibbons one of the great men of his time, declared the immigrating Irish gave America certain habits of speech that persist today—or, they reinforced habits already here. The colonists had brought to America with them certain colloquialisms dating from the days of King James I—*hist* for *hoist*, for example, *bile* for *boil*, *chaw* for *chew*, *jine* for *join*, and *rench* for *rinse*.

As time went on, these usages began to fade from American speech. But the Irish had picked up the same usages at the same time. Being more conservative in speech habits, they clung to them through the years. When they arrived in America, they reinforced these speech habits and insured their survival. Thus *drownded* for *drowned*, *onct* for *once*, *agin* for *against*, and *ornery* for *ordinary* continued in use in America long after they might have been discarded.

Another Celtic habit that America picked up was the frequent use of the definite article before nouns: "I like to climb the trees" instead of "I like to climb trees." As Mencken points out, Americans now say "I have the measles" instead of "I have measles." The British insist on going on holiday or to hospital instead of on *a* holiday or to *a* hospital.

P. W. Joyce in his *English as We Speak It in Ireland* says the use of *dead* as an intensifier, such as "he was dead right," has an Irish origin. He also believes the incorrect use of *them* as a demonstrative pronoun, as in "them are the ones I want," comes from Gaelic, in which such a usage happens to be correct.

The Irish also have contributed to America their good Irish names—names such as *Patrick* and *Michael* and *Dennis*. Generally, they have avoided the Gaelic given names for their English equivalents. For instance, *Peter* instead of *Paedar*, *Cathleen* instead of *Caitlin*, *Eileen* instead of *Eibhlin*, *William* instead of *Liam*.

As for surnames, the telephone directory of every city in America is liberally sprinkled with *Kellys* and *O'Briens*. *Smith* remains the most popular surname in America—someone had figured that one in every eighty-eight Americans bears the name. It is followed by *Johnson*, *Brown*, *Williams*, and *Jones* with the first clearly Irish name, *Moore*, showing up in eleventh place.

However, it's a different story in Boston where the order is *Smith, Sullivan, Brown, Johnson,* and *Murphy.*

In 1928, Howard F. Baker, research associate of the American Council of Learned Societies, estimated that 18,000,000 Americans bore Irish names. Of those, 15,750,000 had gotten them by inheritance, 1,300,000 were Negroes whose forebears had assumed the names, and 950,000 were whites who had, for one reason or another, adopted them. Of course, to a lesser extent, it also has worked the other way around. Occasionally, a *Mac-Shane* has changed his name to *Johnson,* the English equivalent, and an occasional *Padraic* has switched to *Patrick.* But by and large the Irish have stuck with the sturdy names given them.

The Irish have given us so much more than words and songs and great men. They also have helped materially to establish the image of that mythical creature, the typical American. Through the world he has become a character who is at once gay, generous, friendly, with a tendency to make too much, perhaps, of Saturday nights and special occasions, a great joiner but an attentive husband and devoted father nevertheless; hard-working, a man who loves God and is deeply conscious of the fallibility of himself and his fellows. Bless the Irish for that.

12 "OVERSEAS" IRISH:

Ireland Today

Ireland's struggle for maturity in the modern world began, as it had to, with the achievement of Independence—final victory in the centuries-old fight against foreign tyranny.

Over the years, rebellion after rebellion had kept the cause of Irish freedom alive. Even in defeat, there were always those who picked up the pieces and began planning the next step which they were certain would lead to victory. The Young Irelanders, the Fenian movement, the Irish Republican Brotherhood all helped pave the way.

The Irish produced a most eloquent and effective champion in Charles Stewart Parnell, born of Protestant parents in County Wicklow in 1846. His mother's father was a Rear Admiral in the United States Navy. Parnell was no wild, impulsive debater, but a reserved and dignified political leader who knew well the art of political warfare. He was a bold and brilliant leader of the Irish Nationalists in the British House of Commons. Parnell's group helped make William Gladstone Prime Minister in 1886, and Gladstone, in turn, introduced a bill to grant Ireland

Home Rule, but the measure split the Liberals, and Gladstone was replaced as Prime Minister by the Marquess of Salisbury. Parnell failed to hand the gift of freedom to fellow Irishmen, but he gained ground on land reform, and gave the English much pause. For the first time, they had to reckon with a strong, well-directed Irish opposition.

Through the early 1900s, England's Peers continued stalling on Home Rule for Ireland, delaying the expressed intent of the House of Commons. When the House of Lords finally did get around to passing the measure, it excluded Ulster, declaring that it must remain part of the United Kingdom. World War I broke out, and the British government used the conflict as an excuse to postpone the Day of Freedom once again.

Irish patience wore transparently thin, and it was obvious that violence was near. On Easter Monday in 1916, some 1200 volunteers parading along O'Connell Street in Dublin seized the Post Office, hoisted the flag of Independence, and poet Padhraic Pearse read the proclamation of the Irish Republic from the steps.

"Irishmen and Irishwomen," the poet cried. "In the name of God and dead generations from which she receives her old tradition of nationhood, Ireland, through us, summons her children to her flag and strikes for her freedom.

"Having organized and trained her manhood through her secret, revolutionary organization, the Irish Republican Brotherhood, and through her open military organizations, the Irish Volunteers and the Irish Citizen Army, having patiently perfected her discipline, having resolutely waited for the right moment to reveal itself, she now seizes that moment, and, supported by her exiled children in America and by gallant allies in Europe, but relying in the first on her own strength, she strikes in full confidence of victory.

"We declare the right of the people of Ireland to the ownership of Ireland, and to the unfettered control of Irish destinies, to be sovereign and indefeasible. The long usurpation of that right by a foreign people and government has not extinguished the right, nor can it ever be extinguished except by the destruction of the Irish people. In every generation the Irish people have asserted their right to national freedom and sovereignty; six times during the past three hundred years they have asserted it in arms. Standing on that fundamental right and again asserting it in arms in the face of the world, we hereby proclaim the Irish Republic as a Sovereign Independent State, and we pledge our lives and the lives of our comrades-in-arms to the cause of its freedom, of its welfare, and of its exaltation among the nations.

"The Irish Republic is entitled to, and hereby claims, the allegiance of every Irishman and Irishwoman. The Republic guarantees religious and civil liberty, equal rights and equal opportunities to all its citizens, and declares its resolve to pursue the happiness and prosperity of the whole nation and of all its parts, cherishing all the children of the nation equally, and oblivious of the differences carefully fostered by an alien government, which have divided a minority from the majority in the past.

"Until our arms have brought the opportune moment for the establishment of a permanent National Government, representative of the whole people of Ireland and elected by the suffrages of all her men and women, the Provisional Government, hereby constituted, will administer the civil and military affairs of the Republic in trust for the people.

"We place the cause of the Irish Republic under the protection of the Most High God, Whose blessing we invoke upon our arms, and we pray that no one who serves that cause will dishonor it by cowardice, inhumanity, or rapine. In this supreme hour, the Irish nation must, by its valor and discipline and by the readiness of its children to sacrifice themselves for the common good, prove itself worthy of the august destiny to which it is called."

Pearse then read off the names affixed to the courageous document: Thomas J. Clarke, Sean MacDiarmada, Thomas MacDonagh, Eamonn Ceannt, James Connolly, Joseph Plunkett and his own.

The rebels knew when they were outnumbered and realized there would be no general uprising to back them up, but they held other strategic points in Dublin for a week while Irish the world over clenched their fists and cheered them on.

No one expected them to be a match for the British Army or the heavy artillery which pounded the Post Office into a pile of ruins. When the Easter Week rebellion was over, Pearse and sixteen other leaders were led before a firing squad. Others were condemned to die, but public opinion in many countries rose in anger against further blood-letting, and the British spared the lives of several insurgents. Among the lucky ones was an American-born mathematics teacher, Eamon de Valera.

General elections were held after the Armistice ending World War I was signed in 1918, and when the returns were totaled, a curious situation emerged. Nearly all of Ireland's victorious candidates were in jail. Thirty-six new members of Parliament were behind bars, three had been deported, and six others were fugitives in their own country. The few others still at liberty refused to go to London to take their seats. For the second time, the Irish—this time, an Assembly—proclaimed a Republic, and elected as President one of the jailed leaders, Eamon de Valera.

Fighting broke out again and a nerve-shattering guerrilla warfare turned Ireland into a place of sudden death. The British sent the hated Black and Tans and the Auxiliaries to hunt down the rebel fighters, but the police themselves often found they were the hunted instead of the hunters. Ambushes cut them down coldly and quickly. Official cars were ripped by bombs. Barracks went up in flames. Ammunition dumps exploded on dark nights with ground-jarring force. But the police, too, fought back. They had their snipers and informers, their road blocks and search parties. A knock on the door at midnight often meant a quick arrest, quick trial, and quick death.

Again, it was world conscience which helped put an end to this bloody and senseless struggle. The Lord Mayor of Cork, Terence MacSwiney, made himself a martyr of freedom. Jailed, he endured seventy-three days of agony without food and starved himself to death. The world, horrified, shook its head in sorrow.

De Valera was more fortunate. He broke out of jail and escaped to the United States—his birth place—where he appeared at rallies, was cheered wildly by Irish sympathizers, and collected thousands of dollars for the Irish cause.

With such outside pressure building up, England could not long put off a solution. In 1921, Lloyd George invited de Valera to a conference and a truce was signed. But the Irish lost the political negotiations which followed. They were told their island would be divided into two states, with the six counties in the north remaining part of the United Kingdom. The remaining four-fifths of the land, with twenty-six counties, would become the Irish Free State with Dominion status. Lloyd George threatened "immediate and terrible war" unless the Irish envoys agreed to the partition, and the men from Dublin, Arthur Griffith and Michael Collins, believed sincerely that it was the best offer the English would make. They may have been right. But when they returned home, de Valera repudiated them angrily. The envoys replied firmly that the agreement represented a worthwhile first step toward full freedom.

The Irish were as divided over this issue as by Partition, itself, and for nearly two years more, a bitter civil war drained the country of its best brains and muscles. There was strife when, at last, there should have been unity. In 1923, on the seventh anniversary of the surrender of the 1916 rebels, de Valera ordered a cease-fire. The Irish Free State tried to settle down to an uneasy existence, still short of its ultimate goal of freedom with Irish unity, and not at all sure it was within reach.

England and Ireland continued bickering in the 1930s, when a customs war broke out. Then came World War II and old animosities were revived when Ireland was the only English-speaking nation to remain neutral. To many in the Allied world it appeared cynical, if not pro-Nazi. Dublin insisted on maintaining its diplomatic ties with Hitler and its streets were said to "swarm with spies." Irish partisans argued that a Nazi blitz would have destroyed Ireland and that participation in the war would have brought foreign invaders back again—either English or worse. In any case, Irish sympathies were definitely on the Allied side. An estimated 70,000 Irishmen served in the Free World fighting forces, and more than 200,000 workers turned out vital materials in British factories.

By gradual stages, Ireland was drawing away from the Dominion, and finally, the break became complete. The goal of generations of Irishmen was achieved in 1949—again, on an Easter Monday—when the Republic of Ireland was born. The Irish had their long-sought independence, but only in twenty-six counties. A unified Ireland is still in the future, and no one can predict when, if ever, it will become a reality.

Independent Ireland still has problems, and one of them is emigration. Large numbers of her citizens still feel obliged to seek a better life in other countries. In the 1880s, emigrants averaged 60,000 a year. In the 1890s, the figure dropped to 40,000 annually, and in the first decade of this century, to 26,000. The number dipped still further during the years of the Second World War, but has started climbing again. In 1957, 46,000 more people left Ireland than came in. Since 1930, most of the emigrants have sailed for England to find work. Some go to Canada and Australia, and others, of course, follow their ancestors to New York and Boston.

Unfortunately for Ireland, some of the nation's most distinguished citizens have joined the exodus—writers, particularly. Start the list with Oscar Wilde and carry it down the years through James Joyce, Bernard Shaw, Sean O'Casey, and Samuel Beckett. O'Casey, perhaps the world's greatest living playwright, is living in a Devon coastal town. One of his sons, Breon, an artist, settled in London. Another, Niall, served in the British army, and a daughter attended an English school.

In a *Life* article a decade ago, O'Casey was quoted as saying he left Ireland for two main reasons: he was disappointed with the "sober, religious country that had emerged from all the fighting; and he hoped to make a better living in the literary world." He sailed away to England with a promise to "look back now and again to see how the figures looked with a more distant sun shining on them."

In another *Life* article, and subsequently in a book entitled: *The Vanishing Irish*, the distinguished writer, Sean O'Faolain composed a lament on the theme of the small number of marriages in Ireland. He pointed out that the nation is one of the few places on the globe where men outnumber women, and yet, the marriage rate of 5.3 per thousand is one of the lowest in the world. One quarter of the population never marries, and the average age of those who do is thirty-three years for men and twenty-eight for women. The men complain that the young eligible women are only frivolous, empty-headed girls who are hunting millionaires. The young ladies accuse the men of being too interested in sports and clubs and too tied to the apron strings of their families. They're afraid to leave the comfort and safety of their mother's kitchen. Some Irish girls will admit that the chief reason for going to England or America for a job is really to find a husband or a man who is not already a confirmed old bachelor.

The strict rules against divorce, lower living standards, and a shortage of pleasant, modern apartments are often blamed for the lack of interest in marriage, but similar conditions do exist

in other countries and marriage somehow has retained its popularity. O'Faolain believes that a native Puritanism bolstered by
rigid censorship laws must be to blame.

When the Irish do marry—and they do—they raise large families, probably due to Church bans on birth control, but also
due to a natural love for big households with many children.
The birth rate in Ireland is one of the highest in the world—
more than twice that of the United States—so any fear that the
Irish Irish will vanish from the earth in the near future is
probably unfounded.

The writer created something of a furor on March 17, 1960,
with a column written for Hearst Headline Service:

> If the Irish-American paid as much attention to the land
> of his origin as the American Jew pays to Israel, Ireland
> today would be a thriving garden spot. If the Irish-Ameri-
> can lavished in interest and coin what the Italian-American
> shows on Italy, the emptying of the Emerald Isle would
> cease.
>
> These are sobering thoughts on what is always a happy
> day in New York and elsewhere, the honoring of the Patron
> Saint of the blessedly feisty little land.
>
> But sometimes the skirling of the pipes on Fifth Avenue,
> the hearty buckoes in the saloons, the brisk sale of dyed
> carnations and tearful memories of peat fires and the bar
> at the Old Ground in Ennis—God protect it!—are tainted
> with a tinge of hypocrisy which should be mentioned in the
> nearest Confessional.
>
> When an American businessman of Irish extraction
> searches for a place to expand his business interests out-
> side the continental U.S. he is more inclined to build his

plant in, let's say, Puerto Rico or West Germany than in the country that gave him or his family their start. He finds himself growing impatient, even intolerant, of the selfsame Irish independence of spirit and economic posture which he now proudly toasts.

In a world atremble with the "population explosion," Ireland's population remains static or decreases. Its sons and daughters, clean of limb, rosy of jaw and keen of mind, regard emigration as a commendable ambition. There would be even greater drainage if they were not frustrated by the twin devils of the quota system, as imposed by the United States, and by low income at home.

The industrialization of the six counties of Ireland under British rule is but a sample of what Eire could achieve if some of its silk-hatted sons—marching so grandly on Fifth Avenue today—would think of the Ould Sod as worthy of their shekels as it is of their sentimentality.

Happily, the Republic of Ireland seems to be stirring itself a bit more than in the past to rectify this matter. Count Cyril McCormack, director of the Irish Industrial Development Authority in the U.S., upon the occasion of receiving the Archbishop Hughes Gaelic Society of Fordham University Award, made these points:

Ireland is coming around to tax concessions, long-term loans and other competition-meeting incentive systems in its overtures to new industry. Over the past four years, it has attracted about $75,000,000 in foreign capital, which in turn has provided jobs for 10,000 Irish workers. The U.S., alas, is hardly a forerunner in this vitalization of the land that meant so much to Western civilization and Christianity. We have scarcely 20 plants in Ireland. Other countries who are finding it admirably suited for their expansion programs are Britain, Canada, France, Germany, Holland, Israel, Japan, Sweden and Switzerland.

McCormack, son of the immortal tenor, said after accepting his award from Cardinal Spellman:

"Our program is not competitive with industry in the United States. We are not trying to take industries away from here. We are offering to existing American industries an opportunity to expand profitably into lucrative and growing European markets, and are willing to give them all the assistance in our power to enable them to do this." He cited his country's bountiful supply of skilled and semi-skilled labor, her relatively low-wage rates, ample electric power and easy accessibility.

Hope his words aren't drowned out by today's 'Erin-go-Braghs' and the rush to invest in Venezuela.

There is little reason to delay your visit to Ireland. If you're not "fresh over" but have a trickle of the shamrock in you, you should get to know the remarkable country.

When to go? A summer vacation is the best time. Ireland is usually cool, almost never hot. On an extremely warm day, the mercury might hit 80 degrees. Most of the time, the readings will be in the 60's. If you should happen to find yourself there in late fall or winter, you will find the mercury hovering in the 40's. It rarely snows or freezes over, but you may be convinced that the temperature is near zero if you happen to be in a hotel without central heating. Most of them tend to be rather chilly the year round. Best advice—schedule your trip for summer. In any case, be prepared for a goodly portion of Irish dew. Ireland's rain adds a misty softness to the landscape and a definite dampness to the unprepared visitor, so you'd best have your rain garb handy. Ireland also is drenched by sunshine—a pleasant alternative—and the days are long in summer, stretching to more than fourteen hours because of the island's northerly position.

If you should stop there as early as May, you'll find the holiday season already in full swing—begun just after Easter. The Royal Dublin Society's Spring Show and Industries Fair is one of the year's leading events.

In June, fishermen and track fans have their big days. The salmon and trout season are wide open, and Curragh in County Kildare is host to the Irish Derby, a classic for three-year-olds.

July features another top sports event—the Irish Open Golf Championship in County Antrim. The last Sunday in July has a special meaning to those devoutly religious persons who would honor the memory of St. Patrick. This is the day they make their way to Croagh Patrick in County Mayo to climb this sacred mountain.

August opens the hunting season for wild duck, geese, and grouse—and this list should begin to show just how sports-minded the Irish are. The first week of the month brings the fashionable horse show to Dublin. For those with more off-beat interests, there is the Puck Fair at Killorglin in County Kerry. There, as part of 72 hours of uninterrupted fun, a goat is crowned king, and a good time is had by all, including the goat.

September keeps the sports fans happy by bringing back rugby football, and the hurling finals. But the traveler interested in cultural events probably would be most at home in October. It's then that Dublin holds its series of competitions in singing, acting, chess, and Gaelic games. Wexford follows with a festival of art and music.

So much for the formal events. No matter *when* you go, there are *places* you ought to go, regardless of your attitude

toward rugby or grouse shooting. My personal list would begin
with arrival at Shannon Airport, a lovely place of commerce,
then a trip over to nearby Ennis, capital of Clare, and a talk and
maybe a drink with assorted Considines and a night's rest at the
Old Ground, then on across the isle to Dublin by every known
route and devious path.

In Dublin, you should be sure to see the magnificent Book
of Kells at Trinity College—that beautiful record of the ages
which has survived for more than 1200 years. Inspect the old
Parliament House and the Custom House, both prominent landmarks in Irish history. Tour Dublin Castle, St. Patrick's Cathedral, and the National Museum with its collection of reminders
of the nation's earliest days. For a change of pace and sight, note
the ultramodern glass-walled building now housing the Department of Social Welfare and popularly known as the "bus
station."

Night life is all but nonexistent in Dublin, but you might try
an evening or two at the theater. The world-famed Abbey Theater is now housed in the Queens Theater on Pearse Street. There
are others, but it is a good place to start.

If, after a tour of the city, you're in the mood for a few days
at the seashore, then Dun Laoghaire (pronounced Leary) is the
place to go. It's Dublin's most popular resort.

The Lakes of Killarney lie at the southwestern tip of Ireland
and encompass some of the most spectacular scenery to be
found anywhere in the country. There is no single vantage
point and no way to explore this beautiful lake district in a few
hours or a day. It must be seen from a variety of places at different times of day and from a horse-drawn carriage rather than
a bus or auto. In addition to the round hills and silvery lakes,
you will find the ruins of old monasteries and the stone reminders of the tribes who flourished even before the time of St.
Patrick.

Galway is probably Ireland's most "international" city. Ptolemy, who ruled Egypt about 300 B.C., knew of the settlement and called it Magnata. Fifteen hundred years later, it was taken over by the Normans, who chased out the native Irish. Before long, the Spanish were using it as a trading post and when you visit there, you will see the Spanish influence still present in the architecture. These international contributions are also noticeable in the population of Galway. A man may be named Fitz-Stephen or O'Mahoney but have the black hair and the darker skins of the black Irish, and take pride in his Spanish ancestry. Galway also is the gateway to Ireland's "wild west"—Connemara and the Aran Islands—both places well worth exploring.

Limerick is a city rich in history, both landmarks and traditions. It is also one of Ireland's most peaceful cities—so quiet it almost seems to be part of another world. It is an atmosphere I've seldom felt anywhere else and that is the main reason I include it in this brief list. In addition, a visit satisfies a common curiosity. The signs and public inscriptions are *not* written as limericks and the people do not speak in limerick form. No one seems to know how the name happened to be applied from the city to the poetry or what "limerick" means. But there it is —a problem awaiting the brilliant solution of some scholar of the future.

A visit to the Blarney stone at Blarney Castle has been and probably always will be one of the principal tourist attractions of Ireland. I see little reason to resist this popular temptation. In the old days, in order to kiss the stone, you had to be held by some muscular fellow and lowered head first over the edge of the parapet while you wondered whether the risk was worth the accomplishment. Now, the process has been made a lot easier. An opening has been carved in the floor, just over the stone. You slip yourself into the opening, holding onto two iron bars, and while you're in an upside down position, try to give the stone a big smack. It's not so difficult but it is a strange operation. While you are doing it, someone will take your picture to send to the folks back home.

When you finally meet your "cousins" don't be offended if they fail to fall to the ground in adoration of you, the prosperous prodigal returned home. They'll treat you as an equal, and maybe as a bit of an eccentric.

Ireland is not an expensive place by European standards. Food should be available in great variety. There are thick, juicy steaks, game in season, and plenty of fish. Don't pass up the good, old-style bread of the area you happen to be touring, or the famous Irish potato. You'll probably find that your noon meal is the biggest one of the day, and mighty large at that. In the evening, the Irish are likely to want cold cuts, bread, jam, and tea.

When it comes to spending money in Ireland, don't forget the prize quality Irish tweeds and linens. These usually are bargains and are available in shops and department stores all over the country. Other worthwhile gift items include Waterford glass, Connemara marble, lace, briar pipes, walking sticks or shillelaghs.

Note that these goods are hardly the results of great industry. In the south of Ireland, agriculture remains the principal source of national income with tourism second and industry third. More than three-quarters of Ireland's exports are in farm products and nearly all go to one country, the ancient adversary, England. But, in the last twenty-five years, the number of workers in industry has doubled. Electric power developments are increasing in importance. Unemployment has dropped to half what it was before World War II. Now, at least food is plentiful and relatively inexpensive. Wages in Dublin buy about ten per cent more than in England. Heating costs less in the milder climate. Clothing may not be high-fashion, but it is durable.

Certainly, Ireland has improved economically a thousandfold since the dark days of the Famine. Despite its severe losses in manpower over the centuries, it has begun to come to life, nurtured by its newly won independence and the right to stand beside other free nations in the world.

It will make up its own good mind about the nations besides which it chooses to stand.

In defining Ireland's foreign policy, in the wake of its UN delegation's vote for Red China, the influential Jesuit review *America* gave this appraisal:

> Ireland's Frederick H. Boland presides over the United Nations General Assembly. An Irish general, Sean Mc-Keown commands the United Nations forces in the Congo. Ireland has a leading voice among the small countries in the United Nations, and will soon sit as a member of the Security Council. This little nation now exercises an influence which makes her foreign policy a matter of genuine interest to America.

> Ireland's policy is to be neutral without being neutralist. As Premier Sean Lemass said in December (1960), "We do not profess or pretend to be indifferent to the outcome of the East-West conflict, nor present ourselves as neutral on the ideological issues which now divide the world. We are clearly on the democratic side."

> Ireland also realizes that the peace of the world rests on the balance of power, and appreciates the sacrifices made by the great Western states to maintain that balance. But her Government believes that Ireland can render her best service to world peace outside of military alliances, to which she could contribute little in any case.

> As a small nation, Ireland stands for the concept of a world authority which can keep the peace. She has therefor dedicated herself to working through and for the

United Nations. Mr. Lemass says this is the very antithesis to isolation. Irish-Americans might prefer to see their Mother Land lined up solidly behind American foreign policy. But it may be that Ireland can best serve America's highest goals by avoiding identification with American military and diplomatic interests.

As the London *Spectator* has put it: "Ireland, to hold the position she has gained, must be able to demonstrate, even to flaunt, her independence."

A country which is undeniably Western and Christian, yes, indubitably anti-colonial and militarily uncommitted, occupies an unusually favorable position in world councils. Ireland aims to use that place of vantage to serve as a bridge between the West and the new neutral nations of Africa and Asia. It would be rash to conclude that her end or her means are wrong.

Ireland believes it has time. It is in no hurry to surpass the rest of the world. Indeed, it seems content just to make life on the planet as a whole a bit more tolerable. Perhaps that is the wellspring of its strength down through the ages.

BIBLIOGRAPHY

Adamic, Louis, *A Nation of Nations*, Harper & Brothers, New York and London, 1944.

Adams, Leon David, *The Commonsense Book of Drinking*, McKay, 1960.

Bartlett, John, *The Shorter Bartlett's Familiar Quotations*, Permabooks, 1957.

Beard, Charles A. and Mary R., *A Basic History of the United States*, Doubleday, Doran & Co., New York, 1944.

Benham, W. Gurney, *Putnam's Dictionary of Thoughts*, G. P. Putnam's Sons, New York, 1930.

Bourniquel, Camille, *Ireland*, Viking Press, 1960.

Compton's Pictured Encyclopedia and Fact-Index, F. E. Compton & Co., Chicago, 1953.

Creed, Virginia, *All About Ireland*, Duell, Sloan & Pearce, New York, 1951.

Duff, Charles, *Ireland and the Irish.* T. V. Boardman & Co., Ltd. London, New York, 1952.

Duffy, Francis P., *Father Duffy's Story*, Doran, New York, 1919.

Dunaway, Wayland F., *The Scotch-Irish of Colonial Pennsylvania*, University of North Carolina Press, 1944.

Fremantle, Anne, *The Age of Belief*, The New American Library of World Literature, 1955.

Haltigan, James, *The Irish in the American Revolution and Their Early Influence in the Colonies*, Published by the author, Washington, D.C., 1908.

Handlin, Oscar, *Boston's Immigrants*, Belknap Press of Harvard University Press, 1959.

Harris, Frank, *Bernard Shaw*, Simon and Schuster, New York, 1931.

Langer, William L., *An Encyclopedia of World History*, Houghton Mifflin Company, Boston, 1948.

Lunt, W. E., *History of England*, Harper & Brothers, New York, 1938.

Maisel, Albert, *They All Chose America*, Thomas Nelson, 1957.

Mencken, Henry L., *The American Language*, Alfred A. Knopf, New York, 1936.

Morison, Samuel Eliot and Commager, Henry Steele, *The Growth of the American Republic*, Oxford University Press, New York, 1936.

O'Brien, Michael J., *A Hidden Phase of American History*, Dodd, Mead & Co., Inc., New York, 1919.

Potter, George, *To the Golden Door*, Little, Brown & Co., Boston, 1960.

Pratt, Fletcher, *Ordeal By Fire*, William Sloane Associates, 1948.

Roberts, Edward F., *Ireland in America*, G. P. Putnam, New York, 1931.

Schlesinger, Arthur M., Jr., *The Age of Jackson*, Little, Brown & Co., New York, 1945.

Solomon, Barbara Miller, *Ancestors and Immigrants*, Harvard University Press, Cambridge, 1956.

The Columbia Encyclopedia, Columbia University Press, New York, 1950.

The Lincoln Library of Essential Information, The Frontier Press Co., Buffalo, New York, 1935.

Wibberley, Leonard, *Coming of the Green*, Henry Holt & Co., New York, 1958.

Wittke, Carl, *The Irish in America*, Louisiana State University Press, Baton Rouge, 1956.

INDEX